# How to Do *Everything* with

# Microsoft® Office Project® 2007

## Elaine Marmel

GW00542050

New York   Chicago   San Francisco   Lisbon
London   Madrid   Mexico City   Milan   New Delhi
San Juan   Seoul   Singapore   Sydney   Toronto

The *McGraw·Hill* Companies

## How to Do Everything with Microsoft® Office Project® 2007

1234567890 DOC DOC 019876

ISBN-13: 978-0-07-226341-1
ISBN-10:     0-07-226341-5

| | | |
|---|---|---|
| **Sponsoring Editor** | **Copy Editor** | **Illustration** |
| Megg Morin | Bill McManus | International Typesetting and Composition |
| **Editorial Supervisor** | **Proofreader** | |
| Janet Walden | Surendra Nath Shivam | **Art Director, Cover** |
| | | Jeff Weeks |
| **Project Manager** | **Indexer** | |
| Madhu Bhardwaj | Kevin Broccoli | **Cover Designer** |
| | | Pattie Lee |
| **Acquisitions Coordinator** | **Production Supervisor** | **Cover Illustration** |
| Carly Stapleton | George Anderson | Tom Willis |
| **Technical Editor** | **Composition** | |
| Jim Peters | International Typesetting and Composition | |

*To my brother and sister-in-law,*
*Jim and Mariann Marmel.*
*You know why.*

## About the Author

**Elaine Marmel** is president of Marmel Enterprises, LLC, an organization that specializes in technical writing and software training. Elaine has an MBA from Cornell University and has worked on projects to build financial management systems for New York City and Washington, D.C. This prior experience provided the foundation for Marmel Enterprises, LLC to help small businesses implement computerized accounting systems.

Elaine left her native Chicago for the warmer climes of Arizona (by way of Cincinnati, OH; Jerusalem, Israel; Ithaca, NY; Washington, D.C.; and Tampa, FL) where she basks in the sun with her PC; her dog Josh; and her cats Cato, Watson, and Buddy, and sings barbershop harmony with the 2006 International Championship Scottsdale Chorus.

Elaine spends most of her time writing; she has authored and co-authored over 30 books about Microsoft Office Project, QuickBooks, Peachtree, Quicken for Windows, Quicken for DOS, Microsoft Excel, Microsoft Word for Windows, Microsoft Word for the Mac, Windows 98, 1-2-3 for Windows, and Lotus Notes. From 1994 to 2006, she also was the contributing editor to the monthly publications *Peachtree Extra* and *QuickBooks Extra*.

# Contents

# Acknowledgments

Writing a book is a project composed of a team of players—how appropriate for this particular title. I'd like to thank all the folks who contributed to this project: Margie McAneny for hiring me; Megg Morin for jumping in to take over when Margie moved on to explore new opportunities; Jim Peters for keeping me technically accurate; Bill McManus for making sure my writing was clear and understandable; and Janet Walden, Madhu Bhardwaj, and Carly Stapleton for putting it all together to make a book.

The scope of a book-writing project is wide enough that I don't know all the folks who worked on the project by name—to those unnamed people who contributed, I thank you for your dedication.

# Introduction

Project management is a discipline; entire books have been written on the subject, and professional organizations exist to promote project management. Microsoft Office Project 2007 is a powerful piece of software that helps you apply project management concepts to complete projects within time and budget constraints. You define tasks, set task durations and dependencies, and assign resources to tasks, and Project calculates the length and cost of your project schedule. Because Project updates your schedule automatically as you make timing and cost changes, you can focus on the effects of changes to a project rather than on the changes themselves.

This book is for you whether you're new to project management or an experienced user. The book starts with basic concepts associated with computerized project management and continues to build on those concepts to help you master computerized project management. You will benefit most from this book if you are comfortable working in Windows and using a mouse.

This book is divided into six parts:

■ Part I, "Getting Started," introduces the basic project management concepts and terminology that you'll need to learn Project.

■ Part II, "Building a Project," identifies the type of information that Project needs in order to do its job, including working with the project's outline, setting task durations and timing relationships, and assigning people and other resources to your project.

■ Part III, "Viewing Projects," introduces the plethora of ways that you can look at your project information to help you focus on various aspects of a project at various times. In this section, you also learn how to customize views and tables to make them work for you.

■ Part IV, "Resolving Resource and Scheduling Conflicts," identifies the tools that Project provides to help you resolve timing and resource conflicts in your schedule.

- Part V, "Tracking," shows you how to record a baseline for your project—your estimate of how your project will progress—and then enter information that records how things actually progress. Using the tracking information, you can anticipate and address problems before they occur. And, once you complete your project, comparing your baseline to the actual information helps you become a better estimator and ultimately a better project manager.

- Part VI, "Advanced Project Management," shows you how to customize the Microsoft Office Project interface to make using Project easier and more functional in your working environment.

Throughout the book, you'll find a few special elements: Notes, Tips, and Cautions. Notes delve into related topics and provide information that will support you in whatever the main topic of the chapter might be. Tips are short asides that offer information related to the subject at hand; think of tips as having me there next to you, saying, "By the way, here's some information that might help you…" Cautions are my way of helping you avoid common pitfalls and errors that will cause you frustration.

You'll also find "How to…" and "Did You Know?" sidebars scattered throughout each chapter. The text in these boxes explains how to perform a key task or provides helpful information related to the topic at hand.

Whenever I introduce a new term, it appears in italics, followed by a definition or example as explanation. Keyboard shortcuts, such as CTRL-P, are also formatted to stand out against the rest of the text so that you can easily refer to the book as you work through a procedure.

You're ready to dive into the world of computerized project management using Microsoft Office Project 2007. I hope this book makes your experience easy and valuable.

# Part I

# Getting Started

# Chapter 1

# The Basics of Project Management

# How to…

- Define projects
- Understand the process of project management
- Recognize project management terms and tools
- Take advantage of project management software to help you manage project

I believe that understanding the concepts and the terminology of any discipline is the key to your success when working in that discipline. Good singers know how to stand properly and breathe properly to support their sound. Successful investors typically understand the terminology and the approaches used by the pros. An Olympic gold medalist starts with the fundamentals of his or her sport and builds skills by properly using and then expanding on the fundamentals. A successful project manager is no different; to successfully manage a project, you need to understand the basic principles of the discipline.

Project management is, indeed, a discipline; entire books have been written on the subject, and even professional organizations exist to promote project management. It isn't my intent to teach you project management in this chapter; instead, this chapter presents an overview of the basic concepts of the discipline so that you will be able to use the tools Microsoft Office Project offers to help you effectively manage projects. Specifically, I'll define the term "project" and explain the process of project management. Then, I'll introduce some basic terms and tools of project management. Finally, I'll briefly describe how project management software can help you manage projects.

# Defining Projects

Projects are everywhere and in everything you do. In the broadest sense, you can think of a project as a plan established to meet a specified goal. When you wake up in the morning and get ready for work, you follow a routine that includes a set of tasks you must complete before you walk out the front door. You brush your teeth, comb your hair, get dressed, and have breakfast or make coffee to drink on the way to work. You may also walk the dog and make your bed as part of your routine. Each thing you do as part of your morning routine is a *task* in project management terminology, and all of the tasks make up the *project* of getting ready for work. The project isn't complete until you have completed all of its tasks; that is, you can't leave for work until you finish your morning routine.

In the business world, projects tend to be collections of interdependent tasks performed by more than one person, often using equipment, to meet a specified goal within a specified timeframe. Let's look at a simple example.

Suppose that your company, which employs 100 people, has purchased a new telephone system, and your boss has put you in charge of making sure that everyone in the company receives training on using the new system. You start by making a list of the things you need to do to get training for everyone:

- Find and reserve a room for the training.

- Make sure that the room has sufficient telephone equipment in it to accommodate each person in the training class.

- Speak with the trainer to determine how many people should attend training at the same time and how long each training session will take.

- Schedule each person in the company to attend a class.

- Provide lunch for the trainer.

So far, you have a to-do list. But, when you look at your list of tasks, you notice that you can't complete some of them until you have completed others. For example, you can't very well reserve a room if you don't know how big a room you need. And, you can't schedule everyone for training until you know how many people can attend a single training class. So, now you need to organize your to-do list in some semblance of order. And, to make things easier, you name each task. If you drew a picture to represent your project, it might look like the one shown in Figure 1-1.

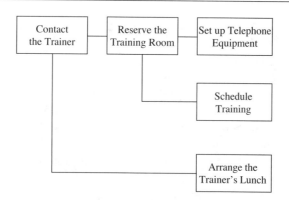

**FIGURE 1-1**   If you were to draw a picture of the telephone training project, it might look something like this.

The picture of the project implies that you must first speak with the trainer before you can complete any of the other tasks. And, you must reserve a room before you can arrange for phone equipment in the room or schedule anyone for training. But the picture also implies that it doesn't matter whether you arrange for equipment setup before or after you schedule training. Similarly, it really doesn't matter when you arrange for the trainer's lunch—as long as you make sure that lunch arrives by the time the trainer needs to eat it.

While you're working on the list of tasks for the telephone training project, your boss drops by and casually asks by when s/he can expect everyone to be trained so that the company can switch to the new phone system, and then tells you that the company would like to start using the new phone system in one week. Your boss just added a new dimension to the project—you need to figure out how long the training project will take to complete to determine if the one-week deadline is realistic. You really can't use a simple to-do list any longer, since timing has entered the picture.

You now turn back to your project and assign estimated times to each task. You estimate that it will take you two hours to contact the trainer and two more hours to find and reserve a room. You then realize that it will take you one hour to arrange for the equipment to be set up. You won't be the person setting up the equipment, so, before you can estimate how long it will take to complete the task of installing the equipment, you need to find out when the equipment installers will arrive and how long it will take them to install the equipment. You also realize that you can schedule training before, during, and after the equipment installers arrive, but you can't really estimate how long it will take to schedule training until you have spoken with the trainer and reserved the room. So, how do you make these estimates? And, what do you do if the estimates are wrong? These are the kinds of questions that project managers deal with regularly.

# Understanding the Process of Project Management

As a discipline, project management examines projects and offers ways to control their progress. Project management attempts to organize the tasks in a project to help you determine if you can complete the project in the time allotted using the available resources, both people and machinery. Further, by organizing the tasks, project management helps to minimize the number of unpleasant surprises that you may encounter during the course of a project—nobody willl be particularly happy if the date to start using the new phone system arrives and only half the people in the company actually know how to use it.

A variety of tools exist to help you plan projects; although the tools include software such as Microsoft Office Project, there are some project management activities that are likely to occur before you ever open a Microsoft Office Project file. Let's examine the process of managing projects.

## Setting a Goal for Your Project

Before you start planning a project, you should identify the project's goal. While that may sound simplistic or even obvious, identifying a project's goal isn't always easy. For example, producing a training guide is a very different goal from actually training. If the team members working on a project define the project's goal differently, they may ultimately work at cross purposes, and the project may fail.

As you determine the goal of your project, be aware that your project may be just one step in a larger project with a longer-term goal. In the example used earlier in this chapter, training staff to use a new telephone system was actually one step in a larger project—that of selecting and installing a new telephone system. Avoid setting a long-range goal that is likely to change before the project ends. Setting a goal of training everyone in the company to use a new telephone system by a specific date isn't realistic if the phone system isn't installed when you set your date; you run the risk of finding out that equipment delivery is delayed and the phone system won't be ready to use until six months after your deadline date.

As you work on identifying your goal, try to include those who will participate in your project. You can use any communication tool that works well in your environment—meetings, e-mail, conference calls—but make sure that you include various levels of management and staff and that you encourage communication among the participants. Many project managers write a goal and scope statement and circulate it among the team members. Writing a goal and scope statement ensures that you've gathered key information and that you and your team agree on the focus of everyone's efforts.

After you understand your goal, you should collect the information you need to define the project's scope. Scope statements contain more specific information or constraints that affect the project's completion. Project constraints usually fall within the areas of cost, time, and quality. Project A's goal may be to find a place to hold a wedding. The project's scope may read something like this: "By June 1, find a room that will seat 250 people for a sit-down dinner in a building with a kitchen for catering the dinner, with a cost of no more than $4000, located near the First Presbyterian Church, where the ceremony will be held." Project B's goal may be to introduce a new automobile model, and the scope of the project might read something like this: "Includes designing the car, crash testing, and creating and launching an advertising campaign. The launch must be completed before the end of the third quarter of 2007 and can cost no more than $500,000."

Project B's scope statement identifies major phases of the project (designing the car, crash testing, and creating an ad campaign). You can use a scope statement like this one as a starting point for planning the tasks in the project. And, reviewing the phases of this project makes it clear that this project would be more manageable if broken into three smaller projects, one for each phase, with new goal and scope statements appropriate to each of the smaller projects.

Once you understand the goal and scope of a project, you can begin to determine the steps that you need to take to reach the goal; you'll find it easiest to plan your project if you look first at the goal and then identify major phases needed to achieve the goal. Within each phase, create tasks that represent a logical sequence of steps.

## Planning and Revising

In addition to planning the phases and tasks in a project and organizing them into a logical sequence of steps, you, as a project manager, must also plan for the resources to complete the project. Resources can include people, equipment, and materials, all of which can be limited in supply. People get sick and take vacations and even are shared among projects at your company. Remember that, in every project, there is a relationship between project cost and project duration. The length of time needed to complete your project may depend on the availability of resources, and you may be able to shorten the length of your project by using more resources. But resources typically cost money, which can increase the cost of your project.

NOTE    *There is also a relationship between cost, time, and quality. The longer a project takes, the more it typically costs because you use resources, which cost money, for a longer period of time. It can be tempting to shorten a project to save money, but you often sacrifice quality when you try to save time. As a project manager, you constantly perform a juggling act, trying to balance time, cost, and quality.*

When you begin to plan a project, you can begin to enter data in Microsoft Office Project. In Figure 1-2, you see an initial Microsoft Office Project schedule. The outline format of a Project schedule clearly shows the various phases of your project. In this sample project, resources have not yet been assigned to tasks, and every task starts at the same time, which typically isn't possible.

It is wise to send an initial project schedule to various managers or coworkers so that you can use the input that you receive to adjust the schedule. You may want to create and save multiple Project files to consider different possible outcomes based on the feedback that you receive. Viewing a variety of plans for the same project is a great way to take advantage of Project's power.

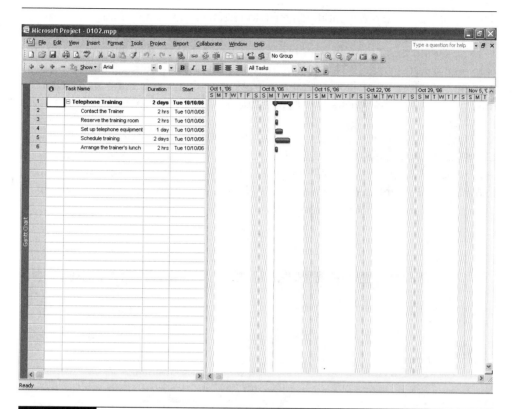

**FIGURE 1-2**   A look at an initial project schedule in Microsoft Office Project

During the planning and revising stage, you typically need to resolve conflicts in timing and resource allocation. For example, you may find that one task is scheduled to start before another task that must be completed first. Or, a team member or resource may be scheduled to work on several projects at once. Or, using expensive equipment excessively in one phase may be hurting your project's budget.

After you resolve these conflicts, and when your project plan seems solid, you can take a picture of it, called a *baseline*, against which you can track actual progress.

## Tracking and Project Management

A large portion of project management focuses on tracking the events of your project as they happen. Tracking project events effectively can play a major role in the success or failure of a project; if you don't track frequently enough, you may miss major events that will delay your project, but if you track too frequently, you may find yourself with no time to manage because you are too busy tracking.

You should try to solidify your tracking methods before your project begins, to help eliminate frustration. You need to determine whether you track each project participant's work or project participants track their own work and merely report their progress to you. You also need to decide how you will report progress to management.

The Microsoft Office Project schedule shown in Figure 1-3 uses the Tracking Gantt view to show the original baseline (the bottom bar of each task) tracked against actual progress (the top bar of each task). The darker portion of each upper task bar and the percentage figure to the right of each upper task bar indicate the percentage of each task that is complete.

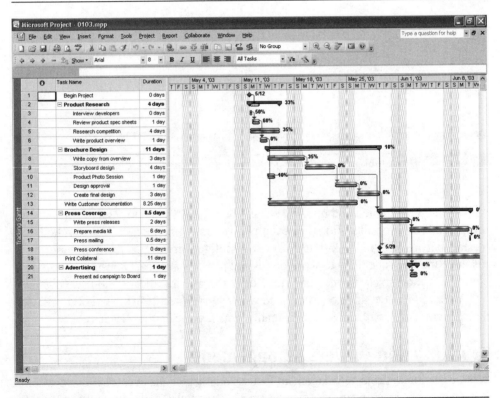

**FIGURE 1-3** The Tracking Gantt view in Project helps you see how much of a task has been completed.

## Revisiting History

Project management deals with concepts that go beyond the tools and features of any project management software package. Many of the most successful project managers will tell you that learning to effectively manage projects comes from trial and error. You have to work through a few projects before you really know the most effective way to enter initial information about your project. You can expect to develop efficient tracking methods over time. If you review the events that happen during your projects, you can avoid repeating mistakes in the future. History, in *any* field, is a most effective teacher.

Using tools available in Microsoft Office Project, you can review your projects and clearly see where tasks were too large to be manageable, where you estimated task duration or resource needs incorrectly, or where you adjusted the project schedule too slowly or too quickly. In a single file, Project stores your original schedule's baseline, interim baselines, and your final tracked schedule. You can use this information when you plan future projects to help you estimate how much time and how many resources you need to complete a task and the cost of a certain material, making you a more successful and efficient project manager. You can even use project history to clarify issues that you face and to help you obtain the support that you need.

# Terms and Tools of Project Management

Project management and project managers are concerned with scheduling, budgeting, managing resources, and tracking and reporting progress; to perform these functions, project managers use tools that have evolved over the years. The following sections introduce some key project management terms and tools.

## Understanding Dependencies

*Dependencies* are the relationships between tasks that affect the overall timing of a project. You can't determine the duration of a project by summing the durations of all tasks, because some tasks in a project happen simultaneously while others happen sequentially. For example, when you build a house, you must pour the foundation before you can frame the walls. But, you can install cabinets and lay carpets at the same time. Project managers anticipate and establish relationships called dependencies among the tasks in a project. After you have created tasks, assigned durations to them, and established dependencies, you can see the overall timing of your project.

## Using the Critical Path

The critical path is a visual representation—usually drawn in red—used to identify the tasks that must be completed on time for the project to be completed by the project's end date. If any task on the critical path becomes delayed, the end date of the project becomes delayed. And, as a project progresses and tasks are completed either early or late, the critical path changes. Knowing where your critical-path tasks are at any point during the project is crucial to staying on track.

Let's look at a simple example to help explain the concept of the critical path. Suppose that you are moving to a new house. The following are some of the tasks that are involved and the time you need to complete them:

| | |
|---|---|
| Shut off telephone, utilities, and other services at the old house | 4 hours |
| Pack the house | 5 days |
| Hire movers | 3 days |
| Forward your mail | 30 minutes |
| Have a garage sale | 1 day |

The shortest task, forwarding your mail, takes only 30 minutes because you can complete the form on the USPS website. Theoretically, you can delay forwarding your mail until 30 minutes before you move. Of course, you might want to give the post office more notice so that you experience no interruption in mail delivery, but for purposes of moving, delaying this task won't delay the move as long as you complete this task by the end of the longest task, which is packing the house. Therefore, the task of forwarding your mail isn't on the critical path. However, you can't delay the task of packing the house, which you estimate will take five days to accomplish, without delaying the move. Therefore, the task of packing the house is on the critical path. In this simple example, only one task appears on the critical path; typically, a whole series of tasks that can't afford delay form an entire critical path.

*Float*, also called *slack*, is the amount of time that you can delay a task before that task moves onto the critical path. In the preceding example, the 30-minute-long task of forwarding your mail has slack. This task can slip a few hours, even a couple of days, and the move will still happen on time. However, if you wait until the last half-hour of the day of the move to forward your mail, that task will have used up its slack and it then moves onto the critical path.

Project helps you identify the critical path. Figures 1-4 and 1-5 show the same schedule; Figure 1-4 shows all tasks, including those with slack, and Figure 1-5 shows the schedule filtered to show only the tasks that are on the critical path.

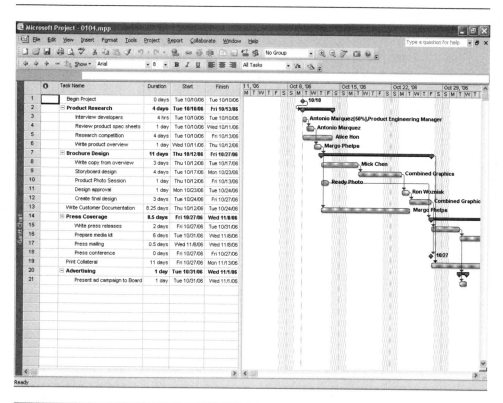

**FIGURE 1-4**    Tasks with slack displayed and tasks on the critical path

NOTE    *Chapter 9 shows you how to work with filters.*

## Distinguishing Between Durations and Milestones

Most tasks in a project take a specific amount of time to accomplish. In the preceding example, forwarding mail took 30 minutes, but packing the house took five days; in larger projects, a task may take months to complete. The length of time needed to complete a task is called the task's *duration*. You will find that you can manage

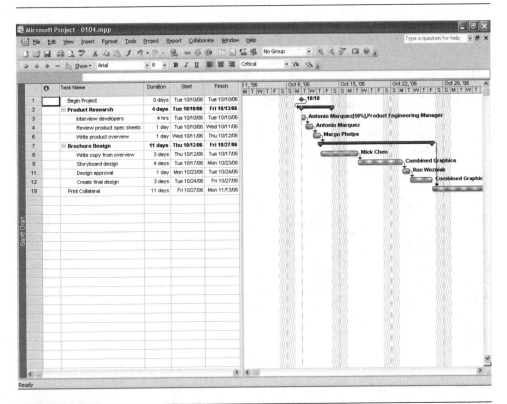

**FIGURE 1-5**  You can filter a Project schedule to display only the tasks that can't afford delay.

progress more effectively if you break long tasks in a project into smaller tasks of shorter durations. For example, consider breaking a six-month-long task into six one-month-long tasks. Monitoring the smaller tasks each month as they are completed reduces the odds of an unpleasant surprise six months down the road and has the added benefit of giving you a sense of accomplishment.

Some tasks are nothing more than points in time that mark the start or completion of some phase of a project. These tasks are called *milestones*, and they have no duration. For example, suppose that your project involves building a new home for a customer, and your company will not begin construction until the customer has signed the contract. Contract signing may be considered a milestone. You can assign a duration to the process of having the customer select all the options to determine the final sale price of the home, but assigning a length of time to the moment when the customer actually signs the contract is probably impossible. Therefore, this task has a duration of 0—that is, contract signing is a milestone that marks a key moment in the project.

## Understanding Resource-Driven Schedules

The number of resources you assign to a task can affect the duration of the task. For example, if one person needs four hours to clean a house, adding a second person will probably reduce the time needed to clean the house by half. Cleaning the house—the project—still requires four hours of effort, but two resources can work simultaneously to complete the task in half the time. In project management terms, a resource-driven task is a task whose duration is affected by adding or subtracting resources.

NOTE     *In reality, people have different skill levels and work at different speeds, so using two people on a resource-driven task doesn't necessarily cut the time of a task in half. And don't forget: when you add more people to a task, more communication, cooperation, and training may be required. Microsoft Office Project handles resource assignments as strictly a mathematical calculation, but you should evaluate the resources involved and modify this calculation if necessary.*

## Understanding Fixed-Duration Tasks

The duration of some tasks is unaffected by the number of people or other resources you devote to them. Driving from Chicago to Cincinnati takes approximately five hours if you obey the speed limit, whether you drive an SUV or a sports car. Pregnancy takes nine months, no matter how many women you have doing the job. Flying from San Francisco to New York is likely to take about five hours, regardless of how many pilots or flight attendants you add. In project management terminology, these tasks have a fixed duration; the timing of a fixed-duration task is determined by the nature of the task.

## Using Drawings to Aid Project Management

Over the years, a variety of picture-based tools, such as Gantt Charts, network diagrams, and work breakdown structures (WBSs) have been developed to aid in the understanding and tracking of different aspects of a project. Figure 1-6 shows

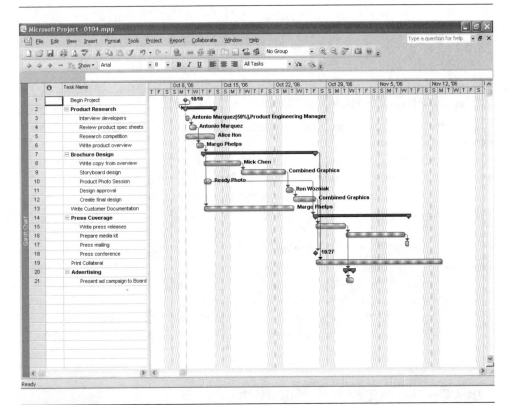

**FIGURE 1-6**    The bars on a Gantt Chart provide a visual representation of the timing of tasks in a project.

a Microsoft Office Project Gantt Chart, and Figure 1-7 shows a Microsoft Office Project network diagram. Figure 1-8 shows a typical WBS, although Microsoft Office Project does not include a WBS chart as one of its standard views.

# How Project Management Software Can Help You Manage Projects

Because project management itself is complex, many people find the idea of using project management software daunting. It probably will take many hours to enter your project data before you can get anything back from the software. It makes sense to expect to provide a certain amount of information about your

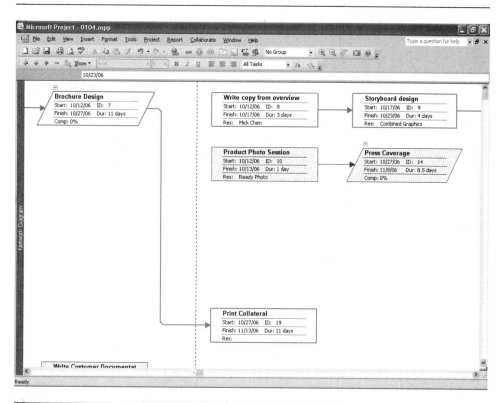

FIGURE 1-7    The network diagram displays the tasks in a project in a diagram similar to a flow chart.

project so that the software package can estimate schedules and generate reports; after all, you can't produce a report, complete with charts, tables, and graphs, without putting in the effort to collect the information and then type it into a word processor or a spreadsheet.

On the bright side, though, after you enter information into Microsoft Office Project, the ongoing maintenance of project data is far easier than generating the handwritten to-do lists that typically become obsolete before you finish creating them. After you enter project data, Project performs its calculations and automatically updates your project schedule. You can easily and quickly spot potential problems such as overallocated resources or tasks falling behind schedule; using tools in Project, you can test alternative solutions. And, the reports that Project generates can make the difference between a poorly managed project and a successful one.

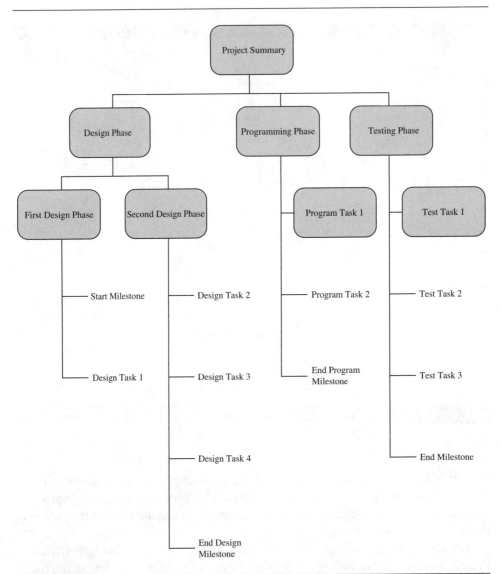

FIGURE 1-8    When you look at a work breakdown structure chart, you might be reminded of a typical company's organizational chart.

To create a project schedule in Microsoft Office Project, you must enter individual task names, task durations, and task dependencies. To track the costs of these tasks, you add the list of human and material resources and their costs for both standard and overtime hours and then you assign those resources to tasks.

1

When you track a project over its lifetime, you need to enter progress on tasks to indicate how complete each task is. You also record changes in task timing or dependencies, resources that are added to or removed from the project, and changes in resource time commitments and costs. Project continually adjusts your schedule as needed with each piece of tracking information that you supply so that you always know where things stand on your project.

In this chapter, you reviewed the basics of project management concepts; in the next chapter, you'll take a look around the Microsoft Office Project interface and learn to open and save projects.

# Chapter 2

## Taking a First Look at Project

## How to...

- Use the screen
- Work with the project calendar
- Add tasks to a project
- Save a project
- Open an existing project
- Get help

In this chapter, you'll start using Project to build a project. First, we'll take a look at the differences between Project Standard, Project Professional, and Project Server. In this book, I assume that you are using Project Professional. Next, we'll examine the parts of the window, and then we'll establish basic scheduling information such as identifying project start and finish dates, reviewing calendar and schedule options, and setting up a project calendar. Then, you'll learn how to enter tasks, save your work, and review how to open existing projects. Last, I'll walk you through using the Help system in Project and the Project Guide, a wizard that can help you set up projects.

# The Versions of Project

Microsoft sells two versions of the desktop product Microsoft Office Project: Project Standard 2007 and Project Professional 2007. These products differ only in their ability to support Project Server 2007. Project Standard is a stand-alone desktop application that cannot interface with Project Server. Project Professional is a desktop application that can interface with Project Server.

What is Project Server? Project Server enables you to work with projects stored in a database that resides on your company's intranet or on the Internet. Only the project manager installs and uses Microsoft Office Project 2007. Everyone else on the project uses Project Web Access, the Web-based interface that connects to the Project Server database. Using Project Web Access instead of Microsoft Office Project, resources can view a project's Gantt Chart, receive, refuse, and delegate work assignments, update assignments with progress and completion information, track issues and risks, manage project documents, and send status reports to the project manager.

Project managers have access to a company-wide resource pool that tracks resource allocations across all projects in the Project Server database. If a project manager finds that a specific resource is unavailable, the project manager can define the requirements for the job and let Project Server tools search the research pool to find another resource with the same skills.

A project manager can use either Project Standard or Project Professional to create and manage projects; if, however, your organization uses Project Server, you must use Project Professional. In this book, I assume that you're using Project Professional 2007.

NOTE    *See Chapter 18 for more information on Project Server.*

If you are not connected to Project Server, you'll see no difference in functionality between Project Standard 2007 and Project Professional 2007. You see commands in Project Professional 2007 that you don't see in Project Standard 2007, but the commands aren't available for use.

# Understanding the Screen

Like understanding the terminology associated with a discipline, understanding the screen of the software package makes it easier for you to follow along in any discussion of the product. To start Project, click the Windows Start button and choose All Programs | Microsoft Office | Microsoft Office Project.

Project's screen uses the classic interface of Office products prior to the release of Office 2007. Like Office 2003 and its predecessors, you'll find menus as well as toolbars; Figure 2-1 identifies the parts of the Project screen.

NOTE    *When you first open Project and view a new, blank project, you'll see the Project Guide, which appears in a task pane down the left side of the screen. Later in this chapter, I'll show you the Project Guide and how to use it. Most screens in this book do not display the Project Guide, to help focus on the pertinent information.*

Some of the parts of screen warrant additional explanation. First, as with other Windows programs, you click menus to open them and display a list of related commands; you click a command to execute it. And, toolbar buttons represent shortcuts to commonly used commands; you click buttons on the toolbars instead of opening menus and clicking commands.

Standard toolbar    Title bar    Formatting toolbar    Menu bar    Entry bar    Timescale

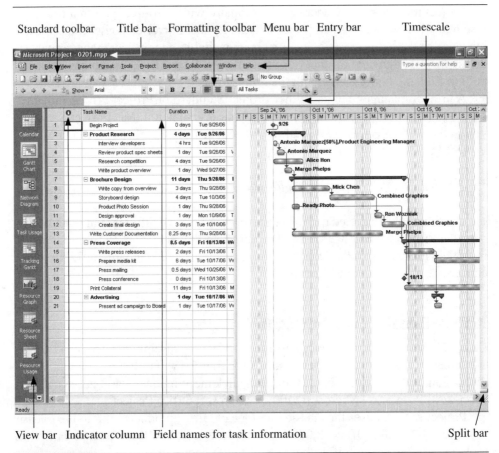

View bar    Indicator column    Field names for task information    Split bar

**FIGURE 2-1**    Understanding the parts of the Project screen

In Figure 2-1, the Entry bar is blank; when you start to enter task information, the information you type appears in the Entry bar, along with a green check mark and red X. You can click the green check mark or press ENTER on the keyboard to accept the information you type, or you can click the red X or press the ESC key to cancel storing the information.

X ✓ Finalize ad campaign using Board input

Project contains a wide variety of *views*, which are different ways to look at project information. The View bar provides you with a handy way to identify the current view and to switch between the most commonly used views. In Figure 2-1, you see the Gantt Chart view; in the View bar, a box surrounds the Gantt Chart icon. Figure 2-2 shows the Calendar view.

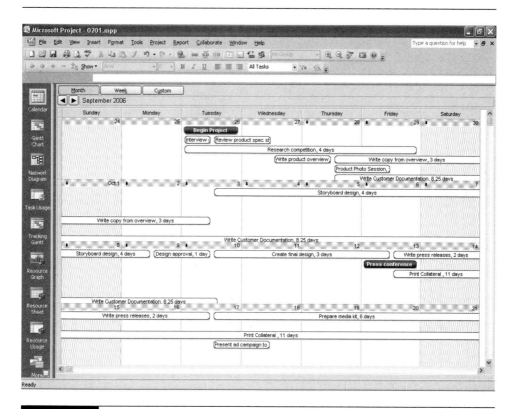

**FIGURE 2-2**    The Calendar view presents your project in a familiar calendar format.

Some of the available views in project are called *combination views*, which are, as you might suspect from the name, a combination of two views appearing simultaneously onscreen. Chapter 7 discusses views in detail; for the time being, note that you can use the split bar to quickly and easily display standard combination views. By dragging the split bar up while viewing the Gantt Chart, you see the combination view that includes the Gantt Chart and the Task Entry view (see Figure 2-3).

*The Gantt Chart view is, by definition, a combination view consisting of a graphic portion on the right and a table on the left. You can drag the vertical split bar to the left or right to display more or less of either side of the Gantt Chart.*

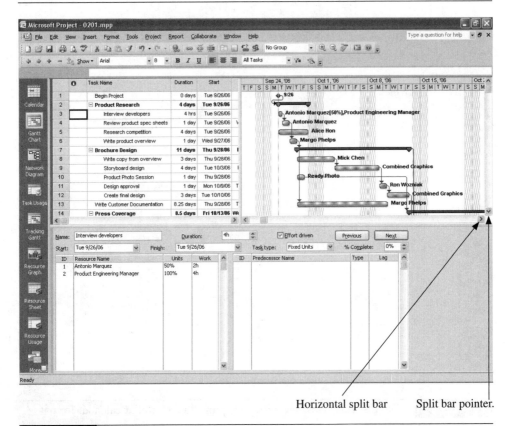

Horizontal split bar     Split bar pointer.

**FIGURE 2-3**  You can drag the split bar to display a combination view.

The timescale appears, in one format or another, on most views. Chapter 3 shows you how to control the appearance of the timescale to view larger or smaller portions of your project.

You cannot type in the Indicator column; however, you will notice icons in the column on occasion to alert you of special circumstances concerning the selected task, typically in response to an action that you've taken. For example, Project may display an indicator for an overallocated resource or because you entered a note about the resource. If you rest your mouse over an indicator, Project displays the information that is associated with the icon in a ScreenTip.

# Establishing Basic Scheduling Information

In the Project Information dialog box, shown next, you supply basic information about a new project that you want to set up. If this dialog box doesn't open automatically when you start a new project, you can open it by choosing Project | Project Information.

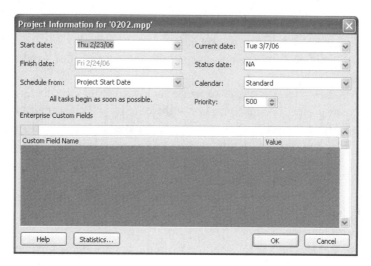

## Display the Project Information Dialog Box When Starting a New Project

You can make the Project Information dialog box appear automatically whenever you start a new project. Choose Tools | Options. In the Options dialog box, click the General tab. Then, check the Prompt for Project Info for New Projects check box.

# Working with Project Start and Finish Dates

If you set a start date for the project, all tasks begin on that date until you assign timing or dependencies to them or you change your scheduling options; later in this chapter, you'll see how you can make new tasks start on the current date instead of the project start date. If the project started before you managed to enter it into Microsoft Office Project, you can set the start date to the real start date—a date in the past. You can also try out different scenarios for your project if you change the project's start date during the planning phase. When you set a start date for a project, Microsoft Office Project adjusts the project finish date using the duration of your tasks and their timing relationships.

Sometimes, however, it's easier to work backward from a project's deadline to schedule your project because you know the date by which something must be completed. For example, suppose that you must plan the annual July 4th celebration sponsored by your company, the Fireworks Company of America. You can schedule tasks by moving backward from the finish date to identify the date by which you need to start the project in order to complete it by July 4. The Finish Date field works hand in hand with the Schedule From field, and you must change the choice in the Schedule From field to Project Finish Date to make the Finish Date field available.

After you decide whether to schedule from the beginning or the ending date of a project, you can enter the date by clicking the down arrow next to the text box and selecting a date from the pop-up calendar that appears.

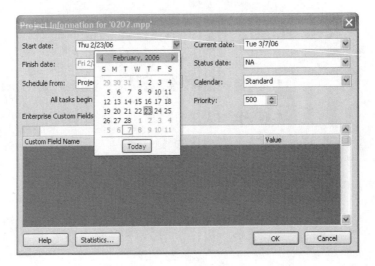

## Scheduling and Constraints

If you schedule your project from its start date, Project uses As Soon As Possible (ASAP) as the default constraint type for all new tasks. Similarly, if you schedule your project from its finish date, Project uses As Late As Possible (ALAP) as the default constraint type for all new tasks. When you schedule backward from a project's finish date, Project can't use tools such as resource leveling to resolve conflicts in your schedule. Chapters 10 and 11 contain information about ways that you can resolve scheduling and resource problems.

## Setting Other Project Information Fields

By default, Project inserts your computer's current date setting into the Current Date field, but you can simply select a different date. You may want to adjust this setting to generate reports that provide information on your project as of a certain date or to go back and track your project's progress from an earlier date.

The Status Date field performs several functions related to project progress:

- It appears as the complete-through date in the Update Project dialog box.

- Project uses it to perform earned-value calculations.

- Project uses it to place progress lines in your project.

If you leave the Status Date field set at NA, Project sets the status date as your computer's current date setting.

From the Calendar field, you can select the calendar on which to base your schedule. The Standard calendar is the default; it schedules work 8 hours a day, 5 days a week, 20 days per month. Later in this chapter, you'll see how to view and change the settings of the Standard calendar and how to create your own calendar.

As you'll see in Chapter 3, you can establish priorities for each task in a project. You also can establish a priority for an entire project. A project priority can be a value between 1 and 1000, and the project level priority plays a role when you use shared resources across multiple projects. In Chapter 11, you'll see how you can use resource leveling to resolve resource problems; setting a project priority helps you to better control how resource leveling adjusts tasks.

Organizations that use Project Server may establish project-level custom fields or outline codes in the Project Server database. If your project is connected to the Project Server database, those project-level custom fields and outline codes appear at the bottom of the Project Information dialog box. An asterisk (*) appears beside any required custom field or outline code to which you need to assign values.

## Setting Up Calendar and Schedule Options

No schedule is valid unless it takes into consideration the calendar used by the organization. Therefore, when you start a project, you typically set up a calendar for the project that reflects your organization's standard working times and holidays or other exceptions. In addition, Project enables you to set a variety of options that affect your project calendar. In this section, we'll explore the available calendar and schedule options and then create a project calendar for a new project.

Using the options on the Calendar tab of the Options dialog box, you can control the way your project calendar works. To view the Calendar tab of the Options dialog box, choose Tools | Options and then click the Calendar tab.

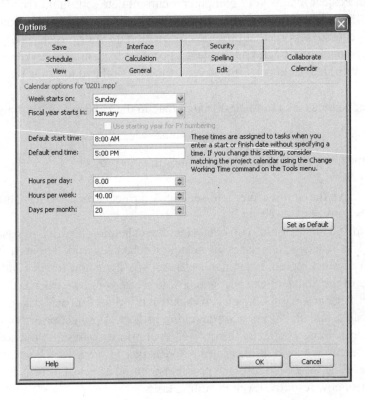

You can see that Project enables you to define your work week and fiscal year, as well as the default starting and ending times for each work day. Although the default starting day of the week is Sunday, your catering business may be closed on Mondays and Tuesdays and your work week might start on Wednesday. The typical project calendar uses a 40-hour work week, consisting of 8-hour days, with approximately 20 days per month, but you can make changes to those settings that better fit your environment. Project uses these settings when you define tasks to calculate how much of a task can be completed on a given day and how many calendar days will be required to complete the task.

On the Schedule tab, shown next, you can control the way Project calculates and stores task information as you enter it. For example, you can change the default unit of time for entering task durations from days to hours for projects that require precise time measurements, such as running chemical tests in a laboratory. In most cases, the default work time setting of Hours works best, but you can alternatively choose to store work in minutes, days, weeks, or months. And, if you prefer to have new tasks begin no earlier than the current date, you can adjust the setting for New Tasks from the default choice of Start On Project Start Date.

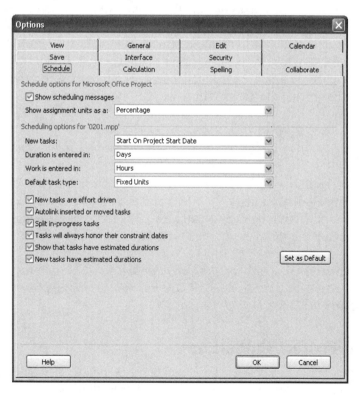

When new tasks are effort driven, Project schedules new tasks so that the work on the task remains constant even as you change assignments. For example, assigning additional resources to an effort-driven task shortens the task duration.

By default, Project automatically creates task dependencies when you insert, cut, or move a task between tasks that have Finish to Start task relationships.

Leaving the Split In-Progress Tasks check box checked enables Project to reschedule remaining duration and work when a task falls behind schedule or reports progress ahead of schedule. If you record progress on a successor task before its predecessor task is completed, the work on the successor task appears split; the portion of the completed work is recorded, and the remaining work continues to use the original dependency you assigned to the predecessor task. If you remove the check from this check box, Project doesn't split the completed work from the remaining work and records the progress information on the originally scheduled dates, regardless of when the actual work is completed. Likewise, remaining work is not rescheduled to maintain the task relationship.

By default, Project schedules tasks according to their constraint dates and will not move constrained tasks outside the range of the constraint. For example, if Task A has a finish-to-start dependency with Task B, but Task B has a Must Start On constraint that's earlier than the finish date of Task A, Project will not reschedule Task B if Task A finishes earlier than expected. If you want to control your project schedule based on task dependencies rather than constraint dates, remove the check from the Tasks Will Always Honor Their Constraint Dates check box.

> NOTE *See Chapter 4 for more information on constraints and dependencies.*

Checking the Show That Tasks Have Estimated Durations check box makes Project display a question mark (?) after the duration unit of any task with an estimated duration. And, by default, all new tasks have an estimated duration of one day, assuming that you set the Duration Is Entered In value to Days.

> NOTE *Any changes you make on the Calendar and Schedule tabs apply only to the current project file. You can save the changes for* all *project files by clicking the Set as Default button.*

## Creating Project Calendars

As you saw earlier in this chapter, Project uses the Standard calendar by default for every project you create. However, the Standard calendar may not work in all situations. You may need to change the project calendar so that it works properly in your working environment.

*Project also enables you to create task calendars and resource calendars; you can read about task calendars in Chapter 3 and resource calendars in Chapter 5.*

You can view the Standard calendar and create your own project calendar. To create a project calendar, choose Tools | Change Working Time. Project displays the Change Working Time dialog box.

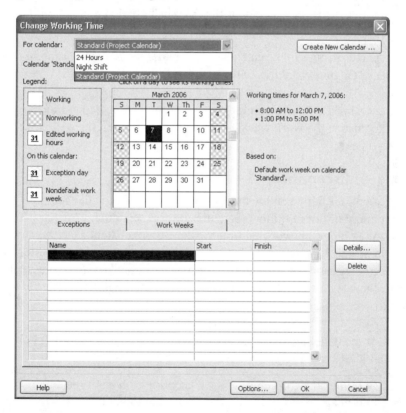

Other calendars that exist appear in the For Calendar list box. To easily create a new calendar, you create a copy of one of the existing calendars and then modify it; follow these steps:

1. Click the Create New Calendar button. Project displays the Create New Base Calendar dialog box.

2. Type the name that you want to assign to the calendar.

3. Make sure that you select the Make a Copy Of *x* Calendar option.

4. Click OK. Project redisplays the Change Working Time dialog box, but the name of the new calendar that you just created appears in the For Calendar box.

5. To make changes to the calendar, click either the Exceptions tab or the Work Weeks tab midway down in the dialog box.

The general process for changing working time varies, depending on whether you want to change the work week or make an exception in the regular schedule, as described next.

## Creating an Exception

Use the Exceptions tab when the block of time you need to change doesn't follow a regular pattern or doesn't affect the entire project schedule. For example, create an exception to block off working time while everyone attends a company-wide meeting on March 7 from 2:00 to 5:00 P.M. Or create an exception to block off every Wednesday morning during the month of March when the project schedule runs from January to June. To create an exception that marks off specific hours as non-working time, follow these steps:

1. Click the date to which the exception applies; in this example, I clicked March 7.

2. Click in the Name column on the Exceptions tab and type a name for the exception and press ENTER or TAB. Project automatically fills the selected date in the Start and Finish boxes.

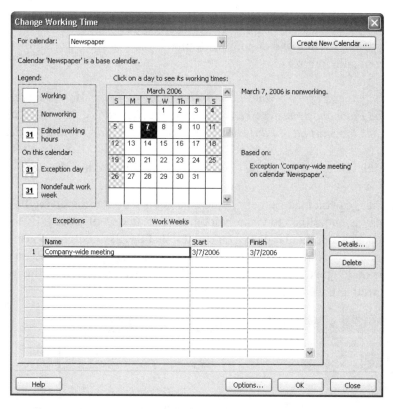

**3.** Click the Details button to display the Details dialog box for the exception.

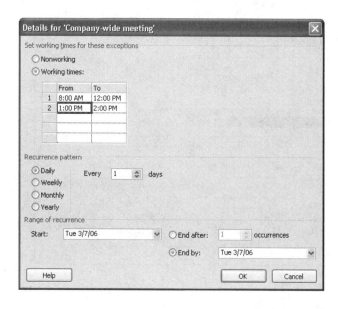

4. Click the Working Times option.

5. Type the starting and ending work times—not for the exception—in the From and To boxes.

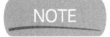

*To mark off every Wednesday morning in the month of March, set the times in the From and To boxes, select Weekly in the Recurrence Pattern section, and click the Start and End By down arrows to select March 1 and March 31.*

6. Click OK to redisplay the Change Working Times dialog box.

The changes you made appear in the calendar section of the dialog box; the selected day is underlined to visually identify it as an exception day. Even if you don't select a particular date, you can tell that the day contains nonstandard working hours by comparing the appearance for the date to the legend on the left side of the dialog box, which identifies working, nonworking, and edited working hours, as well as exception days and nondefault work weeks.

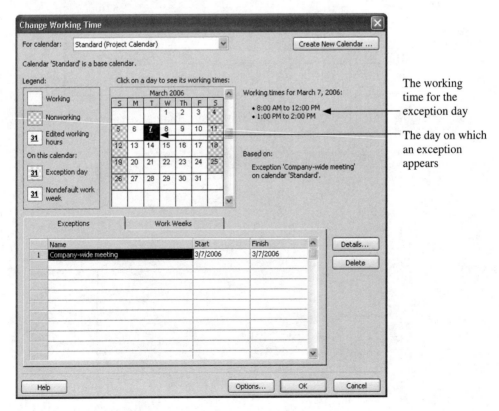

## Creating a Change to the Work Week

Suppose that you run the local newspaper and need to plan the printing of your weekly newspaper based on the articles you're going to publish in each edition. The articles would be tasks on your weekly newspaper publishing project, and each weekly publishing project requires the use of your printing press. But suppose that the press requires cleaning and maintenance each week for three hours on Wednesday afternoon. To schedule your projects accurately, you need a calendar that marks the time needed to maintain the printing press as unavailable. Follow these steps:

1. In the Change Working Time dialog box, click the Work Weeks tab.

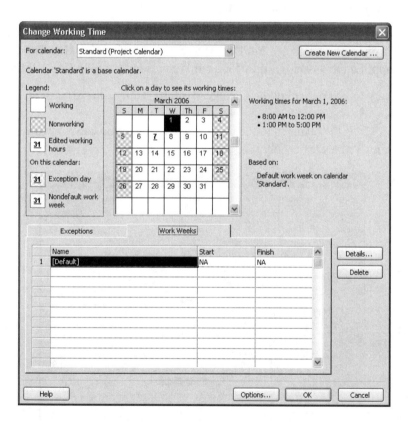

2. Click the Details button. Project displays the Details dialog box for the default work week.

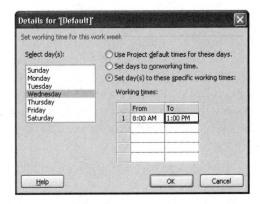

3. Select the day of the week that you want to change.

4. Select an option to specify how you want to change the selected day; for the example, I selected Set Day(s) to These Specific Working Times and supplied the working times for each Wednesday from 8:00 to 1:00 A.M.

5. Click OK to redisplay the Change Working Times dialog box.

Project saves the changes to the default work week; you can view the working time for any Wednesday by clicking it.

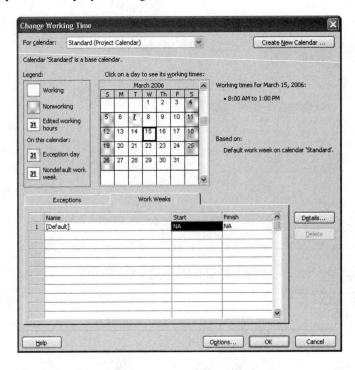

# Working with Tasks

In this section, I introduce adding tasks to a project. Chapter 3 covers working with tasks in detail, including how to enter tasks and subtasks, move and copy tasks, use the outlining features in Project to hide and display tasks, establish task timing by linking tasks together, and set an estimated duration for a task.

In Project, you add tasks simply by typing a name that describes the task in the Task Name column. I like to enter the project name as the first task in the project. As you'll see in a moment, Project uses an outlining feature that enables you to designate tasks and subtasks; by entering the project name as the first task, I can use it as a summary task. For this summary task, Project will display a Gantt Chart bar that represents the duration of the entire project. When you start entering tasks, don't worry about entering them in the "right order." As you'll see in the next section, you can easily move things around.

After you type the task's name, press ENTER or click the check mark in the Entry bar above the task name. Project stores the task, assigning a duration of 1 estimated day—the question mark in the Duration column indicates that the duration is estimated. Project also assigns a start date to the task that matches the project's start date—unless you changed that setting on the Schedule tab of the Options dialog box, as described earlier in this chapter. In addition, Project displays green highlighting in the boxes containing the information Project supplied; this highlighting is called *change highlighting* and appears whenever you make a change to a task's details. Project automatically removes the change highlighting when you make a change to another task.

> *You can hide change highlighting by choosing View | Hide Change Highlighting. You can redisplay change highlighting by choosing View | Show Change Highlighting.*

I typically use the Gantt Chart view for general data entry, since it provides a graphic as well as text representation for tasks. Although Chapter 7 describes views in more detail, most people spend a great deal of time in the Gantt Chart view, so it warrants some additional explanation here.

The left side of the Gantt Chart view is a table called the (many of Project's views contain tables) and contains the text representation for the task. In the right side of the Gantt Chart view, Project displays a bar, the length of which represents the task's duration, as you can tell by examining the timescale. In Figure 2-4, you see the tasks for the telephone training project associated with the new phone system being implemented by ABC Company.

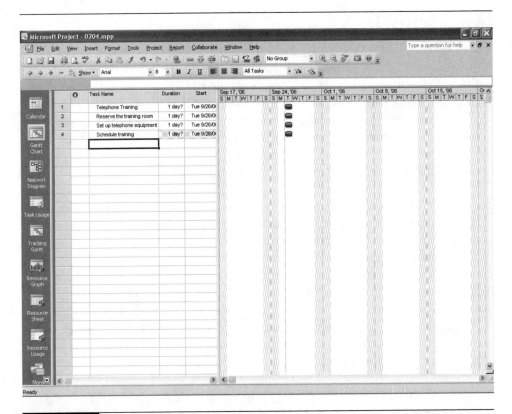

**FIGURE 2-4**  When you enter a task in the Gantt Chart view, you type the task's name in the Entry table on the left; Project fills in default information for the task and displays a bar in the right side of the view that represents the task's duration.

# Saving Your Work

You should save your work frequently. To save a project file, choose File | Save or click the Save button on the Standard toolbar. The first time you save a project, the Save As dialog box appears.

2

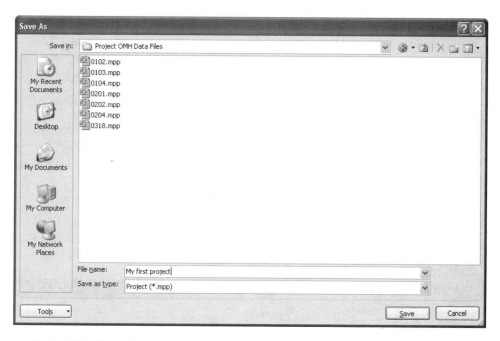

In the File Name box, type a name for the file. You can save the file in a variety of locations:

- Click the arrow at the right edge of the Save In list box to display a hierarchy of your computer's drive and directory organization and navigate to a specific location.

- Click the Up One Level tool to move up one level in that hierarchy.

- Click any of the buttons that appear down the left side of the Save As dialog box to save the file in one of those locations.

- To save a project file in a new folder, navigate to the drive or folder in which you want Project to store the new folder and then use the Create New Folder tool.

By default, Project saves files in Project 2007 format with the extension .mpp. You can save your file to a variety of different formats, including Microsoft Access or an earlier version of Project.

 *The format of Project 2007 files is different from the format of Project 2003, Project 2002, and Project 2000 files. You can, however, save Project 2007 files as Project 2003 files. And, at the time of this writing, Microsoft planned to make a converter available for download so that users of Project 2003 can open Project 2007 files.*

After you enter a name for your file and designate its location and type, click Save to save the file.

## Opening Existing Projects

You open an existing Project file the same way that you open files for other Office programs. You can either click the Open button on the toolbar or choose File | Open. In either case, the Open dialog box appears.

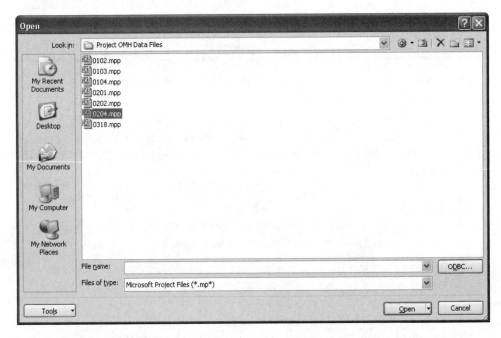

Use the Look In list to navigate to the location where the file is stored. Then, click the file and click the Open button. Project opens the file.

# Getting Help

Project contains a Help system like other Office programs. In addition, Project has a special feature you won't find in other programs: the Project Guide.

## Using Project Help

You can click the Microsoft Office Project Help button located at the end of the Standard toolbar to display the Help window. Project will search both online and offline sources for help. From the Help window that appears, click a subject on which you want help.

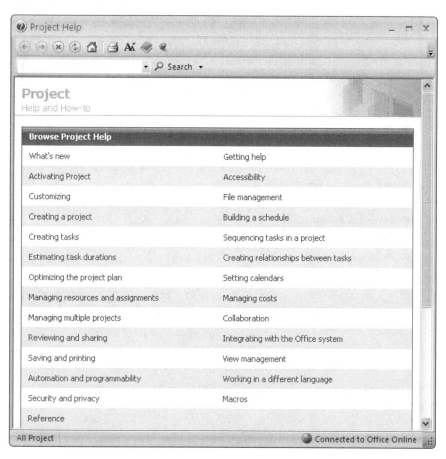

Project then displays the help topics available for that subject.

Click a topic to see the Help text.

You also can search for help; at the right end of the menu bar, type the word or words on which you want help and press ENTER. The Help window opens; your search text appears at the top of the window, and the topics that meet the criteria you typed appear in the window. Click a topic to view its help text.

## Using the Project Guide

When you first open Microsoft Office Project or start a new project, Project initially displays the Project Guide, a wizard of sorts that helps you build projects. The Project Guide is composed of both the Project Guide pane on the left side of the screen and the Project Guide toolbar, which appears just above the Project Guide pane.

Project Guide toolbar

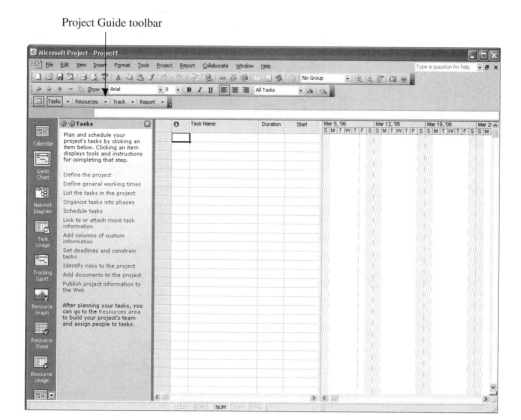

*You can hide or display the Project Guide toolbar at any time if you right-click any toolbar and choose Display Project Guide.*

You can use the Project Guide toolbar and the Project Guide pane to guide you through building a project. The links that appear in the Project Guide pane change, based on the Project Guide toolbar button that you click.

The Project Guide walks you through the process associated with any link you click. Define a Project is the first link that appears in the Project Guide when you click the Tasks button on the Project Guide toolbar. When you click Define a Project, a wizard walks you through three steps associated with starting a project. In the first step, you establish the starting date for your project.

After setting the date, click the right arrow at the top of the pane or click Save and Go to Step 2 at the bottom of the Project Guide pane to continue. In the next step, you indicate whether to set up the project to use Project Server. In the last step, you return to the Project Guide.

You can temporarily hide both the pane and the toolbar if you decide that you don't want to use the Project Guide. Click the X in the upper-right corner of the pane to temporarily hide the pane. Right-click any toolbar and click Project Guide to remove the check mark that appears next to it to temporarily hide the toolbar.

You can turn off the Project Guide feature entirely from the Options dialog box. Choose Tools | Options. On the Interface tab, remove the check mark from the Display Project Guide box.

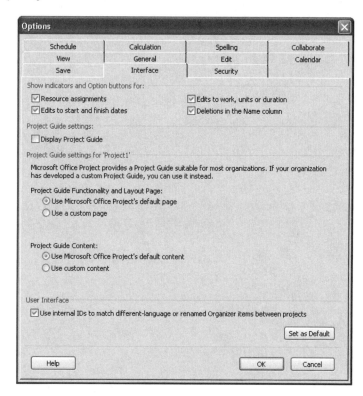

In the next chapter, we'll get into the details of working with tasks in a project. Although you learned how to add a task to a project, there's a great deal more to learn about working with tasks.

# Part II

# Building a Project

# Chapter 3

## Creating Tasks

# How to...

- Insert tasks and create subtasks

- Select, copy, move, hide, or display tasks

- Work with task timing

- Create repeating tasks

- Enter and print task notes

In this chapter, you'll examine the details associated with entering tasks. In Chapter 2, you learned how to add a task to your schedule; in this chapter, you'll learn how to insert tasks you forgot to enter originally, and you'll learn how to create subtasks. You'll learn how to move and copy tasks, as well as hide and display tasks. Then, you'll delve into the details of task timing and how Project handles task durations.

# The Basics of Entering Tasks

In Chapter 2, you learned that you can create a task by simply typing a name for it in the Task Name column on the Gantt Chart view. In this first section, I want to expand on the basics of creating a task and cover some of the other scenarios you might encounter. In this section, you'll learn how to insert a task between two existing tasks, copy tasks, move tasks, and use Project's outlining feature to promote, demote, hide, and display tasks.

## Inserting Tasks

Typically, after you've entered some tasks, you'll realize that you "missed something" and you'll want to insert a task between two existing tasks. When you insert a new task, it appears above the currently selected task. To add the task of contacting the trainer immediately after the Telephone Training task, follow these steps:

1. Click anywhere on the row of the Reserve the Training Room task.

2. Choose Insert | New Task. Row 2 becomes a blank row and all the other tasks move down one row. The cell pointer rests in Row 2, the new task row (see Figure 3-1).

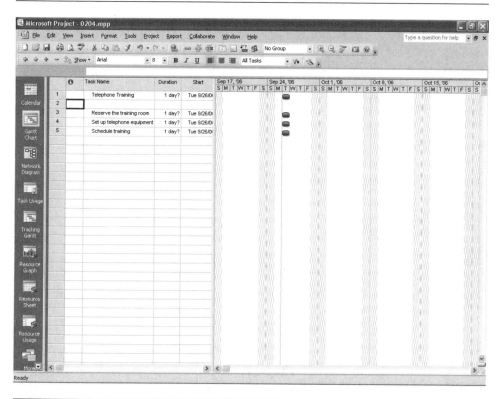

**FIGURE 3-1**   When you insert a new task, Project inserts a blank row.

**3.** Type the name of the task you want to insert—I called it "Contact the Trainer"—and click the check mark button in the Entry bar or press ENTER to accept the new task (see Figure 3-2).

## Creating Subtasks

Often, a task actually consists of several subtasks; the task itself is not big enough to make it a project, but, to complete the task, you must complete a series of steps. For example, after you contact the trainer in the sample project, your company may require that you create a purchase order that authorizes you to hire the trainer.

Start by inserting a blank row below the Contact the Trainer task and then type the task name for the new task—I called mine, "Create Purchase Order"—and save the new task by clicking the check mark in the Entry bar or pressing ENTER. Make sure that the cell pointer rests anywhere on the row of the newly added task

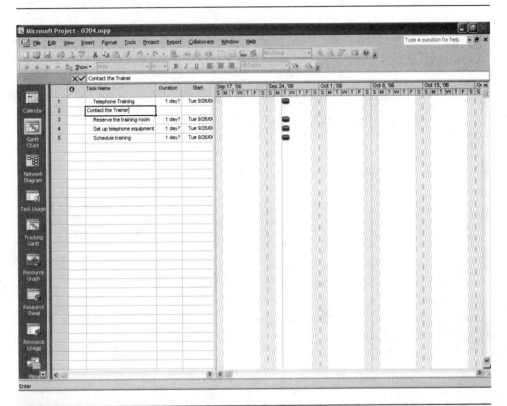

**FIGURE 3-2** Creating a new task

and click the Indent button on the Formatting toolbar to indent the Create Purchase Order task and turn the task into a subtask (see Figure 3-3). In addition, Project displays the task above it—the Contact the Trainer task—in bold and changes the appearance of its Gantt bar; the Contact the Trainer task is now a summary task. Project calculates the duration of the Contact the Trainer summary task using the total durations of all its subtasks.

If you insert additional tasks below a subtask, Project assumes that they, too, are subtasks and indents them accordingly. Click the Outdent button on the Formatting toolbar to return them to the original outline position.

*You can indent and outdent tasks by dragging them. Place your mouse over the first few letters of the task name until the mouse pointer becomes a two-way pointing arrow. Then, drag to the right to indent the task or to the left to outdent it.*

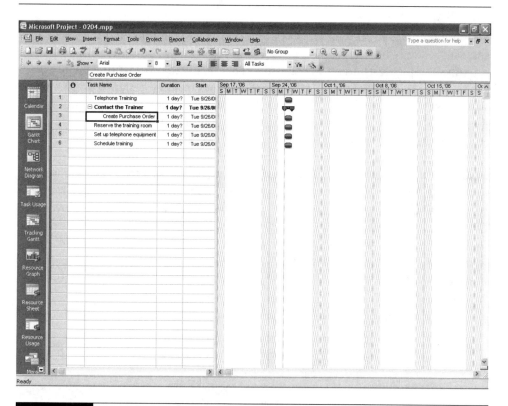

**FIGURE 3-3**   Creating a subtask

## Copying or Moving Tasks

To move or copy tasks, you must select them first. You can select tasks in a number of ways:

- To select a single task, click its ID number or its Gantt bar.

- To select several contiguous tasks, select the first task. Then, hold down SHIFT and click the last task that you want to select.

- To select several noncontiguous tasks, hold down CTRL as you click the ID numbers of the tasks that you want to select.

## Copying Tasks

Suppose that you need to enter tasks to test various versions of a mixture to see which works best as a preservative. You may repeat the same series of tasks (mix the sample, test in various environments, analyze test results, document analysis) several times. Instead of typing the names of those tasks 10 or 20 times, you can save time by copying them. Select them and click the Copy button on the Formatting toolbar; then, click in the cell where you want them to appear and click the Paste button on the Formatting toolbar.

Or, you can use the Fill handle to copy tasks into a contiguous range. To copy using the Fill handle, select the task names—not the IDs—of the tasks you want to copy; the Fill handle is the small black square that appears in the lower-right corner of a selection (see Figure 3-4). When you move the mouse pointer over the Fill handle, it changes to a plus sign (+).

Drag the mouse down until you have selected the group of rows to which you want to copy the selected tasks; when you release the mouse button, Project fills in the cells you selected (see Figure 3-5). Click anywhere outside the selection to cancel the selection.

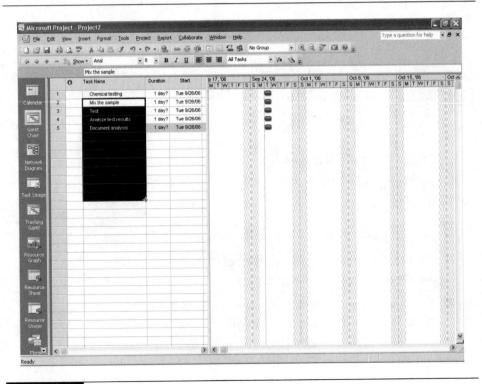

**FIGURE 3-4**   You can use the Fill handle to copy tasks.

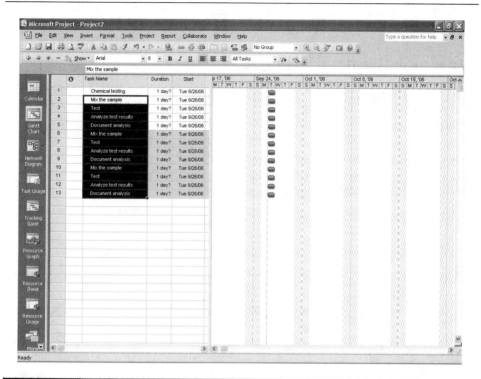

**FIGURE 3-5**    Project copies tasks into the selected range.

 *If the range to which you want to copy already contains information, copying overwrites the existing information. To avoid this problem, insert blank rows in the project before copying.*

## Moving Tasks

To move a task, you can select the task by clicking its row number and then drag it to a new location, or you can use the Formatting toolbar to cut and paste it. However, the task's outline position will be affected when you move it, as follows:

- When you move a summary task, its subtasks move with it.

- If you move a task at the highest level of the outline to a new location just below a task with subtasks, Project demotes the task that you move to make it a subtask.

■ If you move a subtask so that it appears below a task at the highest level of the outline, Project promotes the subtask that you move.

## Hiding or Displaying Tasks

You can take advantage of the outline structure that Project provides to view your project at different levels of detail. By clicking the minus sign (−) that appears beside any summary task, you can hide the subtasks for that summary task; when you click a minus sign, it changes to a plus sign (+), indicating the existence of hidden subtasks. In Figure 3-6, all tasks and subtasks are visible, but in Figure 3-7, I hid the subtasks associated with the Schedule Training summary task. I can redisplay them by clicking the plus sign. When you hide subtasks, Project also hides their Gantt bars.

Using the Show button on the Formatting toolbar, you can control the tasks that appear based on their outline level, and you also can quickly display all the subtasks in your schedule.

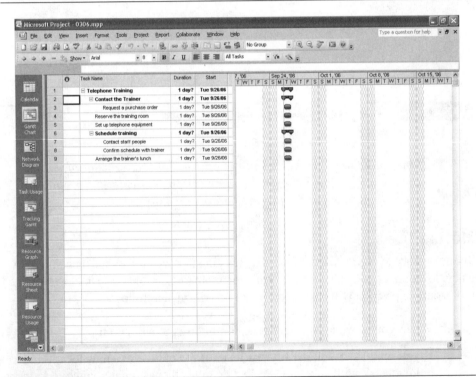

**FIGURE 3-6**  Because no plus signs (+) appear in the outline, you know that Project is displaying all tasks and subtasks.

Using more than three or four levels of outline indentation makes it difficult to see your entire schedule onscreen. In fact, you can use the levels of outline detail as a benchmark to help you define projects of a manageable size. If you find yourself building a very detailed project outline, you should probably re-evaluate the scope of the project and consider breaking it into smaller, more manageable projects.

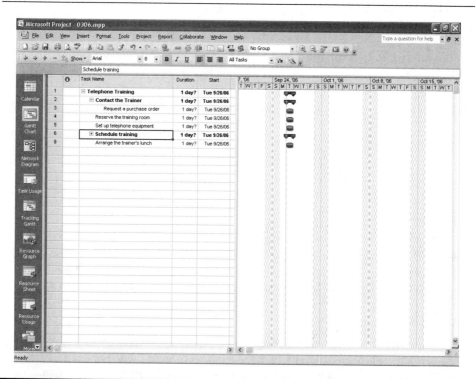

**FIGURE 3-7**  The plus sign (+) beside the Schedule Training task indicates the existence of hidden subtasks.

# Tasks and Timing

When it comes to projects, timing is one of the most critical elements. Initially, every task in a Project schedule is one estimated day long, and all tasks start and end on the same day. In essence, you have listed the steps to get to your goal, but with no related timing. Your schedule is not yet a schedule; at this point, it is just a list.

You have to add durations to your tasks to establish how long—in hours, days, weeks, or months of effort—each task will take. And, in this chapter, we'll examine estimating durations and how Project handles task durations. In Chapter 4, you'll learn how to establish relationships among the tasks.

## Understanding Task Timing

Because you know your business, you're probably pretty good at estimating the time it will take you to complete any given task. When you make an estimate—and you make estimates daily—you analyze the elements of the task that you need to complete, assign an estimated time to each element, and then sum the estimated times. And, you typically allow some extra time, just in case something unexpected comes up.

In addition to your method of estimating task duration, Project can treat the timing of a task in different ways, and you need to understand how Project functions to estimate task durations accurately.

When it comes to timing, Project can create three different types of tasks:

■ Fixed-unit tasks

■ Fixed-duration tasks

■ Fixed-work tasks

In addition, you can affect the behavior of fixed-unit tasks and fixed-duration tasks by using the Effort-driven attribute, which controls the impact on the duration of a task when you add resources to the task. Effort Driven check box (discussed in the 'Establishing Deadline Dates' section, later in the chapter.)

### Fixed-Unit Tasks

By default, each task you create in Project is a resource-driven task that is referred to as a *fixed-unit task*. Suppose that you need to clean a house. One person needs four hours to clean the house. If you add another person (another resource), together they need only two hours to clean the house. Using fixed-unit tasks to create a resource-driven schedule, adding resources reduces task duration, and removing resources increases task duration.

 *The reduction of time required to complete a resource-driven task is strictly a mathematical calculation in Project. Although two people complete the work in half the time mathematically, introducing another resource can increase the task duration because the resources need to communicate.*

3

## Fixed-Duration Tasks

Project also can create *fixed-duration tasks*; for these types of tasks, the number of resources does not affect the task duration. Pregnancy is a fixed-duration task; in humans, pregnancy lasts nine months, and you can't add more women to the job to deliver the baby sooner. In a laboratory experiment, it may take four days to grow a fungus, and you cannot speed up the process by adding lab technicians to the lab.

## Fixed-Work Tasks

For *fixed-work tasks*, you set the duration of the task, and Project assigns a percentage of effort that is sufficient to complete the task in the time that is allotted for each resource that you assign to the task. For example, if you assign four people to work on a one-day task, Project would indicate that each person should spend 25 percent of his or her time on the task to complete it in the time allotted.

## Effort-Driven Tasks

All three task types are effort-driven by default, and, for fixed-work tasks, you have no other choice. But, you can choose to make fixed-duration and fixed-unit tasks effort-driven. If you choose to make these types of tasks effort-driven and you change the number of resources assigned to a task, the amount of work remains the same, but Project redistributes the work equally among all assigned resources. Essentially, Project modifies the percentage of total work that is allocated to each resource based on the number of assigned resources.

I'm going to use Project's default settings; the durations assigned to tasks are resource-driven, and a three-day task requires three days of effort to complete.

# Assigning Task Durations

Assigning durations is simple; you can use one of the following three methods:

- Use the Task Information dialog box
- Use the Duration column of the Gantt table
- Drag a Gantt bar to the required length

 *You don't assign durations for summary tasks, because summary tasks simply roll up the timing of their subtasks and don't have any timing of their own.*

### Assigning Durations from the Task Information Dialog Box

From the Task Information dialog box, you can enter and view information about all aspects of a task, not just its duration. In the Gantt Chart view, double-click a task name to open the Task Information dialog box.

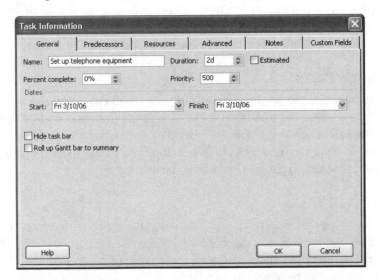

Type a duration in the Duration box. Use the following abbreviations to specify a time frame: m for minutes, h for hours, w for weeks, and mo for months. Click OK to save your settings. The Gantt Chart task bars reflect the new task lengths (see Figure 3-8).

 *If you set start and finish dates for a task, Project uses only working days in that date range when calculating duration. If you enter a duration, Project calculates the beginning and end of the task, taking into consideration weekends and holidays. If you know how many workdays a task will require, but not the days on which the work will occur, use the Duration field to set timing, and let Project calculate the actual work dates based on the calendar.*

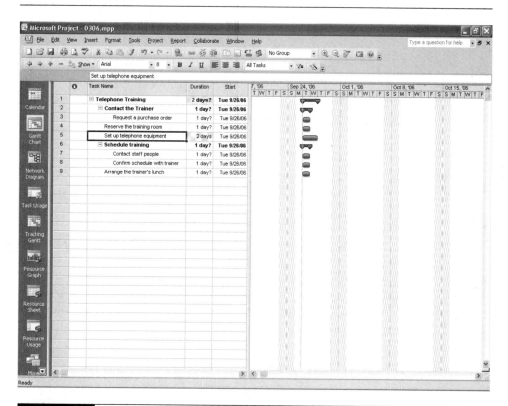

**FIGURE 3-8** Setting a duration updates the task's Gantt Chart bar.

In Project, tasks that have a duration of zero are usually milestones. Managers often use milestones to mark key moments in a project, such as the completion of a phase. The symbol for a milestone on the Gantt Chart is a diamond shape. A task doesn't have to have a duration of zero to be a milestone; you can mark any task as a milestone. On the Advanced tab of the Task Information dialog box, place a check mark in the Mark Task as Milestone check box.

## Entering Durations in the Entry Table

If your focus is to set task durations, entering them on the Entry table of the Gantt View is a quick and easy way to accomplish the task. Simply click in the

Duration column for a task and type in the duration, including an abbreviation (m for minutes, h for hours, w for weeks, and mo for months) to designate the timeframe.

*You can quickly assign the same duration to several contiguous tasks by using the Fill handle. Type the duration for the first task in the group and then drag the Fill handle in the Duration column to copy the duration to the other tasks.*

Project assumes that you are entering planned durations instead of estimated durations unless you type a question mark (?) as you enter the duration.

### Entering Durations by Dragging a Gantt Bar

If you're a visually oriented user, you may find this method the easiest to use. Place your mouse pointer on the right edge of the Gantt Chart until the pointer becomes a vertical line with an arrow extending to the right of it. Click and drag the bar to the right. As you do, Project displays the proposed new task duration and finish date (see Figure 3-9). Release the mouse button when the duration that you want appears in the information box.

## Establishing Deadline Dates

You also can establish a deadline date for a task. Deadline dates would be useful if, for example, you needed to prepare the company's annual report for review at the next board meeting.

Project doesn't use the deadline date when calculating a project's schedule. Instead, a visual cue—a down arrow symbol—appears on the schedule to notify you that a deadline date exists. If you place your mouse over the deadline indicator, Project displays the deadline information (see Figure 3-10).

If the task finishes after the deadline date, you also see a symbol in the Indicators column, but you won't see an indicator if you complete the task prior to the deadline date. Although deadline dates don't affect the calculation of a project schedule, they do affect the calculation of total slack for the project.

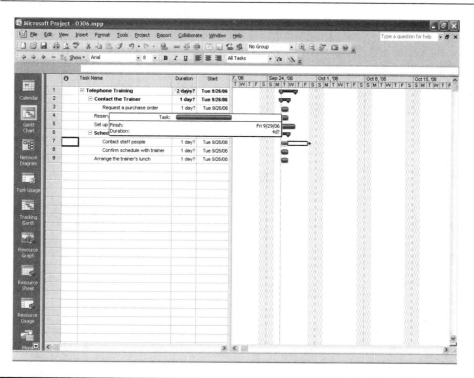

**FIGURE 3-9** You can drag a bar on the Gantt Chart to set a task duration.

You can set a deadline date from the Advanced tab of the Task Information dialog box; double-click the task for which you want to set a deadline.

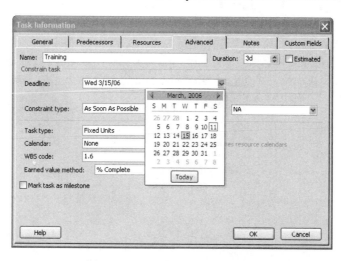

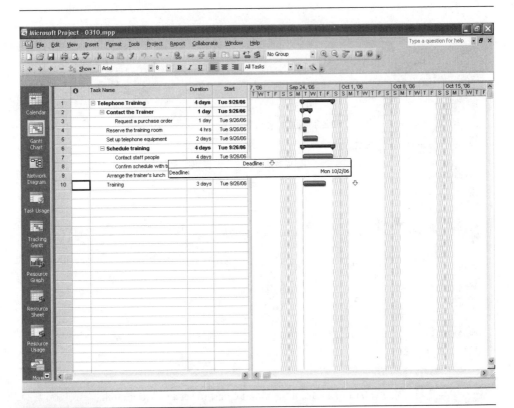

**FIGURE 3-10** The down arrow symbol represents a deadline date.

## Assigning a Calendar to a Task

A task in your project may not follow the project's calendar. You can assign
a different calendar to the task from the Advanced tab of the Task Information
dialog box. Double-click the task name to open the Task Information dialog box
for that task. Click the Advanced tab, and open the Calendar drop-down list to
assign a special calendar for the task.

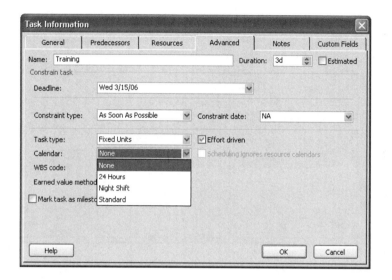

3

*Using the same steps described in Chapter 2 to create the newspaper calendar in the section "Creating a Change to the Work Week," you can create a calendar to assign to a task.*

## Changing the Timescale

After you enter several tasks and task durations, you may want to use different increments of time in the Gantt Chart so that you can concentrate on a particular period in your project or view larger increments with less detail. You can set the timescale to view three levels instead of just two levels.

You can modify the increments of time displayed on the timescale either by double-clicking the timescale or by choosing Format | Timescale to display the Timescale dialog box.

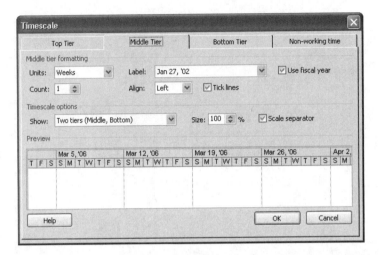

You can change the units for the top tier, the middle tier, and the bottom tier, and you can show more or less of a project, depending on the units you choose for the timescale. By default, Project displays only the middle tier and the bottom tier; the middle tier shows weeks and the bottom tier shows days. To show more of a project, for example, change the middle tier to months and the bottom tier to weeks. To show less of a project—to help you focus on a particular portion of the project—use a timescale that shows days and hours.

# Creating Repeating Tasks

Many projects have weekly staff meetings, monthly budget reviews, or quarterly reports—tasks that occur on a regular basis. Instead of creating 24 weekly staff meeting tasks during the course of a six-month project, you can save time by creating the meeting once and assign a frequency to it. Follow these steps to create a recurring task:

1. Select the task that you want to appear below the recurring task.

2. Choose Insert | Recurring Task to open the Recurring Task Information dialog box.

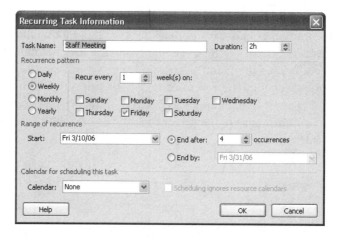

3. Type a name for the recurring task.

4. Set the task duration in the Duration field. For example, you might use a duration of two hours for a staff meeting.

5. Select one of the Recurrence Pattern option buttons: Daily, Weekly, Monthly, or Yearly. Depending on the recurrence that you select, the timing settings to the right change. The figure shows the Weekly settings.

6. Also under Recurrence Pattern, select the settings that describe the frequency with which the task should repeat. For a weekly task, place a check mark next to the day(s) of the week on which you want the task to occur. For a monthly or yearly task, select the day of the month on which you want the task to occur. For a daily task, you have only one choice: whether you want it to occur every day or only on scheduled workdays.

7. In the Range of Recurrence portion of the dialog box, set the period during which the task should recur by entering Start and End after or End by dates. To create a recurring task to prepare a mixture every week for one month of a six-month project, you could set Start and End after or End by dates that designate a month of time.

*By using the End After x Occurrences option, you can ensure that the task will repeat a specific number of times, even if one or more of the designated dates falls on a non-working day. If one of the occurrences falls, for example, on a holiday, Project displays a box that allows you to skip the occurrence or to schedule it on the next working day.*

8. Click OK to create the task.

Project creates the appropriate number of tasks above the selected task and displays them as subtasks under a summary task with the name that you supplied in Step 2. As you can see in Figure 3-11, the recurring task symbol appears in the Indicators column of the Gantt Chart, and the symbol next to each Staff Meeting task in the schedule represents a task with a timing constraint applied. Project applies this constraint automatically as you enter settings for the recurring task. If you move your mouse pointer over one of these symbols, you can see an explanation of that constraint.

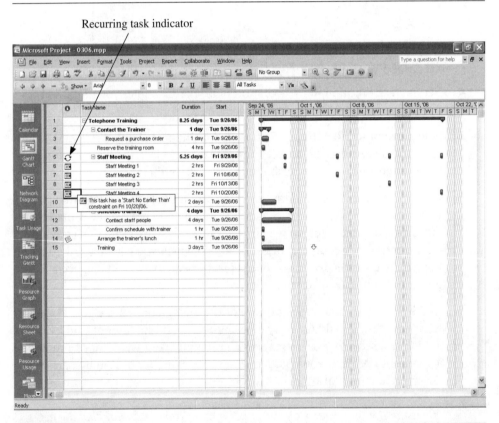

**FIGURE 3-11**    The recurring task symbol appears in the Indicators column beside the Staff Meeting task.

# Entering and Printing Task Notes

As I enter tasks into a project schedule, I find myself thinking about details related to the task—details that I don't want to forget but that I'm not in a position to act on as I create the schedule. For example, suppose that as you set up the task to contact the trainer, you want to be sure to discuss the trainer's lunch during that call. It's also possible that, as you perform one task, you may come upon information that pertains to another task—again, information you don't want to forget but are not in a position to act on at the present time. Suppose that the trainer tells you she'd like a vegetarian lunch.

To ensure that you don't forget to address details such as those in the preceding examples, you can use task notes. Using the Notes tab of the Task Information dialog box, you can store relevant information associated with a task. And, once you've entered a note, Project displays an icon in the Indicators column that serves as a visual reminder; you can slide the mouse pointer over the icon to see the note (see Figure 3-12).

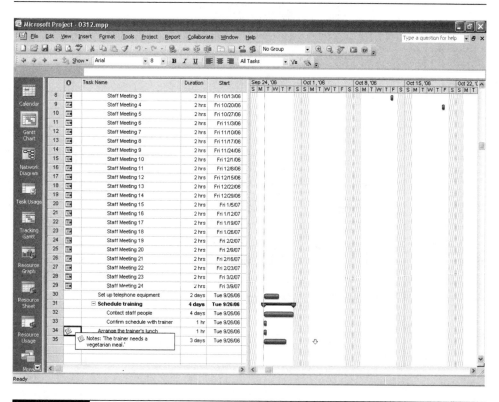

**FIGURE 3-12**   You can see task notes by pointing the mouse at the icon in the Indicators column.

 *You can also attach notes to individual resources and to their assignments, as you find out in Chapter 5.*

To enter a note for a task, follow these steps:

1. Double-click the task to open the Task Information dialog box.

2. Click the Notes tab.

3. Type your note in the area provided. You can use the word processing tools that are above the description box to format your note text.

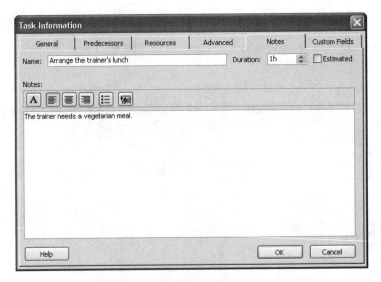

4. Click OK to attach the note to your task.

You also can print notes along with your schedule. Choose File | Page Setup. In the Page Setup dialog box, click the View tab. Check the Print Notes check box and click OK. Notes appear on a separate page after printing your Gantt Chart when you check the Print Notes option.

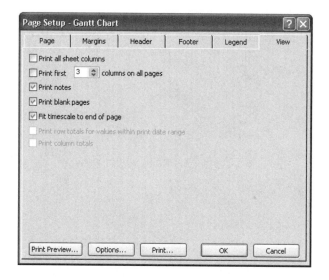

**NOTE** *You find out more about printing schedules in Chapter 7.*

In this chapter, you finished learning the basics of entering tasks, including establishing task durations. Chapter 4 shows you how to establish relationships between tasks—task dependencies.

# Chapter 4

## Working with Dependencies and Constraints

## How to...

- Recognize the types of task constraints available in Project
- Create constraints
- Recognize the types of dependencies available in Project
- Create dependencies
- Create overlaps and delays
- View dependencies
- Delete dependencies

Constraints and dependencies are the major building blocks in a project that control timing. A task constraint affects the timing of the task in relation to either a specific date or the start or end of your project. A task dependency, on the other hand, affects the timing of the task in relation to other tasks in the project. In this chapter, we're going to explore the types of task constraints and dependencies you'll find in Project and how to use them.

# Tasks and Dependencies

You can't know the total time that you will need to complete a project until you establish durations and dependencies. If you set up a project with three tasks, each of which takes five days to complete, and you don't assign dependencies, the project will take five days to complete. But, if the tasks must happen sequentially, then your project will take 15 days to complete.

You set dependencies to specify the order in which tasks must occur on a project. You use dependencies to account for a variety of situations. For example, you may need to get approval from the building inspector before you can move into your new house. So, you may need to order these two tasks so that one follows the other.

In Project, the *predecessor task* is the task that must occur before another task, and the *successor task* is the task that occurs later in the relationship. Any given task can have multiple predecessors and successors, and in Project, you *link* tasks to create dependencies. These links appear on Gantt Charts as lines between task bars, and an arrow at one end points to the successor task. In Figure 4-1, Contact the Trainer is the predecessor task and Request a Purchase Order is the successor task.

Link line

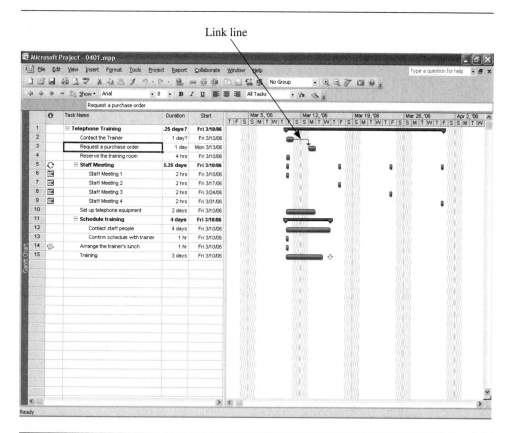

**FIGURE 4-1**   Lines between tasks indicate links and dependencies between tasks.

# Understanding Dependency Types

You can use one of four dependencies to define the relationship between the start and finish of tasks:

- Start-to-finish
- Finish-to-start
- Start-to-start
- Finish-to-finish

The first timing mentioned in each relationship name describes the predecessor task's role in the relationship, and the second timing describes the successor's role. So, a finish-to-start relationship relates the finish of the predecessor task to the start of the successor task. Project refers to these relationships by their initials, such as SS for a start-to-start relationship. The direction of the arrow on the link between the tasks gives you a visual clue describing the type of dependency.

A finish-to-start relationship is the most common type of dependency; you must install software on a computer before you can use the software. The two tasks shown in Figure 4-2 have a finish-to-start relationship.

With the start-to-finish relationship, the successor task cannot finish until the predecessor task starts. For example, employees cannot start using the new telephone system until the system is installed and tested, and employees have been trained to use the system. The two tasks shown in Figure 4-3 have a start-to-finish relationship. Notice the direction of the arrow that connects the two tasks.

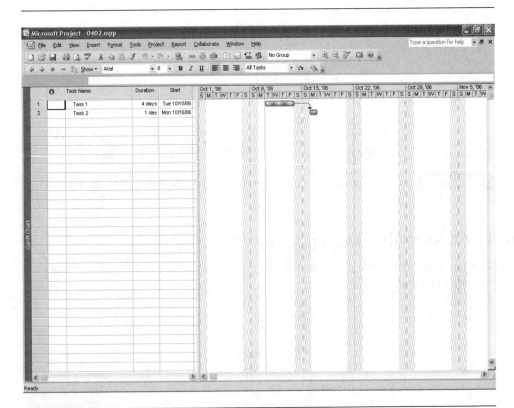

**FIGURE 4-2**   These tasks have a finish-to-start relationship.

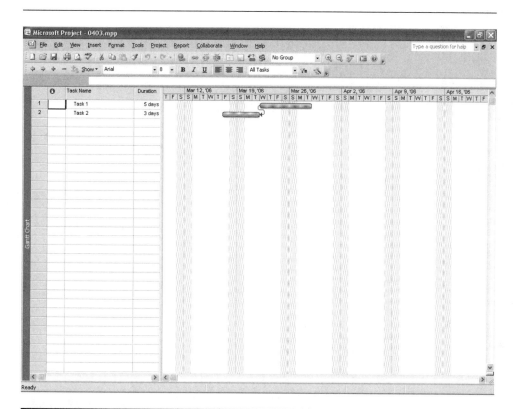

**FIGURE 4-3**    A start-to-finish relationship

In a start-to-start relationship, the successor can't start until the predecessor starts. For example, when horses start a race, you can begin to time them. The two tasks in Figure 4-4 have a start-to-start relationship.

In the final dependency type, the finish-to-finish dependency, the successor task can't finish until the predecessor task finishes. You can finish buying plants at the same time that you finish digging the garden so that you can plant the garden right away. In other words, you do not need to finish buying plants until

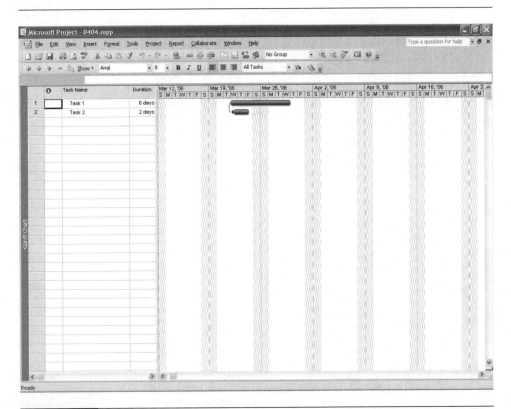

**FIGURE 4-4**    A start-to-start relationship

the digging is complete. The two tasks in Figure 4-5 have a finish-to-finish dependency.

*You can set dependencies between two summary tasks or between a summary task and a subtask in another task group by using a finish-to-start or a start-to-start dependency. You cannot use any other type of dependency, and you cannot set dependencies between a summary task and any of its own subtasks.*

## Creating Dependencies

Project provides several ways to quickly and easily create finish-to-start relationships; because of the ease with which one can create the finish-to-start relationship, I prefer to

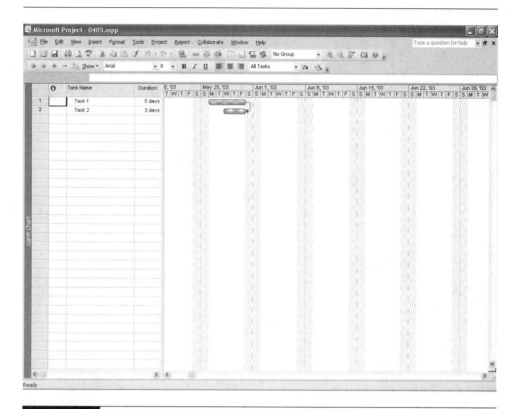

**FIGURE 4-5** A finish-to-finish relationship

link tasks using the finish-to-start dependency and then change the type of dependency from finish-to-start to one of the other dependency types. So, let's start by exploring the ways to create a finish-to-start relationship.

First, you can use the table portion of the Gantt Chart view to type the ID number of a successor's predecessor in the Predecessors column; in Figure 4-6, Task 4's predecessor is Task 3.

Or, you can drag Gantt Chart bars to set finish-to-start dependencies; follow these steps:

1. Place your mouse pointer over the predecessor task until the pointer turns into four arrows pointing outward.

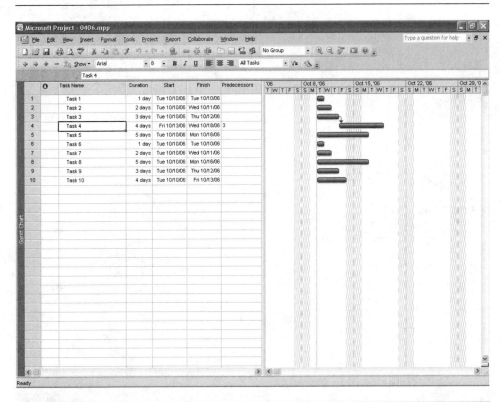

**FIGURE 4-6** You can establish a finish-to-start relationship using the Entry table of the Gantt Chart.

**2.** Drag the mouse pointer to the second task. An information box describes the finish-to-start link that you are about to create (see Figure 4-7).

**3.** Release your mouse button when you're satisfied with the relationship; Project establishes the link.

If you prefer, you can use the Link Tasks tool or menu command. Select the tasks that you want to link. Then, click the Link Tasks tool or choose Edit | Link Tasks. Project establishes the link.

Link Tasks button

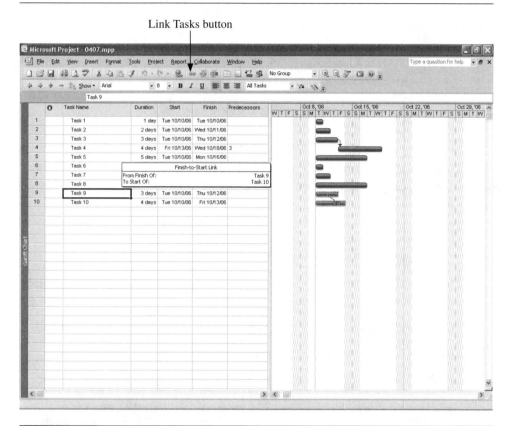

**FIGURE 4-7**    Drag to establish a finish-to-start relationship.

*To select adjacent tasks, drag through their ID numbers in the Gantt Chart table. To select nonadjacent tasks, hold down CTRL as you click the ID numbers of the tasks that you want to link.*

You can use either the Task Dependency dialog box or the Task Information dialog box to set any type of dependency. Use the Task Dependency dialog box to establish dependency types or lag times between tasks. You can open the Task

Dependency dialog box by double-clicking the line that connects the tasks that you want to change.

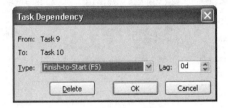

You can use the Task Information dialog box to establish lead times as well as dependencies and lag times. Follow these steps:

*You can read about lag and lead times in the next section.*

1. Double-click the task ID or the task name of the successor task.

2. In the Task Information dialog box that appears, select the Predecessors tab if it's not already displayed.

3. Click in the Task Name column; a drop-down arrow appears at its far end.

4. Click the drop-down arrow to display the drop-down list of task names.

5. Click the task that you want to establish as a predecessor to this task.

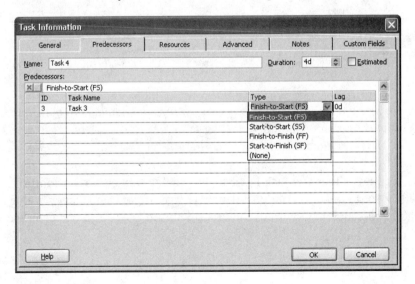

**6.** Click the Type field; a list box arrow appears.

**7.** Click the arrow to display a list of dependency types.

**8.** Click the type of dependency that you want to establish, such as start-to-start or start-to-finish.

**9.** Click OK.

4

## Overlapping and Delaying Tasks

Sometimes, you need to incorporate overlap and delay into task relationships; in Project, you add lag time or lead time to the dependency relationship. Let's look at examples of lag and lead time.

Suppose that your project involves baking bread. In the first task, you mix the ingredients for the dough, and in the second task, you bake the bread. However, you need to allow the bread to rise for four hours before you bake. In this case, you build in a delay between the finish of the predecessor task and the start of the successor task. When you build in lag time, the line between the two tasks that indicates the dependency is longer than usual; the space between the bars represents the gap in time between the finish of one task and the start of the next (see Figure 4-8).

Suppose that you are planning Thanksgiving dinner. In addition to cooking the turkey, you're making sweet potatoes that require 1.5 hours to cook, and you need to start baking the sweet potatoes while the turkey is still roasting. You don't particularly want the sweet potatoes and turkey to finish cooking at the same time, because the turkey needs to sit untouched for 30 minutes after you take it out of the oven before you carve it. So, you want to put the sweet potatoes in the oven while the turkey is still cooking but time the sweet potatoes to finish cooking when you call everyone to the table. The tasks to cook the turkey and the sweet potatoes will overlap, but they won't necessarily finish at the same time.

To let the turkey sit untouched after it finishes cooking, you want to establish some lag time between the time the turkey finishes cooking and the time you call everyone to the table. And, you want to build in lead time to set the table no more than one hour before you call everyone to the table; that way, the ice

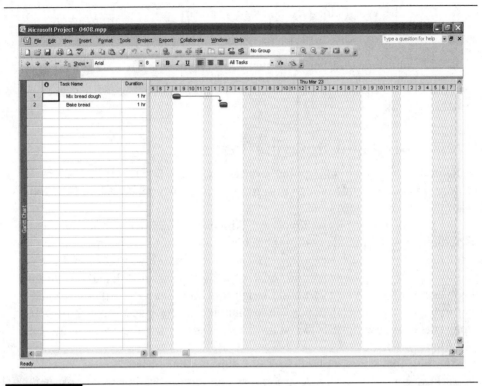

**FIGURE 4-8**    Building in lag time

in the water glasses won't melt. The schedule shown in Figure 4-9 represents
a flexible schedule; if you change the roasting time, all the other tasks will
adjust accordingly.

NOTE    *I changed the timescale so that you can see the hours of the day.*

You create lag or lead time by using the Predecessors tab of the Task Information
dialog box or by double-clicking the link line to display the Task Dependency

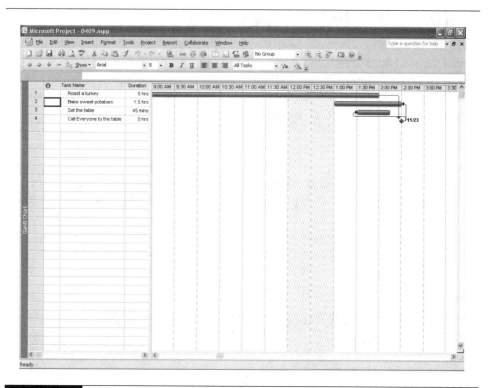

**FIGURE 4-9**    A schedule containing both lag and lead time

dialog box. You create lag time by entering a positive duration in the Lag field, and you create lead time by entering a negative duration in the Lag field.

## Viewing and Deleting Dependencies

After you've established several dependencies in a project, you can study them in several ways. You can, of course, open each task's Task Information dialog box and look at the relationships listed on the Predecessors tab, but that approach can be time-consuming. You can also study the lines drawn between the tasks. Or, you can scroll to the right in the Gantt table, or you can reduce the size of the Gantt Chart to see more of the Gantt table and display the Predecessors column. In this column, you'll see the task number of each predecessor along with two-letter abbreviations for the dependency type and lag and overlap time; if the dependency is finish-to-start and no lag or lead time exists, Project displays only the task ID number of the predecessor.

Perhaps the easiest way to explore dependencies is to use the Task Driver feature in Project. Choose Project | Task Drivers; Project displays a pane along the left side of the screen that contains information related to the factors that affect the start date of the selected task (see Figure 4-10). Select a different task, and the information in the pane changes.

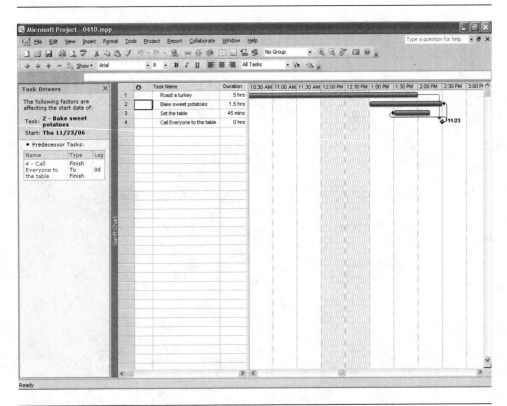

**FIGURE 4-10**   Use the Task Drivers pane to explore dependencies.

You can delete dependencies in several ways:

- Double-click the task ID or task name of the successor task, select the Predecessors tab, click the task name for the link that you want to break, and press DELETE.

- Using the Predecessors column in the Gantt table, press the DELETE key to delete all relationships for a successor task. To change only some of the relationship, click the Predecessors cell then press F2 to edit the information.

- Select the tasks that are involved in the dependency that you want to delete and click the Unlink Tasks tool 🔗, or choose Edit | Unlink Tasks.

- Double-click the dependency line and click the Delete button in the Task Dependency dialog box.

If you delete a dependency, Project adjusts the schedule.

# Establishing Task Constraints

By default, Project assigns an As Soon As Possible constraint to every task, making every task start on the first day of the project. You can set other constraints, as shown in Table 4-1.

| Constraint Type | Explanation |
| --- | --- |
| As Soon As Possible | This constraint forces a task to start on a date as soon as possible. |
| As Late As Possible | This constraint forces a task to start on a date as late as possible without delaying the start date of successor tasks. |
| Finish No Earlier Than/Finish No Later Than | These constraints set the completion of a task to fall no sooner or later, respectively, than a specific date. |
| Must Finish On/Must Start On | These constraints force a task to finish or start, respectively, on a specific date. |
| Start No Earlier Than/Start No Later Than | These constraints set the start of a task to fall no sooner or later, respectively, than a specific date. |

**TABLE 4-1**   Types of Constraints

Only the Must Finish On/Must Start On constraints force a task to start or end on a particular date. All the other constraints force the task to occur within a certain timeframe.

Under what circumstances would constraints other than As Soon As Possible be useful? In the project where your company is implementing a new telephone system, you may want to use an As Late As Possible constraint on the training task.

You set constraints from the Advanced tab of the Task Information dialog box. Select a constraint type from the Constraint Type drop-down list. For all settings in the list other than As Late As Possible and As Soon As Possible, type a date in the Constraint Date field or click its drop-down arrow and select a date from the drop-down calendar that appears.

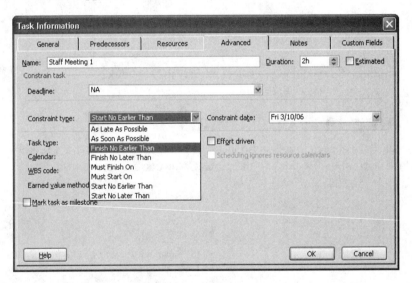

## Constraints, Dependencies, and Conflicts

Because constraints and dependencies both drive the timing of a task, you can unintentionally create a conflict. Suppose that the telephone system project contains two tasks: Task 1, to go live with the new phone system, and Task 2, to test the phone system. You apply a constraint to Task 1 to start the task on April 1. Task 2 is scheduled for completion on April 5. You then try to set up a dependency between Task 1 and Task 2, making Task 2 dependent on

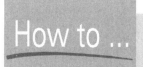

## Insert Columns to Work with Constraints

You can add columns to any table to help you easily work with constraints. For example, you can add the Constraint Type column or the Constraint Date column; follow these steps:

**1.** Right-click the column that you want to appear to the right of the new column you're about to insert.

**2.** Click Insert Column.

**3.** In the Column Definition dialog box that appears, open the Field Name drop-down list and select the field you want to add as a column.

**4.** Click OK, and Project adds a column for the field.

Task 1, and Project displays a Planning Wizard dialog box, notifying you of a scheduling conflict. You'll see this dialog box when a conflict exists among dependencies or between constraints and dependencies.

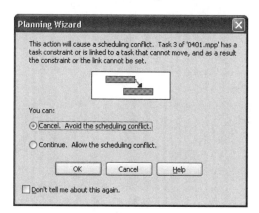

Whenever a conflict exists between a constraint and a dependency, Project uses the constraint to determine the timing of the task, honoring the constraint-imposed date.

*If you prefer to let dependencies determine timing, you can change Project's behavior. Choose Tools | Options. On the Schedule tab of the Options dialog box, remove the check mark from the Tasks Will Always Honor Their Constraint Dates check box.*

In this chapter, you learned about constraints and dependencies, the two tools that affect timing. In the next chapter, you add resources to tasks, in preparation to calculating project cost.

# Chapter 5

# Working with Resources

## How to...

■ Create a list of resources

■ Manage resource availability

■ Assign resources to tasks

■ Remove or replace resource assignments

In Chapters 3 and 4, you learned how to create tasks and assign task constraints and dependencies. To truly manage a project, you need to assign resources—people, materials, or both—to each task. As you create resources, Project lets you assign rates to the resources because resources cost money to use and therefore affect the cost of the project. When you assign the resource to a task in your project, Microsoft Office Project automatically calculates the cost of the task and your project. And the way that you assign resources can change the duration and length of your project and therefore change the project cost.

# Setting Up Resources

Resources are the people, supplies, and equipment that enable you to complete the tasks in your project. In Project, you define work resources, material resources, and cost resources. *Work resources* are equipment or people that spend time working on a task. You define the amount of time that work resources have to spend on a project. For example, for a person who works 40 hours per week, an assignment of 100 percent means that the person will devote all of his time to the task, and a 50 percent assignment means the person will devote half of his time (20 hours per week) to the task.

*Material resources* are items that are used while working on a project. Think of paper, gasoline, or wood as material resources. When you define a material resource, you identify units that are appropriate to measure the quantity of the material resource, and you also indicate whether the amount of material used is based on time or is fixed. For example, the number of gallons of water that are used when filling a swimming pool depends on the amount of time that you run the water and the number of gallons per hour that flow from the faucet. On the other hand, you need two tons of concrete to build a swimming pool, regardless of how long you take to dig the hole and pour the cement.

*Cost resources* give you a way to add a fixed cost to a task without making the cost depend on work performed. If your project requires that you rent a storage unit during part of the project, you can set up the storage unit as a resource that you can assign to tasks during the appropriate periods to account for the cost of the storage unit as part of the task.

## Creating a List of Resources

If you define and assign resources, you can easily identify the tasks that are being performed by various resources because Project displays the resources that are assigned to each task. You also can identify potential resource shortages before you miss a scheduled deadline. And, you can identify underutilized resources that you might be able to reassign to shorten the project's schedule.

When you assign resources to an effort-driven task—the type that Project creates by default—the resource assignments affect the duration of the task. For example, when you assign two people to a task, Project reduces the task's duration by half; when you reduce the duration of a task, you may ultimately reduce the duration of the entire project. If you assign a resource to work part-time on an effort-driven task, you may find that you can complete several tasks at the same time.

On any task with a fixed duration or to which don't assign resources, Project uses only the task duration, task dependency, and task constraint information that you provide to calculate the duration of the project.

I find it easiest to use the Resource Sheet to initially create resources; I can then edit them if I need to make changes to settings. To display the Resource Sheet (see Figure 5-1), click the Resource Sheet button on the View bar or choose View | Resource Sheet.

*If you use the same resources for all your projects, you might want to set up resources in a blank project that contains no tasks, effectively creating a pool of resources in one project. Then you can use Project's resource pool feature to share resources across multiple projects without setting up the resources repeatedly.*

*For more information about resource pooling and managing multiple projects outside Project Server, see Chapter 17. If you use Project Server, you will probably set up enterprise resources, which are resources used across your organization and stored in the Project Server database. Setting up enterprise resources is beyond the scope of this book, but you can read about the concepts in Chapter 18.*

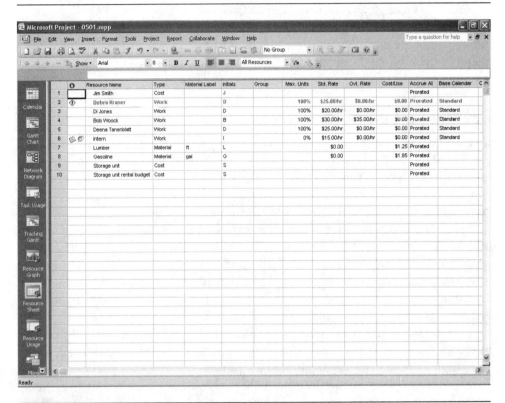

**FIGURE 5-1** By default, Project displays the Entry table of the Resource Sheet.

If you want to add resources that exist in your company address book, you may find it easier to use the Resources page of the Project Guide, which displays a specialized Resource Sheet view. Click the Resources button on the Project Guide toolbar to display the page. Then, click the first link, Specify People and Equipment for the Project, to see the page shown next. Select Add Resources from the Company Address Book, click the Address Book link that appears, and follow the onscreen instructions.

 *The version of the Resource Sheet that appears when you use the Project Guide contains slightly different columns from those in the Resource Sheet that appears in Figure 5-1.*

Using the Resource Sheet helps you avoid accidentally creating the same resource twice. For example, Project sees Debbie and Debi as two resources, even though you may have simply misspelled the name the second time.

Each column in the Resource Sheet represents a piece of information you supply for a resource as you create the resource. Simply press TAB to move from column to column for each resource. Table 5-1 describes the information you enter into the Resource Sheet.

*You can customize the Resource Sheet to show other information that you may want to store for each resource. See Chapter 8 to find out how to insert a column in a table.*

| Field Name | Type of Information |
|---|---|
| Indicators | You don't type in this column; instead, icons appear in this column from time to time to alert you to various conditions or situations. For example, you may see an indicator for an overallocated resource (in Figure 5-1, Debra Kraner is overallocated) or an indicator that you entered a note about the resource. If you point at an indicator with your mouse, Project displays the information that is associated with the indicator icon. |
| Resource Name | Type the name of the resource. For a human resource, you can type their name or a job description, such as Product Analyst 1 or Intern. |
| Type | Use this column to specify whether you're defining a human (work), material, or cost resource. |
| Material Label | Type the unit of measure for a material resource. For example, you can use feet to measure lumber and gallons to measure gasoline. |
| Initials | Project enters the first letter of the resource name by default. |
| Group | You can classify resources that share some common characteristic, such as job function, using the Group field so that you can filter or sort project information about a group. Just type a name to create a group, making sure that you spell the group name the same way each time you use it; otherwise, filtering and sorting won't work. |
| Max. Units | Use this column to define the maximum amount of a resource you have available. For work resources, use a percentage, with 100 percent representing one person's full-time effort and 200 percent representing two full-time resources. |
| Std. Rate | Enter the rate that you charge for the resource during regular business hours for a resource. For a material resource, type a rate per unit based on the Material Label column. For a work resource, Project assumes you charge by the hour (and calculates cost by multiplying number of hours by the rate per hour), but you can charge in minutes, days, weeks, months, or years. To specify a time increment other than hours, type a forward slash and then the first letter of the word representing the time increment. For example, to charge for a resource by the day, type /d after the rate that you specify. |
| Ovt. Rate | The overtime rate is the rate that you charge for using a resource outside regular business hours. |
| Cost/Use | Think of the cost per use as a fixed fee for using a resource; it may cost you $50 to rent a room. Project will calculate a resource's cost using a combination of the cost per use and the standard rate. Project uses the formula *cost per use + (standard rate × number of units)*. That same room rental may cost you $50 as a setup fee (the Cost/Use value) and then $25/hour (the Std. Rate value) for each hour you use it. |

**TABLE 5-1**   Resource Sheet Fields

5

| Field Name | Type of Information |
|---|---|
| Accrue At | Use the choices in this list field to specify how and when Microsoft Office Project charges resource costs to a task. By default, Project accrues the resource cost of the task on a prorated basis; a five-day task costing a total of $1000 will accrue at $200/day. But you also can select Start to have Project calculate the resource cost for a task as soon as the task begins, showing a cost of $1000 for the first day and $0 for days 2 through 5 of our five-day task. Or, you can select End to have Project calculate the resource cost for the task when the task is completed, showing a cost of $0 for the first four days and $1000 for the fifth day of our five-day task. |
| Base Calendar | This field identifies the calendar that Project should use when scheduling the resource to identify working and non-working time. By default, Project assigns the Standard calendar to each resource, but you can create calendars, for example, to handle shift work. |
| Code | Use the Code field as a catchall field to assign any information. Typically, you use an abbreviation of some sort. For example, you may want to track the company department to which each resource is assigned in your project. You can sort and filter information by the abbreviations that you supply in the Code field. |

**TABLE 5-1**    Resource Sheet Fields (*continued*)

NOTE *It is easy to confuse a cost resource with a resource with a cost per use rate. I distinguish them this way: A cost resource's cost may change each time you use it, whereas a resource with a cost per use costs the same amount each time you use it. The cost of airline tickets (a cost resource) depends on when and where you fly. The cost for using a printing press (a cost per use material resource) includes a setup fee that remains the same each time you run the press plus a standard fee based on the standard rate per hour or the standard rate per page.*

After you create a resource, Project displays the resource's ID number on the left edge of the Resource Sheet, to the left of the Indicators column.

## Modifying Resource Information

You can modify information for a resource on the Resource Sheet or in the Resource Information dialog box. To display the Resource Information dialog box, double-click any resource on the Resource Sheet or choose Project | Resource Information. You already provided most of the resource information on the Resource Sheet; Project displays that information on the General tab of the Resource Information dialog box.

Let's look at some of the fields that are available on the General tab of the dialog box that don't appear on the Resource Sheet.

*Remember, if you store the following information for most resources, you can add these fields to the Resource Sheet view; see Chapter 8 for details on adding a column to a table such as the Resource Sheet.*

First, you can type the e-mail address of a resource in the Email field. If you use Outlook, you can click the Details button to find the resource's information in the Outlook Contacts list and copy and paste it.

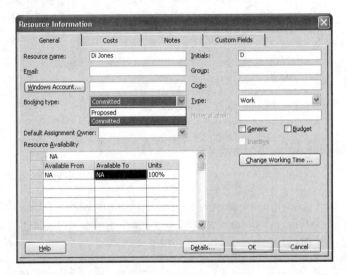

If you use Windows authentication, you can click the Windows Account button in the Resource Information dialog box to import the Windows Account information for the user.

The Default Assignment Owner field is also a Project Server-related field that enables you to identify a resource to serve as the owner of any assignments made to the selected resource. In Project Server, assignment owners have privileges that others do not.

## Understanding Booking Types

Booking types are most useful if you use Project Server. In the Booking Type field, you can select either Committed or Proposed. You officially assign a resource to a project when you choose Committed. Proposing a resource does not officially assign the resource to the project; if another project manager commits the resource to a different project for the same timeframe, Project will not indicate that the resource is overallocated. If you assign a booking type to a resource, Project applies that booking type to all tasks in your project to which you assign the resource.

## Using Generic Resources

You can set up a resource as generic by placing a check mark in the Generic box on the General tab of the Resource Information dialog box. Generic resources are descriptions of the skills that you need to complete a task instead of specific people, equipment, or materials. Although the generic resource feature was designed primarily for use with Project Server, you can use generic resources when you don't care who does the work—you simply need to account for the cost of getting the work done on the project. The Intern resource shown earlier in figure 5-1 is a generic resource. It's a job description, not a person.

## Setting Up Budget Resources

You also can set up a resource to act as a budget resource. Budget resources can be assigned only to the project summary task and give you the opportunity to specify how work or costs will be allocated during the project. Suppose, for example, that you want to budget for the cost of the storage unit required during the life of your project. You would create a cost budget resource for the storage unit and assign the budget resource to the project summary task. Then, you can assign a value to the budget resource either as a lump sum by adding the Budget Cost field to the Gantt table or over time by adding the Budget Cost field to the Task Usage view or the Resource Usage view. After you start recording actual values, you can compare budget amounts to actual amounts.

*Project doesn't display the project summary task by default. From the Gantt Chart view, choose Tools | Options. At the bottom of the View tab, click Show Project Summary Task and then click OK.*

You also can set up a work budget resource and assign it to the project summary task. Then, you can add the Budget Work field to the Task Usage view or the Resource Usage view and record the number of hours of work you want to budget for the entire project. As you track the work for your project's tasks, you can compare the work performed with the budgeted work.

*The Resource Availability table of the General tab of the Resource Information dialog box is described in the next section, "Setting Up Resource Availability."*

## Working with Resource Notes

On the Notes tab of the Resource Information dialog box, shown next, you'll find a free-form text box in which you can type any information that you want to store about the resource, such as a reminder about a resource's upcoming vacation, an explanation about resource availability, or notes concerning the purpose of a resource cost. After you type text in this box and click OK, a Note indicator icon appears in the Indicators column on the Resource Sheet; if you place your mouse pointer over the icon in the Indicators column, Project displays the contents of the note.

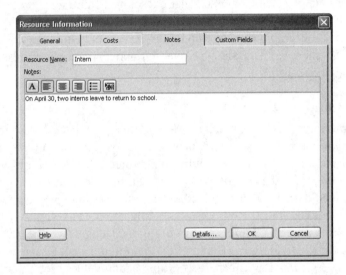

# Setting Up Resource Availability

Not all resources are available 100 percent of the timeframe of a project. Resources might not be available for a variety of reasons. In this section, we explore various reasons why a resource might not be available and how to account for the unavailability in Project.

## Setting Project Start and Finish Dates

Suppose that you intend to use a resource with a type of Work who will not be available during the entire timeframe of the project; your resource will be available for a three-month period, from April 1 to June 30. You can use the Resource Availability table in the Resource Information dialog box to identify the period of time that a resource will be available.

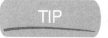

*You also can use the Resource Availability table to specify periods of time when the resource is available only part-time.*

Double-click the resource in the Resource Sheet view and click the General tab. In the Resource Availability table, click in the Available From and Available To boxes and select starting and ending dates. In the Units box, specify the percentage of time the resource will be available; for example, if the resource will be available only half of the time, type 50%.

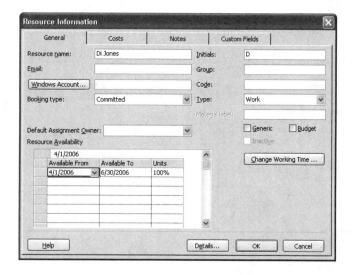

## Setting Work Hours

As you read in Chapter 2, Project uses the Standard calendar to calculate the timing of the project. By default, Project assumes that each resource works according to the workday hours defined in the Standard calendar. But it isn't necessary for all resources to follow the schedule defined by the Standard calendar. You can create a calendar for a resource so that Project can continue to accurately predict the completion of tasks and your project while taking into account varying resource work schedules.

*Having accurate resource calendars can make a major impact on a project schedule. For example, if your project involves running an experiment that requires monitoring, and the resource who monitors the experiment is never available on Wednesdays, you don't want Project to schedule the experiment for a Wednesday.*

Suppose that your Standard calendar defines a 40-hour work week as Monday through Friday from 8:00 A.M. to 5:00 P.M. with one hour for lunch from 12:00 P.M. to 1:00 P.M. And suppose that Di Jones actually works her 40-hour week by working 7:00 A.M. to 6:00 P.M. (10 hours a day) on Monday through Thursday, taking an hour for lunch between 12:00 P.M. and 1:00 P.M. To create a resource calendar for her, follow these steps:

1. Double-click her entry on the Resource Sheet to open the Resource Information dialog box.

2. On the General tab, click the Change Working Time button.

3. In the Change Working Time dialog box, click the Work Weeks tab.

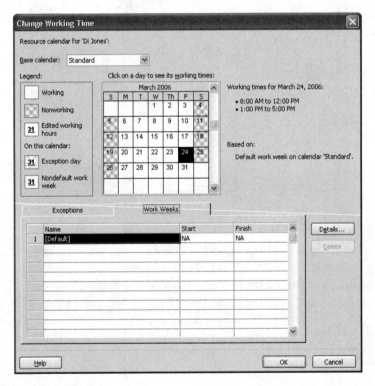

4. Select the [Default] entry.

5. Click the Details button.

**6.** Click the Set Day(s) to These Specific Working Times option.

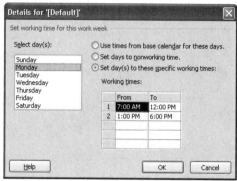

**7.** Click Monday and set the times for Di's schedule.

**8.** Repeat Step 7 for Tuesday, Wednesday, and Thursday.

**9.** Click Friday.

**10.** Click the Set Days to Nonworking Time option.

**11.** Click OK. Project redisplays the Change Working Time dialog box.

Click any Monday, Tuesday, Wednesday, or Thursday on the calendar to view Di's work schedule to the right of the calendar. Click any Friday, and Project indicates that Friday is a non-working day. Click OK to save Di's resource calendar.

*To avoid overallocating a resource that works part of a day, level the resource on a day-by-day basis. Read more about handling overallocations in Chapter 11.*

## Blocking Off Vacation Time

It's inevitable; human resources take vacation time. If you mark vacation days on the resource's calendar, you can help Project to track schedule dates more accurately and avoid overallocating a person by assigning work during a vacation period. Consider vacation days as an exception to the resource's calendar. Follow these steps:

**1.** Double-click the resource's entry on the Resource Sheet to open the Resource Information dialog box.

**2.** On the General tab, click the Change Working Time button.

**3.** In the Change Working Time dialog box, click the Exceptions tab.

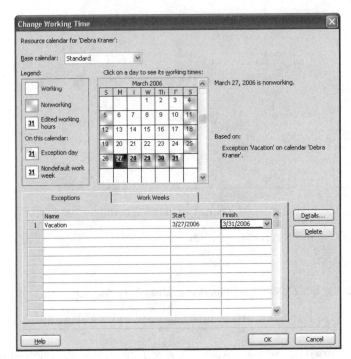

*You can identify the vacation days using the calendar. If necessary, use the scroll bar on the calendar to find and click the first day. Then press SHIFT and click the last day that you want to select. If you use this approach, press the RIGHT ARROW key after Step 4 and skip Step 5.*

**4.** In the Name box, type a name for this calendar exception—I called mine Vacation.

**5.** In the Start and Finish boxes, select the starting and ending dates of the resource's vacation time.

*You can click to move from field to field or use the RIGHT ARROW key to move from the Name field to the Start field and from the Start field to the Finish field. To select a date, you can type it or use the drop-down arrow that Project displays in the field.*

**6.** Click OK twice to save the exception.

Project marks the selected days as non-working time.

# Assigning Resources

Once you get your resources set up, you can begin to assign them to tasks. You can easily assign resources to tasks from the Gantt Chart view. From the View bar, click Gantt Chart or choose View | Gantt Chart. Then, follow these steps to assign resources to tasks:

**1.** Select the task to which you want to assign a resource. You can click the task bar on the Gantt Chart, or you can click any column for the task in the Gantt table.

**2.** Click the Assign Resources button or choose Tools | Assign Resources to open the Assign Resources window, shown in Figure 5-2.

Assign Resources button

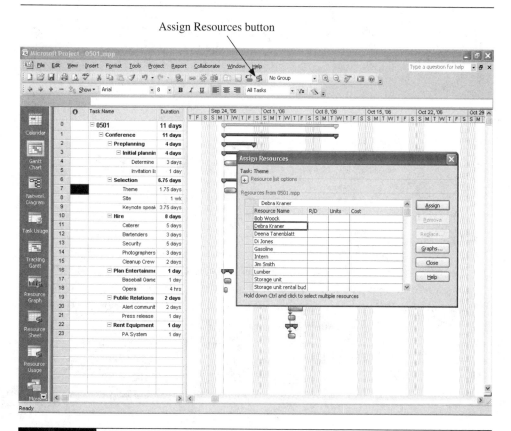

**FIGURE 5-2**    The Assign Resources window

3. In the Assign Resources window, click the resource that you want to assign from the Resource Name list. If you forgot to define the resource you want to assign, just type the name of the resource in the Resource Name column.

**NOTE** *Use the R/D column only if your organization uses Project Server and you intend to use the Resource Substitution wizard. Type R for Request to indicate that you can use any resource with the required skills to work on the task. Type D for Demand to indicate that you specifically require the selected resource to work on the task.*

4. Project assigns 100 percent of the resource by default; if you want to assign 100 percent of the resource, go on to Step 5. Otherwise, type the quantity of the resource as a percentage in the Units column and move to Step 6. Project assumes percentages, so you don't need to type the percent sign (%).

5. Click the Assign button. Project places a check mark in the leftmost column of the Assign Resources window to indicate that the resource is assigned to the selected task.

## Assigning Material Resources

By their nature, you can use material resources in fixed or variable ways. When you use a material resource in a fixed way, you use the same quantity of the material, no matter how long the task lasts; to pour the foundation of a house, you'll need five tons of concrete, and the time to pour the concrete doesn't matter. When you use a material resource in a variable way, the length of the task does affect the amount of the material that you will use; when you water the lawn, the amount of water that you use depends on how long you run the sprinkler system. When you supply the rate at which you use a material resource, Project recognizes the variable usage. By *not* supplying a rate for a material resource, you indicate the fixed usage of the resource.

6. Repeat Steps 3, 4, and 5 to assign additional resources to the selected task. To assign resources to another task, simply click that task in the Gantt table or chart and then repeat Steps 3, 4, and 5.

7. Click Close when you finish assigning resources. Project displays the names of resources assigned to tasks next to the task bar on the Gantt Chart (see Figure 5-3).

If you click the Graphs button in the Assign Resources window, you can view three graphs that may help you select the best resource to assign to the job. None of these graphs relates particularly to the task to which you're assigning resources;

**5**

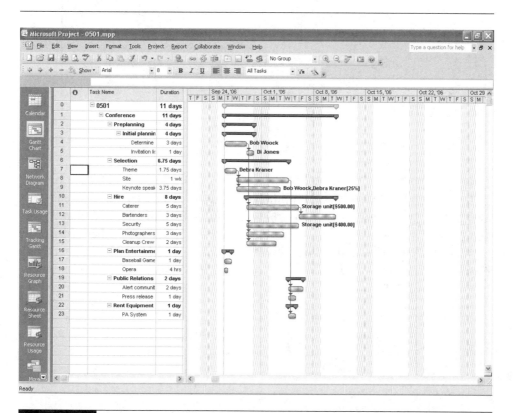

**FIGURE 5-3**    Resources assigned to tasks appear next to the task bar on the Gantt Chart.

instead, the graphs focus on the resource. To view the graphs, click a resource in the Assign Resources window and then click Graphs. Project displays the Work graph, which shows the amount of work that is assigned to the selected resource on a day-by-day basis. Remember, this graph doesn't refer to any task specifically.

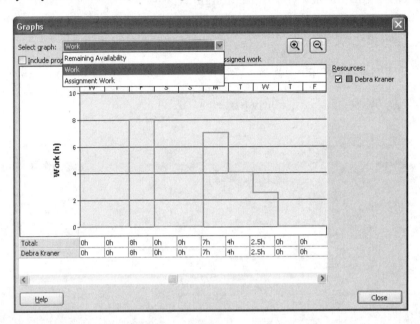

If you click the Select Graph drop-down arrow, you can select the Assignment Work graph. This graph breaks down the total workload of the resource that you're considering. You see the resource's workload on the selected task, other tasks, and the resource's total availability. You can use this graph to see if assigning the resource to the selected task will result in an overallocation.

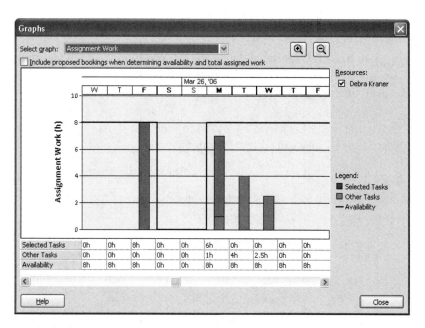

You can use the Remaining Availability graph to view the resource's unassigned time. If you've overallocated a resource, you don't see a negative availability; the resource's availability appears to be 0.

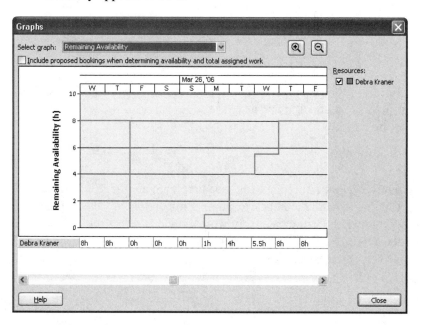

# Removing or Replacing Resource Assignments

Sometimes, you need to switch around resource assignments; you can remove a resource from a task or replace one resource with another resource. To remove a resource assignment, follow these steps:

1. Display the Gantt Chart view by clicking the Gantt Chart button in the View bar or by choosing View | Gantt Chart.

2. Select the task from which you want to remove the resource assignment.

3. Click the Assign Resources button or choose Tools | Assign Resources to display the Assign Resources window.

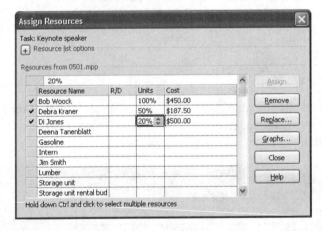

4. Highlight the resource that you want to remove from the task. You should see a check mark next to the resource in the leftmost column of the window.

5. Click Remove.

Alternatively, you can replace one resource with another. Follow Steps 1 to 4 in the preceding list and then click Replace. Project displays the Replace Resource dialog box, shown in Figure 5-4, from which you can select replacement resources. Highlight each resource that you want to assign, supply units, and click OK to see the changed resource assignment.

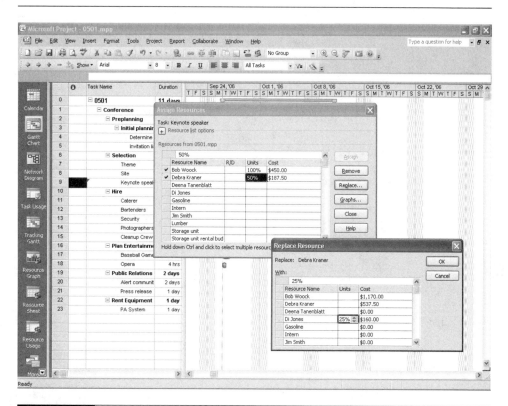

**FIGURE 5-4**    Replacing a resource assignment.

In this chapter, you've learned how to create resources, modify resource calendars, assign resources to tasks, and change resource assignments. In the next chapter, you'll learn how to estimate project costs.

# Chapter 6

# Estimating Project Costs

## How to...

- ■ Assign fixed costs to tasks
- ■ View a project's estimated cost
- ■ Handle rate changes for resources

Among the most important responsibilities you have as a project manager is to constantly monitor project costs to ensure that your project doesn't exceed its planned budget. And, when you create a project in Microsoft Office Project, you can create an estimate of your project's cost. If you assign costs to each resource and then assign resources to tasks in your project, Microsoft Office Project uses the duration of a task and the cost of the resources assigned to it to calculate the cost of each task and, therefore, the cost of the entire project. The amount of time a resource spends on a task, however, is not necessarily the only cost associated with a task and project. For example, projects, tasks, and resources can have fixed costs associated with them. This chapter starts with a quick look at overall project costs and then focuses on handling fixed costs; finally, at the end of the chapter, we look at handling resource rate changes during a project.

# Understanding How Project Collects Cost Information

While assigning a cost to a resource is not a requirement in Project, identifying a rate per hour or per use for each resource enables Project to calculate the estimated and actual cost of a project. Microsoft Office Project calculates the estimated and actual cost of a task by using the cost of the resources you assign to a task. The calculation is basic math—the resource's rate multiplied by the number of hours the resource spends on the task. Project than adds up the cost of each task to produce an estimated and actual cost for the project. In Chapter 5, you learned how to assign costs to resources on the Resource Sheet.

If you assign costs to resources, you can use Project to monitor and control the money that you're spending on a project. You can even control when costs accrue, which can help you schedule payment for bills related to your project. By assigning costs, you can identify the cost of resources and materials for any task, the cost of any phase of your project, and the cost of the entire project.

But you don't collect cost information just to try to keep a project's costs under control; you can use the cost information that you gather on one project to calculate bids your company may make on future projects.

# Working with Fixed Costs

Project handles the variable costs for a task by multiplying a resource's rate by the task's duration. Project also allows you to assign a cost per use to a resource, such as the price per gallon of gasoline you pay to run the mower as part of your lawn service.

In some cases, though, part or all of the costs associated with a task do not change in relation to the task's duration or the number of resources assigned to the task. Every time your printing company runs a job, for example, you need to set up the press, and the cost for setting up the press doesn't depend on how long it takes to print the material or how many employees work on the printing job. The setup cost may depend on the size of the job—and be smaller for smaller jobs and larger for larger jobs. To accurately calculate the cost of a job, you must add the fixed cost to the variable costs. For example, the fixed cost to set up the printing job must be added to the variable costs of the employees who manage the job and the time the job takes to complete.

Project can handle these fixed costs in either of two ways:

- ■ You can assign the fixed cost generically to a task.

- ■ You can set up a cost resource and assign the cost resource to the task.

I prefer the method that uses the cost resource because it has some added benefits; using this method, you can document the purpose of the cost using the Notes tab of the task to which you assign the cost resource, and you can distribute the cost using time-phased fields in either the Task Usage view or the Resource Usage view.

> NOTE
>
> *To add a fixed cost generically, switch to the Gantt Chart view and use the Cost table. You can enter the task's fixed cost and assign an accrual method. This technique doesn't give you the opportunity to document the purpose of the cost or to distribute the cost over time.*

To use a cost resource to assign a fixed cost to a task, first set up the cost resource on the Resource Sheet; see Chapter 5 for details. In Figure 6-1, the Press Setup resource is a cost resource. When you set up a cost resource, you do not assign a rate or cost per use to the resource; instead, you assign the cost when you assign the resource, as you'll see in a moment. But, you can control

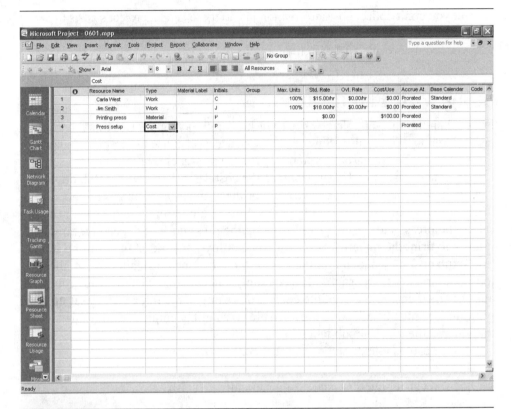

**FIGURE 6-1**    The Press Setup resource is a cost resource.

the timing Project uses to apply the cost. If you set the Accrue At field to Start or Prorated, Project charges the cost at the beginning of the task. If you set the Accrue At field to End, Project charges the cost at the end of the task.

*To control the way that Project accrues all fixed costs, use the Calculation tab of the Options dialog box; to display the Options dialog box, choose Tools | Options.*

To assign a fixed-cost resource to a task, follow these steps:

1. Click the Gantt Chart button in the View bar or choose View | Gantt Chart.

2. Select the task to which you want to assign a resource. You can click the task bar on the Gantt Chart, or you can click in any column for the task in the Gantt table.

3. Click the Assign Resources button or choose Tools | Assign Resources. Project displays the Assign Resources window.

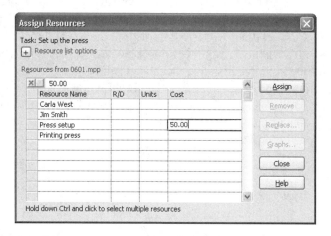

4. In the Assign Resources window, click in the Cost column of the cost resource that you want to assign.

5. Type the cost you want to assign to this task.

6. Click the Assign button. Project assigns the cost resource to the task; the resource's cost appears next to the Gantt bar for the task (see Figure 6-2).

7. Assign other resources using the techniques described in Chapter 5 or click the Close button.

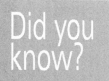

# Choosing Between a Cost Resource and a Cost/Use Resource

You may be wondering how to choose between using a cost resource and a cost per use resource; both seem to be methods of adding fixed costs to a task. And, they are. There are no "hard and fast" rules that dictate when you should use one or the other.

I use a cost resource when the cost of using the resource will change each time I use it in a project; that way, I can assign the appropriate cost as I assign the resource. In my printing press example, the setup cost of the press—a fixed cost essential to calculating the cost of the job—can change each time I set up the press, depending on the size of the print job.

*(continued)*

I use a resource with a cost per use when the cost of using the resource is always the same on the project. The cost for running the printing press (a cost per use material resource) is always $100, regardless of the number of employees working on the job, the length of time the job takes, or the size of the job. By using a cost/use resource, I don't have to worry about assigning the cost each time I use the resource, because Project will assign the cost for me. And, when the cost of a resource is the combination of a fixed price plus a variable price, I use a cost per use resource and establish both a cost/use amount and a standard rate.

Assign Resources button

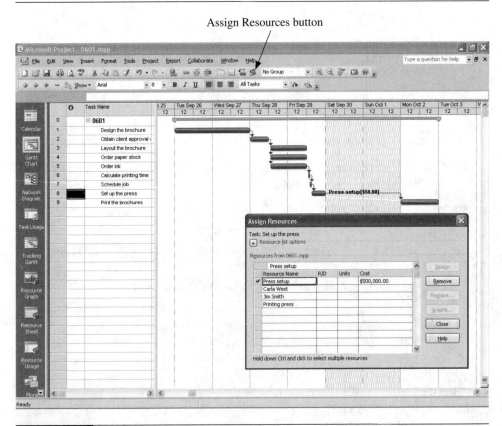

**FIGURE 6-2** Resources and their costs appear beside Gantt bars.

# Viewing a Project's Estimated Cost

You can see your project's estimated cost most easily by viewing the project's statistics. Although we're going to look at the Project Statistics dialog box now, before you set a baseline and begin recording progress on the project, you can see that viewing the Project Statistics dialog box from time to time can give you good overview information.

| Project Statistics for '0604.mpp' | | | | |
|---|---|---|---|---|
| | Start | | Finish | |
| Current | Tue 3/28/06 | | Tue 4/25/06 | |
| Baseline | NA | | NA | |
| Actual | NA | | NA | |
| Variance | 0d | | 0d | |

| | Duration | Work | Cost |
|---|---|---|---|
| Current | 21d | 54.5h | $2,307.50 |
| Baseline | 0d | 0h | $0.00 |
| Actual | 0d | 0h | $0.00 |
| Remaining | 21d | 54.5h | $2,307.50 |

Percent complete:
Duration: 0%    Work: 0%

Close

While viewing either the Gantt Chart view or the Resource Sheet view, choose Project | Project Information. In the Project Information dialog box that appears, click the Statistics button to open the Project Statistics dialog box.

 *In Part V of this book, we'll look at tracking projects, recording work done, and analyzing and reporting on progress.*

# Handling Resource Rate Changes

There is one last unusual cost situation that we need to consider: how to handle resource rate changes. Suppose that your company changes resource rate costs at the beginning of each year and your project runs from November to March. For the first two months of the project, you need to charge resources at one rate, and from January through March, you need to use a different rate for the same resources. Or, it's possible that a resource costs one amount when performing one task and a different amount when performing another task. Project uses cost rate tables to accurately reflect resource costs as they change.

Using cost rate tables, you can identify the effective dates for each rate and you can create up to 125 rates for any one resource. Using cost rate tables, you can account for cost increases or decreases to resources during the life of your project and you can simultaneously use different rates for the same resource, depending on the task.

To assign multiple rates to a resource, display the Resource Sheet view. Then, double-click the resource for which you want to assign multiple rates and click the Costs tab in the Resource Information dialog box.

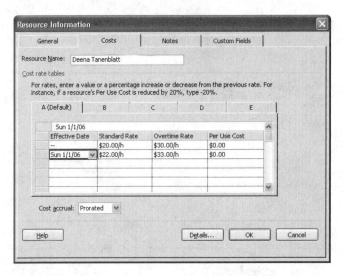

On the Costs tab of the Resource Information dialog box, you see five cost rate tables—tabs A through E. On each tab, you can assign different rates to a resource for use on different starting dates throughout a project's life. Each cost rate table accommodates up to 25 rates. Project uses the effective dates that you supply to apply the correct rate to a resource at different times during the project.

*You can let Project calculate percentage rate increases or decreases for you. Instead of typing the new rate amount, type in the percentage increase or decrease, such as +10% or −10%, and Project will calculate the rate for you.*

But let's look at the other example I cited: suppose that you use one resource on two tasks and charge one rate for work on one task and a different rate for work on another task. In this case, you can use each cost rate table tab to represent the rate for different kinds of work and set up values on cost rate tables A and B. To assign the correct resource cost rate table to a task, follow these steps:

**1.** Assign the resource to the task using the Assign Resources window. For details, see Chapter 5.

Assignment Information button

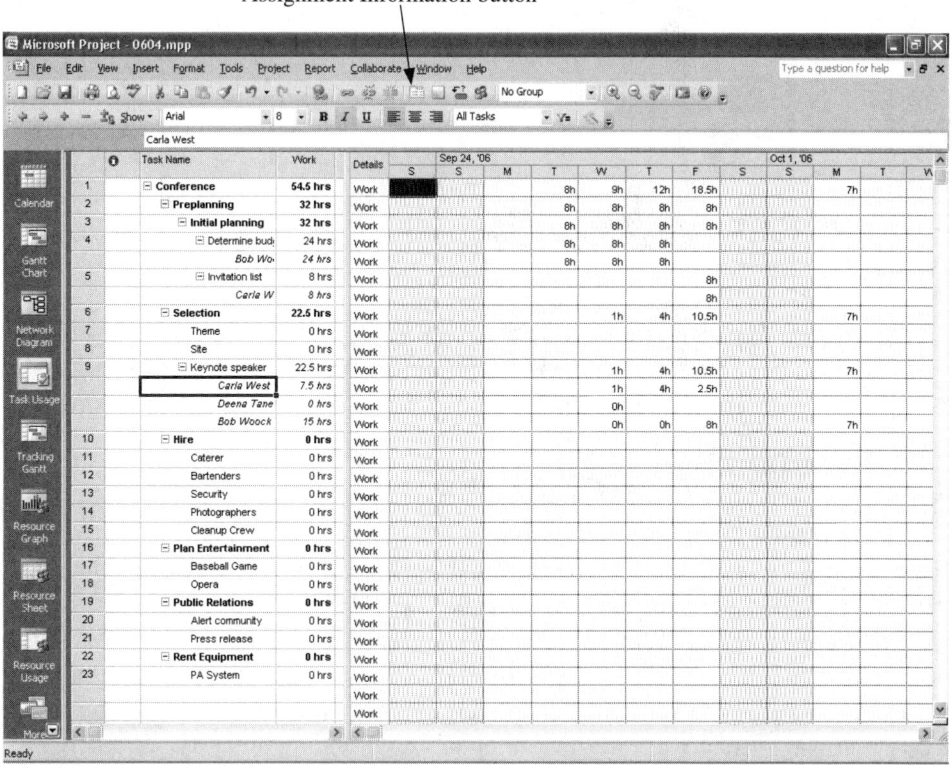

**FIGURE 6-3**    The Task Usage view

2. On the View bar, click Task Usage or choose View | Task Usage (see Figure 6-3).

3. In the Task Name column, select the resource for which you want to select a cost rate table.

4. Click the Assignment Information button on the Standard toolbar. Project displays the Assignment Information dialog box.

5. Click the General tab to select a cost rate table.

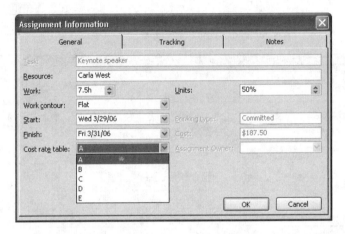

**6.** Open the Cost Rate Table drop-down list and select the correct cost rate table.

**7.** Click OK.

In this chapter, you've seen how Project calculates project cost and handles fixed costs. You've also seen how you can use the Project Statistics dialog box to view a lot of good overview information about your project. Last, you learned how to use different rates for different resources at various times during a project. In the next chapter, we'll focus on the views available in Project; views help you look at a project in a variety of ways, and each view can help you analyze your project in a different way so that you can stay on top of things and avoid nasty surprises.

# Part III

# Viewing Projects

# Chapter 7

# Working with Views

## How to...

- Switch views

- Create or edit views

- Share views between projects

- Work with combination views

- Change the Details section of a view

- Print a view

By their very nature, projects are multifaceted; you, as project manager, need to be concerned about making sure you identify all the tasks that need to be done, assign resources to tasks, and determine the estimated cost and completion date of tasks and the project...and all of that happens just in the planning stage. Once you complete the project plan, you need to start monitoring the project to make sure that tasks complete on time, resources aren't overallocated, and the project stays within the projected cost.

You can't focus on all areas simultaneously; in fact, to do your job effectively, you need to focus on different areas individually. That's where *views* enter the picture—they help you concentrate on different aspects of your project. In this part of the book, we're going to focus on the mechanics of viewing your project from different perspectives. And, because views are very flexible, Chapters 8 and 9 will expand upon using views effectively.

# The Purpose of Views

Project contains around 30 views that you can use to enter, organize, and examine project information; each view helps you focus on a different aspect of your project. You can classify Project's views into three groups, and many views in Project are actually combinations of two views:

*When you don't display the View bar down the left side of the screen, the view's name appears at the left edge of the view.*

# Did you know?

# Indicators in Views

Sometimes, you see icons in the Indicators column, the leftmost column of a table view. These icons are called *indicators*, and their appearance means that additional information exists for the row in which they appear. For example, a Notes indicator appears in the Indicators column on the Resource Sheet if you assign a note to a resource. The following table explains the meaning of the various kinds of indicator icons. When you see one onscreen, you can identify its purpose by pointing your mouse pointer at it, which causes balloon-style help information to appear.

7

| Type of Indicator | Meaning |
|---|---|
| Constraint indicators | Identify that a constraint, other than the default As Soon As Possible constraint, applies to a task. Constraint indicators can also show that the task hasn't been completed within the timeframe of the constraint. |
| Task type indicators | Typically identify special conditions about a task, such as whether the task is a recurring task or whether the task has been completed. |
| Workgroup indicators | Provide some information about the task and its resources. For example, a workgroup indicator can tell you that a task has been assigned but that the resource hasn't yet confirmed the assignment. |
| Contour indicators | Identify the type of contouring assigned to the task. Project uses contouring to distribute the work assigned to a task; you'll read more about contouring in Chapter 11. |
| Miscellaneous indicators | Identify items that you created, such as a note, a hyperlink, a calendar that's been assigned to a task, or a resource that needs leveling. |

■ **Chart or graph views**    Present information by using pictures. The Gantt Chart view is a chart view. It is also a combination view, displaying a table—the Entry table in Figure 7-1—on the left side of the view and a chart on the right side of the view. Later in this chapter, we'll explore combination views in greater detail.

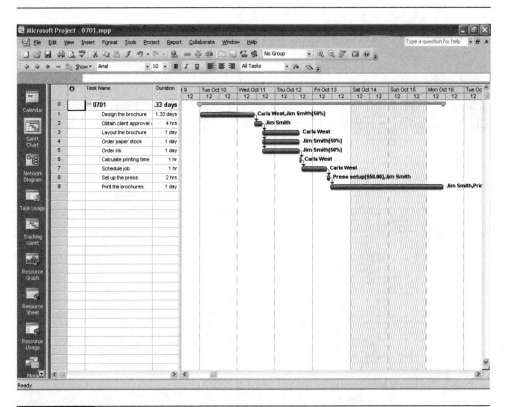

**FIGURE 7-1** The Gantt Chart view combines a table and a chart.

■ **Sheet views** Present information in rows and columns; think "spreadsheet" and you'll be visualizing a sheet view. The Resource Sheet view, shown in Figure 7-2, is a sheet view. Each row on the sheet contains all the information about an individual resource in your project, and each column represents a field that identifies the information that you're storing about the resource.

■ **Form views** Display information about a single task or resource in your project. An example is the Task Form view, shown in Figure 7-3.

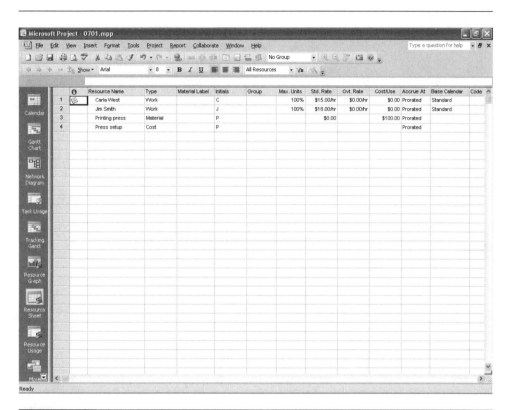

**FIGURE 7-2**    The Resource Sheet is a sheet view, presenting information in rows and columns.

## Switching Views

You can easily change the view by clicking the More Views icon in the View bar (you may need to scroll down in the View bar to see it) or choosing View | More Views. Project displays the More Views dialog box, which provides dozens of views you can use.

The best way to become familiar with each view is to apply it to your project and analyze what you see. Each view helps you focus on some particular aspect of your project.

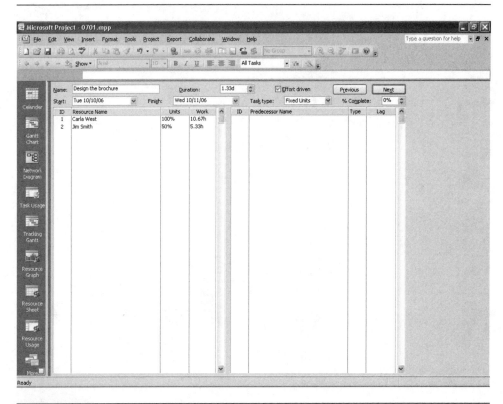

**FIGURE 7-3** A typical form view.

# Creating or Editing a View

You can create a new view quickly and easily in Project; as you create a view, you select an existing view on which to base the new view, and you identify the table to attach to the view. You also identify how you want information grouped in the view; you learn more about grouping information in views in Chapter 9. You also can set filters to remove information from the view that doesn't meet the filtering criteria, or you can set filters to simply highlight the tasks that meet the criteria; Chapter 9 also contains more information about filtering a view. Follow these steps to create a new view:

1. Choose View | More Views; the More Views dialog box appears.

2. Click the New button. The Define New View dialog box appears.

**3.** Select the Single View option and click OK. The View Definition dialog box opens.

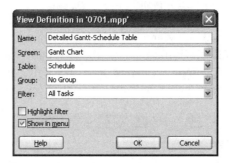

**4.** Enter in the Name box a name for the new view that describes the information that you'll show in the view.

NOTE *You'll read about combination views later in this chapter.*

**5.** Open the Screen drop-down list and select an existing view on which to base the new view.

**6.** Open the Table drop-down list and select an existing table to include in the new view. See Chapter 8 for more information on tables.

**7.** Open the Filter drop-down list and choose a filter to apply to the view. To avoid filtering the view, select the "All" filter—All Tasks for a task-related view, and All Resources for a resource-related view. To filter the view by highlighting information that meets the filter criteria, check the Highlight Filter check box at the bottom of the View Definition dialog box.

**8.** Check the Show in Menu check box to make the new view appear on the View bar and on the View menu. If you don't check this box, you can display the new view only by selecting it from the More Views dialog box.

**9.** Click OK. The new view appears in the More Views window.

**10.** Click Apply to display the new view onscreen.

7

Although you can edit a built-in view, I don't recommend it; by editing a built-in view, you change the defaults that most people expect to see when using a particular view. If you share your project with someone else and you've edited a default view, you may cause confusion. So, instead of editing a built-in view, I suggest that you make a copy of the view and edit the copy. Using this technique places only one restriction on the view: you cannot change the view on which you base the copy; the Screen list box won't be available. Typically, this restriction doesn't present a problem.

Copying a view is simple; choose View | More Views to display the More Views dialog box. Highlight the view you want to copy and then click the Copy button. Project displays the View Definition dialog box, with all the options selected that apply to the view you are copying. Change the name of the view and make any other changes you need to the options in the dialog box; then, click OK.

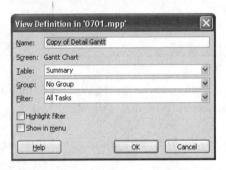

    *You delete views—and you can copy a view that you create to another project or make it appear in all projects—using the Organizer. See Chapter 20 for details.*

# Combination Views

In Project, you can display two views simultaneously onscreen—and Project refers to this phenomenon as a combination view. In this section, I'll show you how to easily create a combination view and change either of the two views to a different view. You'll also learn how to create your own combination view.

## Displaying and Changing Combination Views

To get an idea of what a combination view looks like, Figure 7-4 shows the Network Diagram view and the Task Form view; in this combination view, the top portion

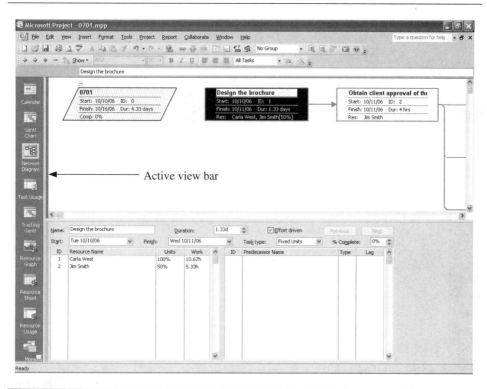

**FIGURE 7-4** In a combination view, detailed information appears in the bottom of the view about whatever you select in the top of the view.

shows task relationships and some overview information about each task and the bottom portion shows details of the task selected in the top portion of the view. When you click a new task in the top portion of the view, new information appears in the bottom of the view.

If you focus your attention on the left edge of the view (between the view and the View bar, if you've displayed the View bar), you'll notice a dark line that appears beside one of the views. The dark line is the Active view bar, and it provides a visual clue that identifies the view in which you are working. When you click in either of the views, the Active view bar appears beside the view in which you clicked.

The default Network Diagram is a single view (see Figure 7-5), but you can turn any view into a combination view by using your mouse pointer and the split bar. When you point your mouse pointer at the split bar, the mouse pointer becomes two horizontal lines with arrows. If you double-click, Project

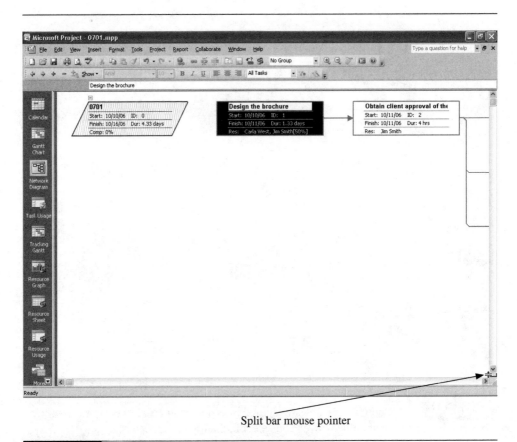

Split bar mouse pointer

**FIGURE 7-5** You can double-click the split bar to create a combination view.

automatically splits the screen, displaying the original view in the top of the screen and another view in the bottom of the screen.

*You also can drag the split bar toward the top of your screen, or choose Window | Split.*

To redisplay only the Network Diagram view, double-click the split bar again, drag the split bar down, or choose Window | Remove Split.

 *If you switch views while displaying a combination view, the new view also appears as a combination view.*

## Creating a New Combination View

Suppose that you regularly like to view the Calendar view combined with the Leveling Gantt view and you'd like to save that combination view. Follow these steps:

1. Choose View | More Views to display the More Views dialog box.

2. Click New to display the Define New View dialog box.

3. Click the Combination View option and then click OK. Project displays the View Definition dialog box, in which you can create a combination view.

4. Name the view.

5. Use the Top and Bottom drop-down lists to select the views that should appear in those portions of the combination view.

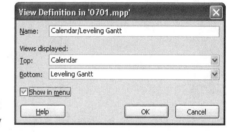

6. Check the Show in Menu check box to make the view appear in the View bar and on the View menu.

7. Click OK to save the combination view, and then click Close to close the More Views dialog box.

# Changing the Details in a View

The Task Usage view and the Resource Usage view contain a Details section that appears on the right side of those views (see Figure 7-6).

You can change the information that appears in the Details section. Right-click anywhere in the Details section and click an option on the shortcut menu.

Details section

The right side of the Task Usage view is called the Details section.

Project adds a row to the Details section each time you select a choice from this menu (see Figure 7-7). To remove a row, right-click the Details section and click the item that you want to remove.

If the field you want to add to the Details section of a usage view doesn't appear on the shortcut menu, you can add it by using the Detail Styles dialog box. Choose Format | Detail Styles to display the dialog box.

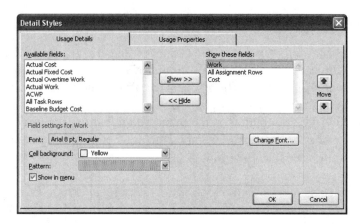

Click a field in the Available Fields list on the left side of the box and then click the Show button. Click OK to save your selection.

**7**

FIGURE 7-7   You can add rows to the Details section to display additional information.

# Printing a View

You can print your project from any view. Start by selecting the view that you want to print. Project prints only those columns of a sheet view that appear onscreen. If your project doesn't fit on one page, Project prints the entire left side of your project before it prints the right side.

You can click the Print button on the Standard toolbar to print or you can open the Print dialog box to control, for example, the number of pages you print or the portion of the timescale that you print.

NOTE    *You can also preview before printing, by clicking either the Preview button in the Print dialog box or the Print Preview button on the Standard toolbar.*

From the Page Setup dialog box, you can control a large variety of options; to display this dialog box, choose File | Page Setup.

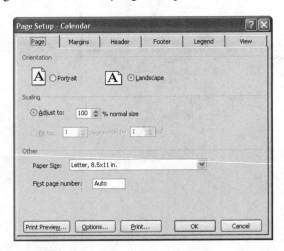

The following list describes what you can do on the six tabs of the Page Setup dialog box:

- **Page tab**    Set orientation and scaling. Scaling may help you fit the printed text onto one page.

- **Margins tab**    Change the page margins and specify whether Project should print a border around the pages.

■ **Header tab**   Control the content and alignment of the information that appears on the top of every printed page.

■ **Footer tab**   Control the content and alignment of the information that appears on the bottom of every printed page.

> TIP
>
> *You can include Project-level fields in the header, footer, or legend of your printed product. From the appropriate tab of the Page Setup dialog box, use the Project Fields list box to select the field that you want to include and click the Add button.*

■ **Legend tab**   Control the content and alignment of the information that appears in the legend of every printed page. This tab is available in the Page Setup dialog box only when you're printing a Calendar, Gantt Chart, or Network Diagram view.

■ **View tab**   Control what Project prints; the options that appear on the View tab vary from view to view. When you print the Task Usage view or the Resource Usage view, two check boxes appear on the View tab that are not available in any other view:

   ■ **Print Column Totals**   When you check this box, Project adds to the bottom of the printed page a row that shows column totals for timephased fields.

   ■ **Print Row Totals for Values Within Print Date Range**   When you check this box, Project adds to the printed page a Total column that shows row totals for timephased data in the specified date range. These totals lines print on the same page as the last rows or columns of data, before any Notes pages.

> TIP
>
> *In many cases, you can add to a table a column that gives you the same information that you can get in the row totals. The column prints where you place it, while the row totals print on a separate page.*

In this chapter, you learned the basis of working with views; in the next chapter, we'll continue the exploration of views by focusing on the tables that appear in most views.

# Chapter 8

# Working with Tables and Views

## How to...

- ◼ Switch tables
- ◼ Create or edit a table
- ◼ Adjust table settings

In the last chapter, you learned the basics about views; some views contain tables, and in this chapter, we're going to focus on working with tables in views. You'll learn how to switch from one table in a view to a different table; how to create or edit tables; and how to adjust tables, changing row height and column width, and adding and hiding columns.

# Understanding Tables

Most views in Project display a table on the left side of the view that presents information in rows and columns. In Figure 8-1, I've expanded the table portion of the view so that you can see the entire table.

The tables available to you depend on the view you select. For example, while viewing the Gantt Chart, you can use any of the following tables:

- ◼ Cost
- ◼ Entry
- ◼ Hyperlink
- ◼ Schedule
- ◼ Summary
- ◼ Tracking
- ◼ Usage
- ◼ Variance
- ◼ Work

Each table stores different kinds of information, and you use tables to enter information into your project or view information about your project.

Table portion of the view

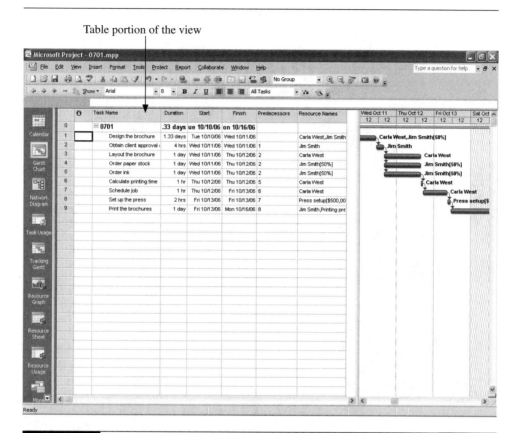

**FIGURE 8-1**    Tables often contain more columns than you can see when you initially display the view.

# Switching Tables

Not all views contain tables; you won't find tables in the Calendar view, the Network Diagram view, or the Resource Graph view, among others. But if a table does appear in a view, you can switch to another table while using the same view.

To switch to the most commonly used tables for a view, right-click the Select All button, which appears in the upper-left corner of the table portion of the view, to display a shortcut menu (see Figure 8-2). Then, click the table you want to apply to the view.

TIP

*If you click (instead of right-click) the Select All button, Project selects all information in the table portion of the view.*

Select All button

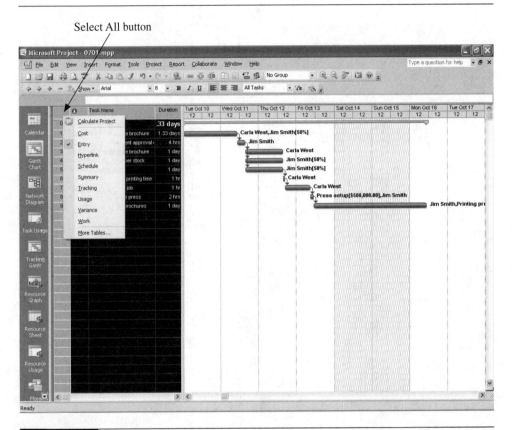

FIGURE 8-2     Switching tables

Remember, the choices that appear on the shortcut menu change depending on the view you displayed before you right-clicked the Select All button. If the table you want to use doesn't appear on the shortcut menu, click More Tables; Project displays the More Tables window, which displays all the tables that are available in Project.

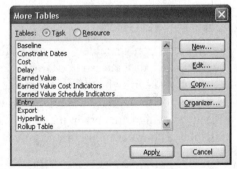

Notice that you can display tables appropriate for task views and tables appropriate for resource views by clicking the corresponding option button at the top of the More Tables window.

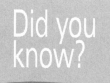

# Project and PERT Analysis

PERT analysis (PERT stands for Program Evaluation and Review Technique) was devised by the Special Projects Office of the U.S. Navy in the late 1950s to track the flow of tasks and estimate probable outcomes. Project contains views that support PERT analysis, and many project managers use these views to estimate the probable duration of a task, its start date, or its end date. Using the tables associated with the various PERT views in Project, you specify the optimistic, pessimistic, and expected durations of tasks in your project. Then Microsoft Office Project uses a weighted average of the three durations and calculates probable start and end dates.

To display a PERT view, you use the PERT toolbar; right-click any toolbar and then click PERT Analysis. Initially, the three PERT views—Optimistic Gantt, Expected Gantt, and Pessimistic Gantt—don't appear in the More Views window. Similarly, the four PERT tables—one for each PERT view plus the PERT Entry Sheet—don't appear in the More Tables window. However, once you display the PERT views and tables using the PERT Analysis toolbar, the views will appear in the More Views window, and the tables will appear in the More Tables window.

**8**

## Creating or Editing a Table

The technique you use to create a new table in Project is very similar to the technique you use to edit an existing table. If you cannot find an existing table in Project that is similar to the table you want to use, create a new one. Otherwise, look for an existing table that has several of the fields that you want to include; then, make a copy of it and edit the copy. That way, you leave the original table untouched so that anyone else who uses your project will find the default tables.

Suppose that you feel the table would work better if the columns appeared in a different order than the order in which Project shows them. For example, suppose that you want to view the Total Cost column first on the Cost table. Or perhaps you want to add a table to the list of tables that appear on the shortcut menu that

Project displays when you right-click the Select All button. In the following steps, I'll show you how to copy a table and edit it; then, I'll show you the differences if you want to create a new table.

1. Right-click the Select All button and click More Tables. Project displays the More Tables window.

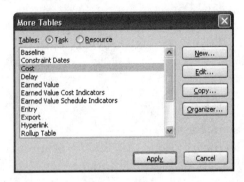

2. Click Task or Resource to identify the type of table you want to create or edit.

3. Click a table that you want to copy.

4. Click the Copy button to create a copy of the table to edit. Project displays the Table Definition dialog box.

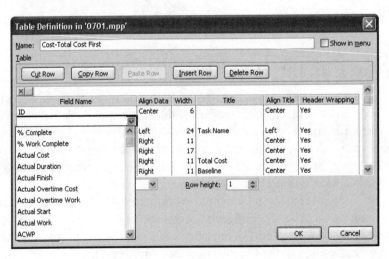

5.  In the Name box, supply a name for the table that means something to you. If an ampersand appears, as it does in the illustration, remove it. An ampersand to the left of a character tells Project which character in the table title serves as a "hot key" so that you can display the table using the keyboard instead of the mouse.

6.  To display the table in the shortcut menu that appears when you right-click the Select All button, place a check in the Show in Menu check box.

> **TIP**    *Project will also display the table in the side menu that appears when you choose View | Table.*

7.  To add a field to the table, click the title of the field name that you want to appear to the right of the new field that you add. Then, click the Insert Row button.

8.  Click the drop-down arrow in the blank field to display the list of fields, and select a field name.

9.  In the same row, click in the Align Data column. Project displays the default alignment settings for the data and the title as well as the width of the column. You can change the alignment for either the data or the title by clicking the arrow on the right side of the field.

10. If necessary, click in the Width column and modify the width of the column to accommodate the type of information that you think will typically go there. If you aren't sure about the ideal column width, just accept the default.

11. To remove a field from the table, click anywhere in the row of the field you want to remove and then click Cut Row. You also can move the row you cut by clicking the title of the field name that you want to appear to the right of the new field that you add and then clicking Paste Row.

12. (Optional) You can click the Title field and enter a title for the column if you don't want to use the default field name.

13. Repeat Steps 7 through 12 to add more fields to your table.

8

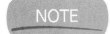

*Use the Header Wrapping field—a Yes or No choice—to specify whether long field titles wrap within the column heading. If you set the Header Wrapping field to No, Project hides that portion of a column title that doesn't fit within the allotted space for the column.*

**14.** Check the Lock First Column check box to keep the first column of your table onscreen when you scroll across the table. Typically, the Task ID column is locked in place in a table.

**15.** Click OK when you are finished to redisplay the More Tables window.

**16.** Click Apply in the More Tables window to display the new table onscreen.

If you have included any date fields in the table, such as Start Date or Finish Date, you can modify the date format by using the drop-down list of choices in the Date Format field below the list of fields in the table. You can also modify the height of all the rows with the Row Height setting that appears beside the Date Format field.

You create a new table by skipping Step 3 and clicking New in Step 4. When the Table Definition dialog box appears, no fields will appear; complete Steps 5 through 16 to finish the process.

*You delete tables—and you can copy a table that you create to another project or make it appear in all projects—by using the Organizer. See Chapter 20 for details.*

# Adjusting Tables

In views containing tables, you can change the height of the rows or the width of columns or switch to a different table. Or, you can move columns around, hide columns, or add columns. When you save your project, Project saves changes you made to tables.

## Displaying More of a Table

Tables appear most often in combination views, where the right side of the screen is a chart or graph; in these views, most of the table appears hidden initially. But you can display as much of the table as will fit on your computer screen. Drag the

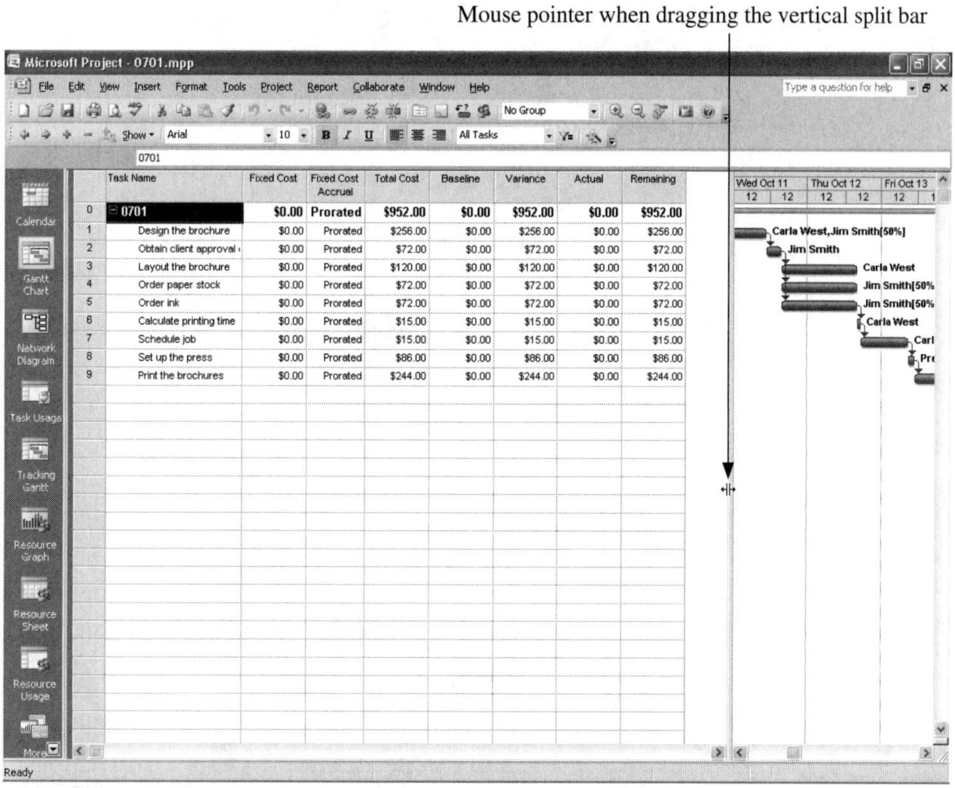

Mouse pointer when dragging the vertical split bar

**FIGURE 8-3**    Drag the vertical split bar to display more of a table.

vertical split bar to the right to display more of a table; drag it to the left to display more of the other portion of the view (see Figure 8-3).

## Changing Row Height

When information is too wide to fit within a column, you can change the height of a row, and Project will wrap the data to fit within the taller row. Notice that the name for Task 2 in Figure 8-4 doesn't fit within the Task Name column.

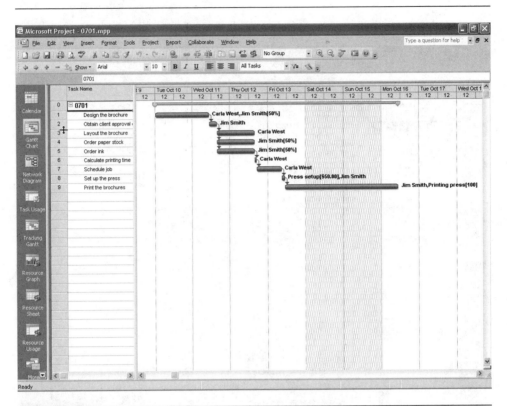

FIGURE 8-4 You can widen a row to display more text in the Task Name column.

If I increase the height of that row, the name wraps so that it is visible. To change the height of a row, move the mouse pointer into the Task ID number column at the bottom of the row; the mouse pointer changes to a pair of arrows pointing up and down. Drag down; when you release the mouse button, Project increases the height of the row and wraps any text in that row that didn't fit within its column (see Figure 8-5).

You can change the height of multiple rows simultaneously. Press and hold CTRL while you click the ID of each row you want to change. Then drag the bottom of any selected row.

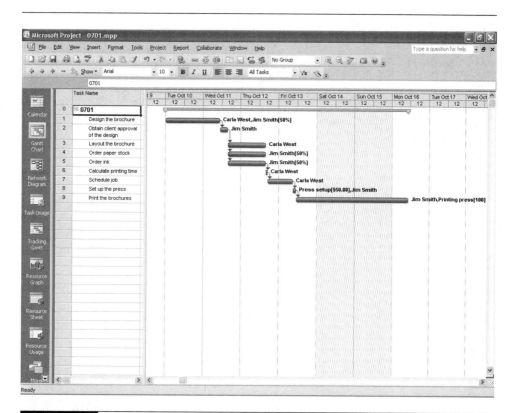

**FIGURE 8-5**    You can drag a row to change its height.

## Changing Column Width

Each column in a table has a default width assigned to it, but you can change that width. Move the mouse pointer to the right edge of the title of the column that you want to change; the pointer changes to a pair of arrows pointing right and left. Drag to the right to make a column wider or drag to the left to make the column narrower. If you make a column narrower than its title, Project automatically wraps the column title (see Figure 8-6).

## Inserting and Hiding Columns

You can remove a column from a table by hiding it; if you save your project after hiding a column, Project remembers the setting. When you close and then reopen the project, the hidden column remains hidden.

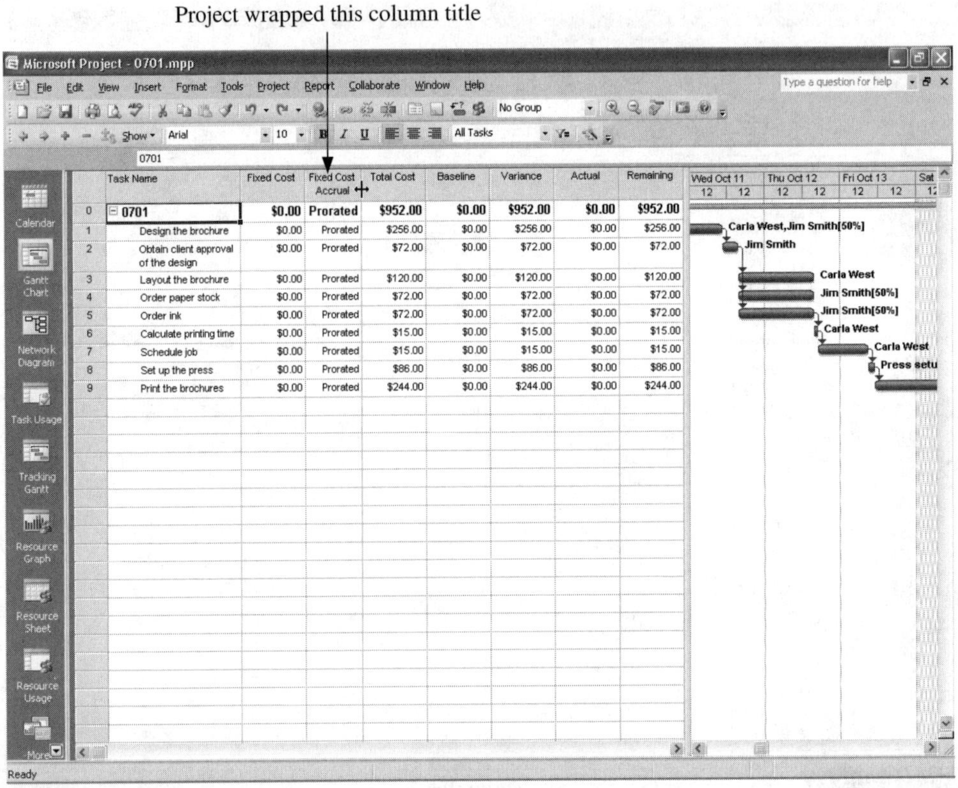

Project wrapped this column title

FIGURE 8-6    You can drag a column to widen it.

To hide a column, right-click the heading of the column and click Hide Column from the shortcut menu that appears (see Figure 8-7). Project hides the column, but the data stored in the column remains a part of your file. You simply don't see it because you have hidden the table column that would display the data.

You can redisplay the column or add a different column to your table. When you insert a column in a table, Project adds it to the left of a column you select. To redisplay a hidden column or insert a new column into a table, right-click the

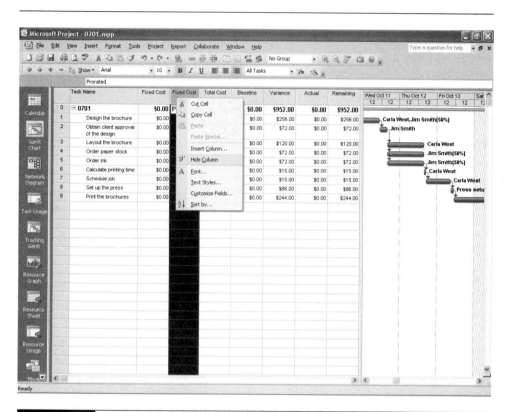

**FIGURE 8-7**    Hiding a column

column heading that should appear to the right of the column that you're going to insert. Then, click Insert Column from the shortcut menu that appears. Project displays the Column Definition dialog box.

In the Field Name drop-down list box, select the name of the column that you want to add. You don't need to make any other changes—you don't even need to type anything in the Title field. Just click the Best Fit button to make sure that Project provides enough space for the column title, and Project will insert the column to the left of the selected column.

In this chapter, you learned how to work with tables that appear on the left side of most views. In Chapter 9, you'll finish your exploration of views and tables by learning how to sort, filter, and group information in a view.

# Chapter 9

# Organizing Information in a View

## How to...

- Sort tasks
- Filter views
- Group information on views

Organization is instrumental to effectively managing a project. To truly understand what's going on in a project, you often need to view the project information in a variety of ways—and you already know, from the previous two chapters, how views can help you look at information from various perspectives.

But viewing from various perspectives may not be sufficient; you may find that you'd understand the information in the view better if you could refine it further—by sorting it, filtering it to focus on certain tasks or resources, or grouping it. In this chapter, you'll learn how to take these additional steps to help you fully evaluate a project.

NOTE    *Work breakdown structure codes and outlining codes can help you organize a project; see Chapter 19 for more information.*

# Sorting Tasks

In Project, you can sort a project from most views in almost any way that you want. For example, in the Gantt Chart view, Project automatically sorts tasks by ID. But you may find it useful to view your project information if you sort by cost (see Figure 9-1).

To reorder the information in the Gantt Chart view so that tasks are ordered by start date, choose Project | Sort | By Start Date (see Figure 9-2).

When you display the Sort menu, you see five common sort keys. You can sort by almost any field if you use the Sort window; click the Sort By command at the bottom of the Sort submenu to open the Sort window.

Using this window, you can set up a three-level sort. If Project finds a "tie" at the first sort level,

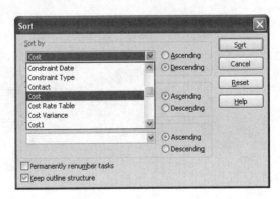

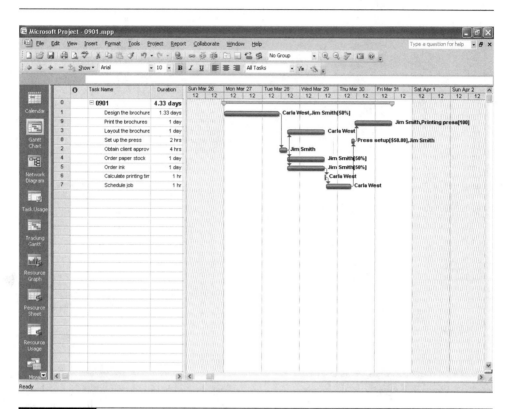

FIGURE 9-1 A schedule sorted by cost

it uses the second sort field to break the tie and determine the order of appearance. Similarly, if Project finds a tie at the second sort level, it uses the third sort field that you specify to break the tie. Using the check boxes at the bottom of the dialog box, you can make your sort choices permanent by reassigning task IDs, and you can choose to retain the outline structure of the project.

# Working with Filters

Filters reduce the information that appears in the view so that you can more easily focus on specific aspects of your project. For example, you can apply filters to view only those tasks that are assigned to a specific resource. Project uses two kinds of filters. Using task filters, you can view specific aspects of tasks. Using resource filters, you can view specific aspects of resources.

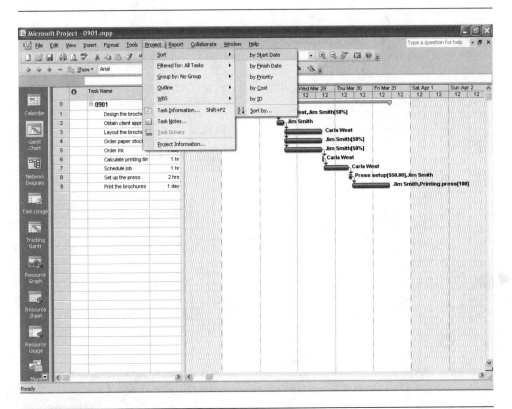

**FIGURE 9-2**    Changing the sort order

# Applying a Filter

When you filter a view, you provide conditions that Project uses to identify the
tasks or resources to display in that view. When you filter a view, you can choose
to highlight the information that meets your conditions or you can hide the rest of
the information. To apply a filter and hide all other information, follow these steps:

1. Display onscreen the view that you want to filter.

2. Choose Project | Filtered For (see Figure 9-3).

3. Click the filter that you want from the Filtered For submenu. Project
   applies the filter and hides all tasks or resources that don't meet the
   condition of the filter.

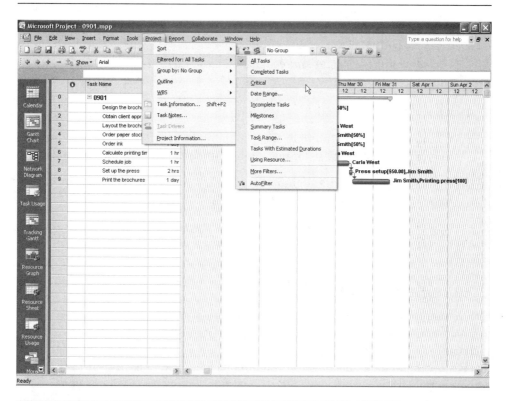

**FIGURE 9-3** Filtering a project

To apply a filter that doesn't appear on the list, or to apply a filter that highlights the tasks that meet a certain condition, follow these steps:

1. Display onscreen the view that you want to filter.

2. Choose Project | Filtered For | More Filters to display the More Filters window.

3. At the top of the window, click either Task or Resource to apply a task filter or a resource filter.

*Remember that you can't apply a task filter to a resource view or a resource filter to a task view.*

4. Click a filter from the list.

5. (Optional) Click Highlight to apply a highlighting filter. Project changes the text color of the tasks or resources that meet the condition of the filter.

6. If you did not click Highlight in Step 5, click Apply. Project displays only those tasks or resources that meet the condition of the filter.

*To turn off a filter, choose Project | Filtered For, and then click All Tasks or All Resources, as appropriate.*

## Creating or Editing a Filter

The technique you use to create a new filter is very similar to the technique you use to edit an existing filter. If you cannot find an existing filter in Project that is similar to the filter you want to use, create a new one. Otherwise, look for an existing filter that has several of the fields that you want to include; then, make a copy of it and edit the copy. That way, you leave the original filter untouched so that anyone else who uses your project will find the default filters. In the following steps, I show you how to copy a filter and edit it; then, I'll show you the differences if you want to create a new filter.

1. Display onscreen the view that you want to filter.

2. Choose Project | Filtered For | More Filters to display the More Filters window.

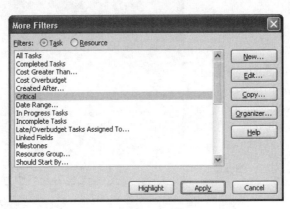

3. Click either Task or Resource to identify the type of filter you want to create or edit.

4. Click a filter that you want to copy.

5. Click the Copy button to create a copy of the filter. Project displays the Filter Definition dialog box.

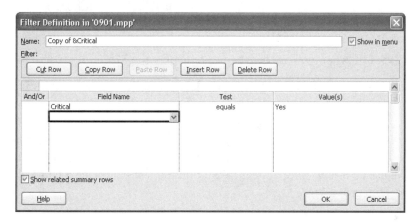

6. In the Name box, supply a name for the filter that means something to you. If an ampersand (&) appears, as it does in the illustration, remove it. An ampersand to the left of a character tells Project which character in the filter title will serves as a "hot key" so that you can display the filter using the keyboard instead of the mouse.

7. Click a blank line in the Field Name column, and Project displays a drop-down arrow to the right of the field.

8. Click the drop-down arrow in the blank field to display the list of fields. Select a field name.

9. Click in the Test column cell for the new row and then click the drop-down arrow to display the list of operators. Select a comparison operator.

10. Click in the Value(s) column cell for the new row and then either enter a value or click the drop-down arrow to display the list of values appropriate for the field.

11. Repeat Steps 7 through 10 to add more fields to your filter. If you supply additional criteria, also supply an And/Or operator. "And" is the default operator and means that the filter displays information only if the task or resource meets all criteria. "Or" means that the filter displays information if a task or resource meets any of the criteria.

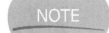

*Each line that you add in the Filter Definition dialog box is called a statement. You can have Project evaluate certain statements together, but separate from other statements in your filter, by grouping the statements into a set of criteria. To group statements, leave a blank line between sets of criteria, and select either operator in the And/Or field for the blank row. If your filter contains three or more statements within one criteria group, Project evaluates all And statements before evaluating Or statements.*

12. Click OK when you are finished to redisplay the More Filters window.

13. Click Apply in the More Filters window to display the new filter onscreen.

You create a new filter by skipping Step 4 and clicking New in Step 5. When the Filter Definition dialog box appears, the name Filter 1 appears in the Name box and no fields will appear; use Steps 6 through 11 to create the filter and add fields to it. To make your new filter appear in the Filtered For list, place a check in the Show in Menu check box.

*You delete filters—and you can copy a filter that you create to another project or make it appear in all projects—by using the Organizer. See Chapter 20 for details.*

## Using AutoFilters

You can use AutoFilters to quickly and easily filter a view by any field in the view. You work directly on the sheet of any sheet view instead of using a menu or a window. When you click the AutoFilter button on the Formatting toolbar, a drop-down arrow appears at the right edge of every column name in a sheet view. When you open any drop-down list, Project displays filters that are available in the column (see Figure 9-4).

You can hide the AutoFilter drop-down arrows by clicking the AutoFilter button again.

*You can set options in Project so that AutoFilter drop-down arrows appear automatically for each new project that you create. Choose Tools | Options. On the General tab, place a check in the Set AutoFilter On For New Projects check box.*

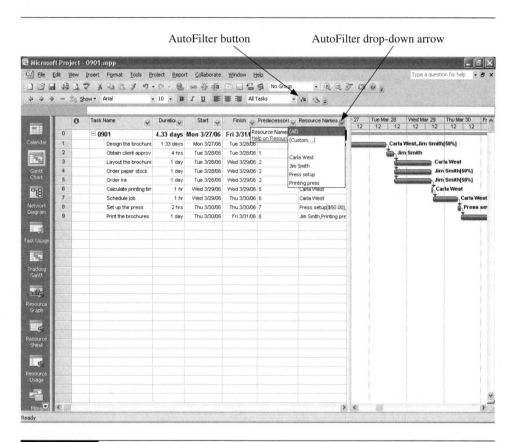

**FIGURE 9-4** Click a drop-down list entry to filter the schedule by that entry.

# Grouping Information

You may be able to solve a problem if you group tasks in a view by some common denominator. For example, you might want to group complete and incomplete tasks to more easily focus on incomplete tasks. When you group tasks, Project places yellow highlighting at the top of each group (see Figure 9-5).

## Assigning a Group

You can quickly and easily group tasks in one of the more common groups if you display the view that you want to group. Then, choose Project | Group By and click a grouping.

Group By button

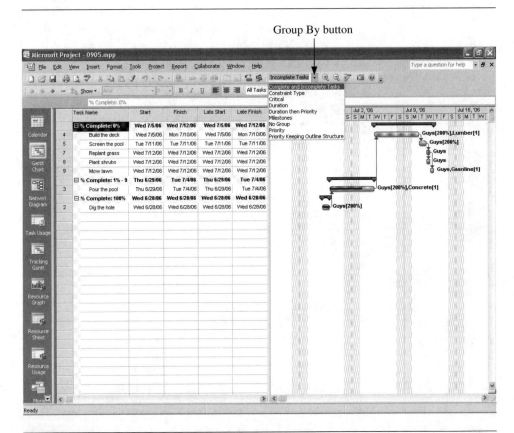

**FIGURE 9-5**    You can also select one of the common groupings by using the Group By button on the Standard toolbar.

    *You can group tasks only in task views and resources only in resource views.*

## Creating or Editing a Group

You can group by almost any field, even if that grouping doesn't appear on the Group By menu or in the list that appears when you click the Group By button on the Standard toolbar. To group in a way that doesn't appear on the menu, create a copy of an existing group and edit it to suit your purposes; follow these steps:

**1.** Display the view that you want to use to group.

**2.** Choose Project | Group By | More Groups. Project displays the More Groups window.

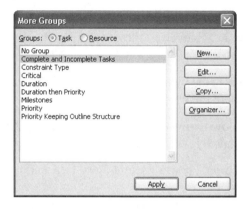

**3.** Click either Task or Resource to apply a task grouping or a resource grouping.

**4.** Select a group name from the list.

**9**

**5.** Click the Copy button to create a copy of the grouping. Project displays the Group Definition dialog box.

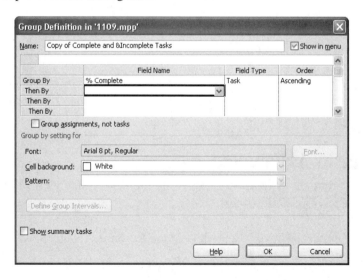

**6.** In the Name box, supply a name for the group that means something to you. If an ampersand appears, as it does in the illustration, remove it. An ampersand to the left of a character tells Project which character in the filter title will serve as a "hot key" so that you can display the filter using the keyboard instead of the mouse.

**7.** Click the Show in Menu check box to display the group on the Group By menu.

**8.** Click a blank line in the Field Name column, and Project displays a drop-down arrow to the right of the field.

**9.** Click the drop-down arrow in the blank field to display the list of fields. Select a field name by which you want to group information in the view.

**10.** In the Order column, choose Ascending or Descending.

 *You can optionally select a font for the grouping title information and change the cell background and the pattern that Project displays for the field. You also can include summary tasks in groups if you place a check in the Show Summary Tasks check box.*

**11.** Click OK to save your choices and redisplay the More Groups dialog box.

You can click Apply to apply the group that you just defined. To turn off grouping, choose Project | Group By | No Group.

 *You delete groups—and you can copy a group that you create to another project or make it appear in all projects—using the Organizer. See Chapter 20 for details.*

## Grouping by Assignment

You also can group on assignment fields using the Task Usage view or the Resource Usage view. Follow these steps:

**1.** Select either the Task Usage view or the Resource Usage view.

**2.** Choose Project | Group By | Customize Group By. You see the Customize Group By dialog box.

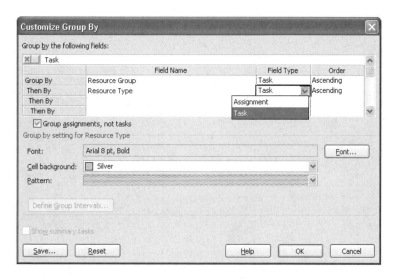

**3.** Select the fields by which you want to group.

**4.** Check the Group Assignments, Not Tasks check box.

**5.** In the Field Type column, select whether to group by assignment or by task.

NOTE

*For this example, I displayed the Task Usage view in Step 1. If you select the Resource Usage view in Step 1, the name of the check box changes to Group Assignments, Not Resources, and, in the Field Type list, you choose whether to group by assignment or by resource.*

**6.** Click OK.

To turn off grouping, choose Project | Group By | No Group.

In this final chapter on working with views, you learned to sort, filter, and group information in views. In the next chapter, we'll begin a new section of the book that focuses on resolving conflicts.

9

# Part IV

# Resolving Resource and Scheduling Conflicts

# Chapter 10

# Resolving Scheduling Problems

## How to...

■ Adjust task duration using various techniques

■ View and change the critical path

As you use the various views in Project to evaluate your project's proposed schedule, you may find that you have trouble completing the project in the expected timeframe with the available resources. You can use a variety of techniques to try to adjust the schedule; most of the approaches involve changing a task's duration in some way. In this chapter we'll look at the methods you can use to try to resolve a scheduling problem, including shortening the critical path.

# Adding Resources to Tasks

If you set a task's type to Fixed Units and check the Effort Driven check box, you can add resources to the task to reduce the time needed to complete the task. In the Gantt Chart view, double-click the title of the task to display the Task Information dialog box.

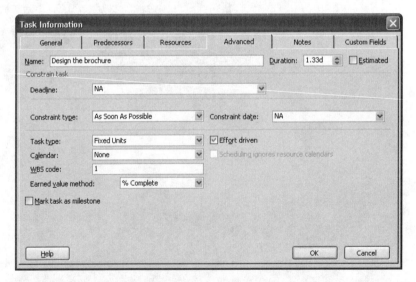

Click the Advanced tab and set the Task Type field to Fixed Units. Make sure that a check appears in the Effort Driven check box. When you subsequently add resources to the task, Project will reduce the task's duration.

*When you create a task, Project checks the Effort Driven check box on the Advanced tab of the Task Information dialog box by default; using the Effort Driven option allows Project to reallocate the work among the resources you assign to the task when you add a new resource to the task.*

# Increasing a Task's Duration

Odd as it may seem, sometimes increasing a task's duration can resolve a scheduling conflict because you may find that once-scarce resources are now available to complete the task if you change a task's timing.

You can change the duration from several different views, including the Gantt Chart view and the Task Usage view, or you can use the Task Information dialog box. Double-click the task and, from any tab in the dialog box, use the Duration box to change the duration.

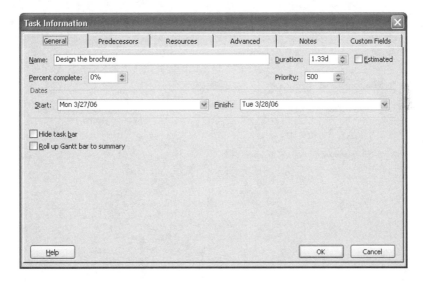

# Using Overtime

Project defines overtime as the amount of work that is scheduled beyond an assigned resource's regular working hours, and Project charges overtime hours to the project using the resource's overtime rate. For example, suppose that you assign 40 hours of work and 15 hours of overtime to a task. The total work for the task remains at 40 hours, with 15 hours being worked during regular business hours and charged to the project at the resource's standard rate. The 12 hours of overtime are worked outside of regular working hours and charged to the project at the resource's overtime rate. So, using overtime reduces the time that a resource takes to complete a task, but increases the cost of your project.

To enter overtime, follow these steps:

1.  Display the Gantt Chart view using the View bar or by choosing View | Gantt Chart.

2.  Choose Window | Split to display the Task Form in the bottom pane (see Figure 10-1).

3.  Click the Task Form to make it the active pane.

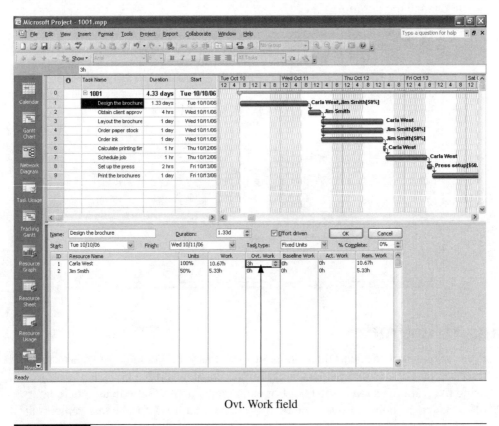

Ovt. Work field

**FIGURE 10-1**    Setting up a combination view

4. Choose Format | Details | Resource Work. Project adds the Ovt. Work column to the Task Form.

5. In the top pane, click the name of the task to which you want to assign overtime.

6. In the bottom pane, fill in the overtime amount for the appropriate resource.

*After you finish entering overtime, you can hide the Task Form by dragging the split bar down to the bottom of your screen or by choosing Window | Remove Split.*

# Taking Advantage of Slack

Most projects contain noncritical tasks with slack that can start late without affecting the schedule. Slack time is the amount of time that a task can slip before it affects another task's dates or the finish date of the project. Free slack is the amount of time that you can delay one task without delaying another task. If your schedule contains slack, you may be able to move tasks around, using tasks with slack to compensate for tasks that take longer than planned.

*Typically, when you use the Must Start On constraint, you create slack time. To avoid creating slack time, use the As Soon As Possible constraint whenever possible. You set constraints on the Advanced tab of the Task Information dialog box. Read more about constraints in Chapter 4.*

To find tasks with slack time in a schedule, follow these steps:

1. Choose View | More Views to open the More Views window.

2. Select Detail Gantt from the list and click Apply.

3. Right-click the Select All button and select Schedule from the list of tables.

4. Drag the divider bar to the right to view more of the table. Now you can see the Free Slack and Total Slack fields.

You also can identify slack on the Gantt bars; Project represents slack with a thin line that extends from the bottom of regular Gantt bars (see Figure 10-2).

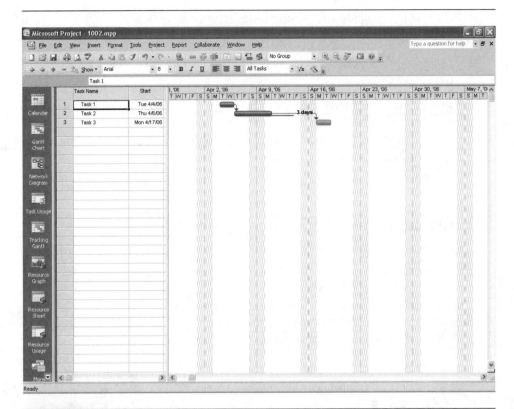

**FIGURE 10-2**    Slack appears as a thin line that extends from the bottom of regular Gantt bars.

*If you see negative slack in your schedule, the schedule contains an inconsistency. For example, negative slack appears when Task 1 has a finish-to-start dependency with Task 2, but Task 2 has a Must Start On constraint that is earlier than the end of Task 1.*

# Reviewing Task Constraints and Dependencies

When projects appear to fall behind schedule, review the task constraints established for each task. By default, when you take an illogical action—like setting a start date for Task 2 that is earlier than Task 1's start date, when Task 2 is linked to and follows Task 1—Project displays the Planning Wizard. Or, if you are about to take an action that is likely to lengthen the project schedule—like setting a Must Start On constraint on a task with no slack time and with other tasks linked to it—the Planning Wizard warns you.

You can turn off the Planning Wizard warnings by checking the Don't Tell Me About This Again check box at the bottom of the Planning Wizard dialog box. If you turn off the Planning Wizard, Project still warns you if you take actions that cause scheduling problems. Instead of the Planning Wizard warnings, Project displays a message like the following, which makes suggestions concerning actions that you can take on the predecessor task to avoid these kinds of conflicts.

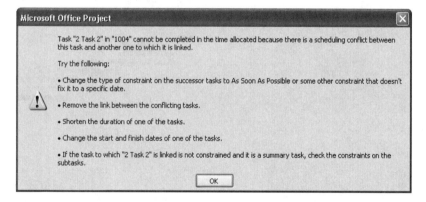

This message box doesn't give you the option of canceling your action, but you can undo the action after you click OK. If you prefer the opportunity to cancel an action that may lengthen the project schedule or create an illogical schedule, you may want to continue to use the Planning Wizard.

*If you already turned the Planning Wizard off and want to turn it back on, choose Tools | Options. On the General tab, check the Advice from Planning Wizard check box, and then check the Advice About Errors check box.*

# Splitting Tasks

When you split a task, you schedule the work to fall at nonconsecutive times. You schedule work to start on the task, schedule work to stop on the task for a period of time, and then schedule work to begin again on the task. Splitting a task creates a gap in the task's scheduled progress, which you can identify by the dotted lines appearing between the two portions of the split task in the task's Gantt bar (see Figure 10-3).

Follow these steps to split a task:

1. Click the Gantt Chart view in the View bar or choose View | Gantt Chart.

2. Click the Split Task button on the Standard toolbar. The mouse pointer changes shape and a screen tip tells you how to split a task (see Figure 10-4).

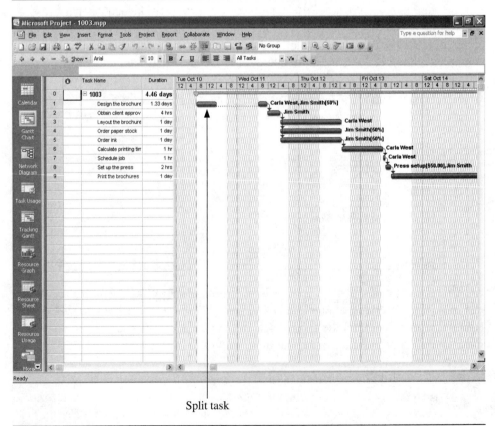

Split task

**FIGURE 10-3**  Splitting a task schedule's work to fall at nonconsecutive times

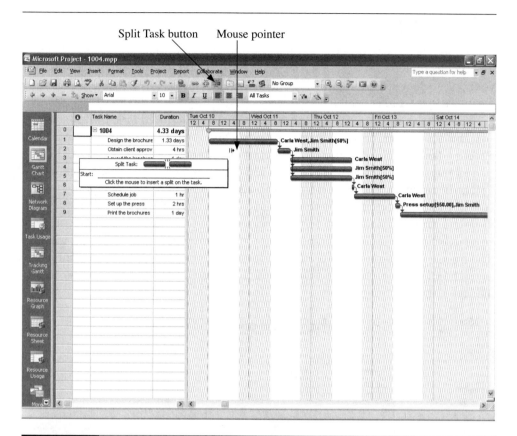

Split Task button   Mouse pointer

**FIGURE 10-4**   A screen tip guides you through splitting a task.

**3.** Move the mouse pointer along the bar of the task that you want to split. As the mouse pointer moves, dates representing the split date appear in the screen tip.

**4.** Click when the screen tip shows the date on which you want to split the task; Project inserts a split.

*You can create a larger split by dragging the Gantt bar to the right instead of clicking.*

If you decide that you want to remove a split, drag the two portions of the split task's Gantt bar together so that they touch.

# Working with the Critical Path

Shortening the critical path of your project is another way that you can shorten the timeframe allotted for the entire project. The *critical path* is that set of the tasks in your project that must not fall behind schedule; if they are not completed on time, the entire project falls behind schedule.

The tasks that appear on the critical path are called *critical tasks*. Most tasks in a project have some slack, and you can delay these noncritical tasks some without affecting the project finish date. However, if critical tasks become delayed, the project finish date changes to accommodate the delay. As you use the techniques described earlier in this chapter to modify tasks to resolve scheduling problems, you may or may not affect or even change the critical path.

Some managers like to use slack to help make them aware of tasks that are close to being on the critical path. You can have Project treat all tasks with less than a specified number of days of slack as if those tasks were on the critical path, using the Calculation tab of the Options dialog box. Choose Tools | Options and then click the Calculation tab.

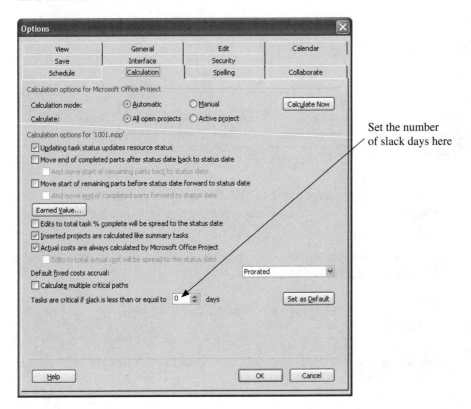

Set the number of slack days here

At the bottom of the tab, in the Tasks Are Critical if Slack Is Less Than or Equal To box, enter a number of days. Project will define a task as critical if the task's slack is less than or equal to the value you enter. And don't forget: noncritical tasks can become critical if they slip too much.

Before you can shorten the critical path, you need to identify the tasks on the critical path, and you can do that using formatting or filtering. When you use formatting, you can manually apply formatting or you can use the Gantt Chart Wizard.

## Filtering to View Critical Tasks

Alternatively, you can identify the critical path by filtering for it. You can apply the Critical filter to any task view to display only critical tasks. First, display the view that you want to filter. Then, select Critical from the Filter list box on the Formatting toolbar (see Figure 10-5) or choose Project | Filtered For| Critical.

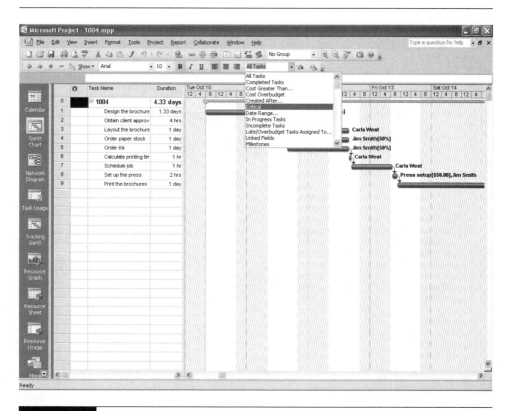

FIGURE 10-5    Filtering to view critical tasks

Filtering is an effective tool to display only certain aspects of the project, but sometimes you need to identify the critical tasks while viewing all the tasks in your project. So, as an alternative, you can use formatting. When you use formatting, you distinguish between critical and noncritical tasks while you are viewing all the tasks in your project.

## Formatting to Identify Critical Tasks

You can format task bars to distinguish critical tasks from noncritical tasks. The formatting you apply to critical and noncritical tasks appears in all views in which you can see task bars and identifies critical tasks with a Yes in or near the bar of the tasks and identifies noncritical tasks with a No.

To format task bars, follow these steps:

1. Click Gantt Chart in the View bar or choose View | Gantt Chart to display the Gantt Chart view.

2. Choose Format | Bar Styles to display the Bar Styles dialog box.

3. Select Task from the list at the top of the Bar Styles dialog box.

4. Click the Text tab at the bottom of the dialog box.

5. Select a position for the formatting: Left, Right, Top, Bottom, or Inside. When you click a position, a drop-down arrow appears.

6. Click the drop-down arrow and scroll to select Critical.

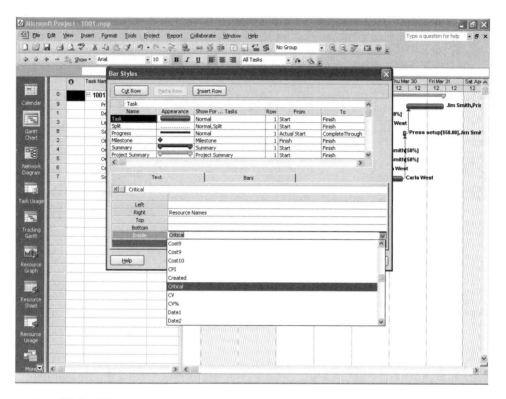

**7.** Click OK.

After you apply the formatting, the Gantt Chart shows critical and noncritical tasks. In Figure 10-6, I placed critical information inside task bars, so Project displays No inside noncritical tasks and Yes inside critical tasks.

## Using the Gantt Chart Wizard to View the Critical Path

If you prefer, you can use the Gantt Chart Wizard to display the critical path in your project. A wizard walks you through a process, asking you questions or prompting you to make selections. When you use the Gantt Chart Wizard, Project uses your input to modify the formatting of your Gantt Chart; in this example, we'll use it to make critical tasks stand out.

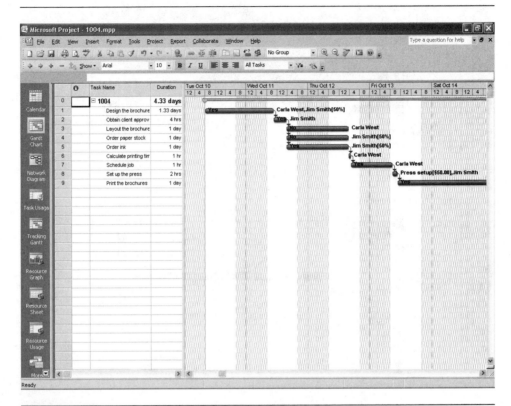

**FIGURE 10-6**    Using formatting to identify critical tasks

You can use the Gantt Chart Wizard from either the Gantt Chart view or the Tracking Gantt view; in this example, I'll work in the Gantt Chart view. Follow these steps to use the Gantt Chart Wizard to display the critical path:

1. Choose View | Gantt Chart.

2. Click the Gantt Chart Wizard button at the right edge of the Formatting toolbar or choose Format | Gantt Chart Wizard. The first Gantt Chart Wizard dialog box welcomes you to the Gantt Chart Wizard.

## Did you know?

## Other Uses of the Gantt Chart Wizard

Although we're using the Gantt Chart Wizard to view the critical path, you can use the wizard to apply a variety of formatting to the Gantt Chart. The second screen of the wizard presents you with five options, described in the following table. Although you can select only one item, try clicking each of the choices to see a preview of its style on the left of the dialog box.

| Option | Description |
| --- | --- |
| Standard | Shows the Gantt Chart you typically see—blue taskbars, black summary taskbars, and a black line superimposed over the taskbars to indicate progress on tasks. |
| Critical path | Uses the Standard layout, but displays critical-path tasks in red. |
| Baseline | Displays baseline taskbars and planned taskbars separately. You can read more about baselines in Chapter 12. |
| Other | Controls the appearance of the view; using a drop-down list, you can select from several alternative, predefined chart styles for the categories of Standard, Critical Path, Baseline, and Status. |
| Custom Gantt Chart | Makes additional Gantt Chart wizard boxes appear to allow you to create a highly customized Gantt Chart. |

**10**

**3.** Click Next and select Critical Path to describe the kind of information that you want to display on the Gantt Chart.

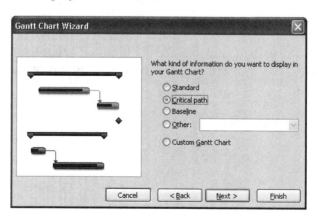

**4.** Click Next and identify task information to display with your Gantt bars: Resources and Dates (the task end date only), Resources, Dates (task start and end dates), None (no information), or Custom Task Information.

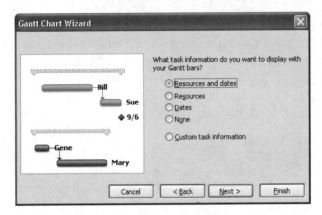

**5.** Click Next and indicate whether you want to show link lines between dependent tasks.

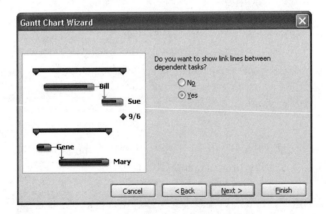

**6.** Click Next and then click the Format It button to apply your choices. Project displays a final dialog box to tell you that your formatting is complete.

**7.** Click the Exit Wizard button to view the formatting changes.

When you view the Gantt Chart, all tasks in the project still appear, but tasks on the critical path appear in red.

If you save your file and later want to remove Gantt Chart Wizard formatting, you need to run the Gantt Chart Wizard again, selecting Standard on the first screen where you can select the kind of information that you want to display on the Gantt Chart.

## Shortening the Critical Path

Once you've identified the critical tasks, you can focus on shortening the critical path. Shortening the critical path on a project is often a project manager's goal, because reducing the duration of a project typically reduces the cost of the project.

To reduce the time that is allotted on the critical path, you can reduce the duration of critical tasks, overlap critical tasks to reduce the overall project duration, or both reduce the duration of critical tasks and overlap critical tasks.

To reduce the duration of critical tasks, you can do the following:

- Add resources to a critical task if the task is a fixed-work task or an effort-driven fixed-unit task. Adding resources to these types of tasks reduces the time it takes to complete the tasks.

- Add overtime to an effort-driven critical task.

- Use the PERT Analysis views to reassess your estimates and use a more optimistic task time.

To overlap critical tasks, you can do one of the following:

- Adjust dependencies.

- Add lead time to overlapping tasks.

- Redefine a finish-to-start relationship to either a start-to-start or a finish-to-finish relationship.

Now that you know *what* you can do, you need to identify tasks that you want to change, and then make the changes. Select a view, and filter it for critical tasks only; I prefer the Task Entry view, which is a combination view of the Gantt Chart and the Task Form view, because the top pane displays a graphic representation of your project and the bottom pane displays most of the fields that you may want to change (see Figure 10-7).

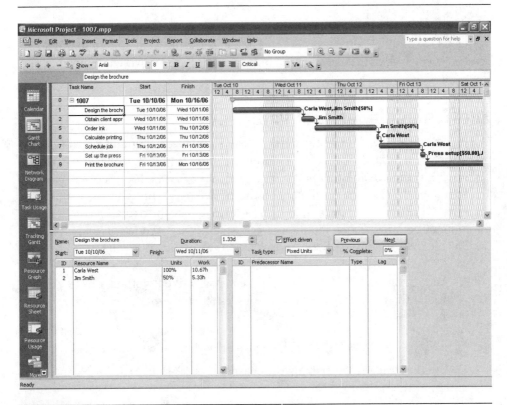

FIGURE 10-7    The Task Entry view works well when you want to make changes to your schedule.

To set up this view, follow these steps:

1. Click Gantt Chart from the View bar or choose View | Gantt Chart.

2. Right-click the Select All button and select a table. The table that you apply to the Gantt Chart is a matter of personal preference; I like the Schedule table because it shows slack information.

3. Choose Window | Split. The Task Form appears in the bottom pane.

4. Right-click the Task Form window and click Resources & Predecessors from the menu that appears.

5. Choose Project | Filtered For | Critical.

6. Click each critical task to evaluate it, and make changes in the Task Form at the bottom of the screen.

You also can sort your critical tasks by duration so that critical tasks appear in order from the longest to the shortest. Then, you can try to shorten longer tasks. Choose Project | Sort | Sort By. In the Sort window that appears, select Duration from the first Sort By list and click Sort.

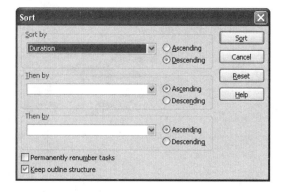

## Displaying Multiple Critical Paths

In many large projects, you may find that you actually have more than one critical path. You can view multiple critical paths simultaneously; when you have lots of tasks that are driving other tasks and you want to find out which ones are truly critical, viewing multiple critical paths can help you.

By default, when you view only one critical path, you're viewing the tasks that must be completed to finish the project on time (see Figure 10-8).

The project shown in the illustration contains four groups of tasks. Task IDs 2, 3, and 4 make up one group; task IDs 6 and 7 make up a second group; task IDs 9 through 13 make up a third group; and task IDs 15 through 18 make up the fourth group. I've formatted the critical path for the project so that it is red and appears with a cross-hatched pattern; notice that it involves tasks in the first two groups.

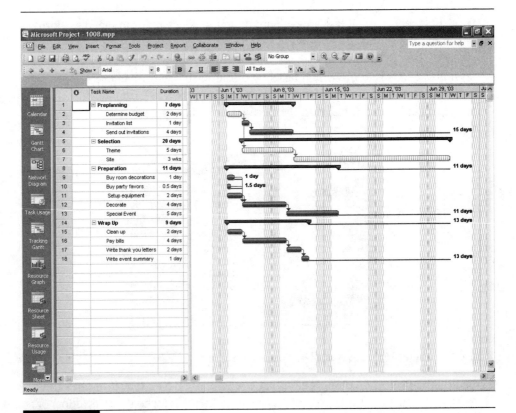

**FIGURE 10-8**    By default, you see only one critical path.

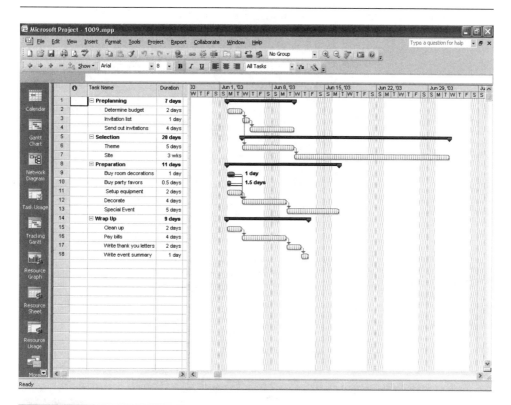

**FIGURE 10-9**   Displaying multiple critical paths

When you display multiple critical paths, Project displays a critical path for each group of tasks (see Figure 10-9). Project identifies the critical path for each group of tasks by setting each task's late finish date equal to its early finish date. Tasks with no dependencies are critical because their late finish dates are equal to their early finish dates. In groups where some tasks contain slack—like the third group—then some tasks are not critical while others are critical. By viewing multiple critical paths, you can determine which tasks within any group of tasks must be completed on time to avoid delaying the group.

10

To view multiple critical paths, choose Tools | Options. Then, click the Calculation tab and check the Calculate Multiple Critical Paths check box.

**Options**

| View | General | Edit | Calendar |
| Save | Interface | Security | |
| Schedule | Calculation | Spelling | Collaborate |

Calculation options for Microsoft Office Project

Calculation mode:      ⦿ Automatic      ○ Manual      [ Calculate Now ]

Calculate:      ⦿ All open projects      ○ Active project

Calculation options for '1019.mpp'

☑ Updating task status updates resource status
☐ Move end of completed parts after status date back to status date
   ☐ And move start of remaining parts back to status date
☐ Move start of remaining parts before status date forward to status date
   ☐ And move end of completed parts forward to status date
[ Earned Value... ]
☐ Edits to total task % complete will be spread to the status date
☑ Inserted projects are calculated like summary tasks
☑ Actual costs are always calculated by Microsoft Office Project
   ☐ Edits to total actual cost will be spread to the status date
Default fixed costs accrual:      [ Prorated      ▼ ]
☑ Calculate multiple critical paths
Tasks are critical if slack is less than or equal to  [ 0  ⬍ ]  days      [ Set as Default ]

[ Help ]      [ OK ]    [ Cancel ]

Check this box to display multiple critical paths

In this chapter, you looked at ways to adjust your project schedule to try to complete the project within the allotted timeframe using the available resources. In the next chapter, we'll review ways to resolve resource conflicts in a project schedule.

# Chapter 11

# Resolving Resource Conflicts

## How to...

- Identify resource conflicts
- Resolve resource conflicts using a variety of techniques

Whenever you assign resources to tasks in a project, Project checks the resource's calendar to make sure that the resource is working during the scheduled assignment. But, Project doesn't look at the other assignments the resource may already have, creating the possibility of overallocating the resource. When a resource is overallocated, you have assigned more work to the resource than the resource can accomplish in the time allotted. In this chapter, we'll look at resolving resource overallocation using a variety of techniques.

# Understanding and Identifying Resource Conflicts

Suppose that resources at your company work a standard five-day week, 8 hours per day. You cannot assign a resource to work full-time on two tasks that start on the same day without overallocating the resource; such an assignment means that you expect the resource to perform 16 hours of work in an 8-hour day—and, while some jobs seem to require 16 hours of work a day, that isn't an accepted project management technique and isn't an example of good planning. Figure 11-1 shows two tasks that begin on the same day. By assigning the same resource to them, I cannot avoid an overallocation.

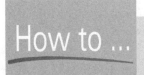

How to ...

# Display the Resource Management Toolbar

You can easily display the Resource Management toolbar shown below. Right-click any button on any toolbar to display a list of available toolbars. Toolbars that already appear onscreen have a check beside them. Click the Resource Management toolbar.

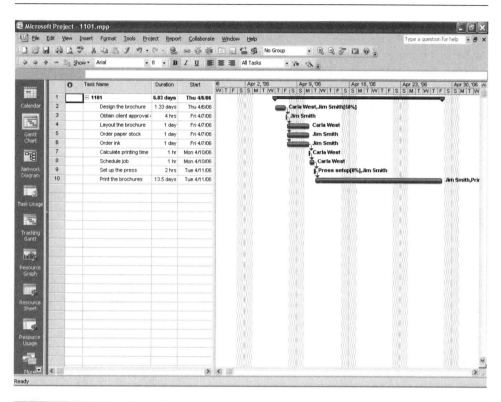

**FIGURE 11-1**   Jim Smith is overallocated because of his assignments to Tasks 5 and 6.

Before you can resolve resource conflicts, you need to spot them. You can use views and filters to help you identify resource overallocation problems. You also can use the Resource Management toolbar to help you spot and resolve overallocations.

In resource views like the Resource Sheet view or the Resource Usage view, overallocated resources appear in red, boldface type (see Figure 11-2) and a Caution icon appears in the Indicators column; you can view the caution message if you point at the icon with your mouse. Later in this chapter, I'll talk about resource leveling—the thrust of the caution message.

To display the Resource Usage view, click Resource Usage in the View bar or choose View | Resource Usage.

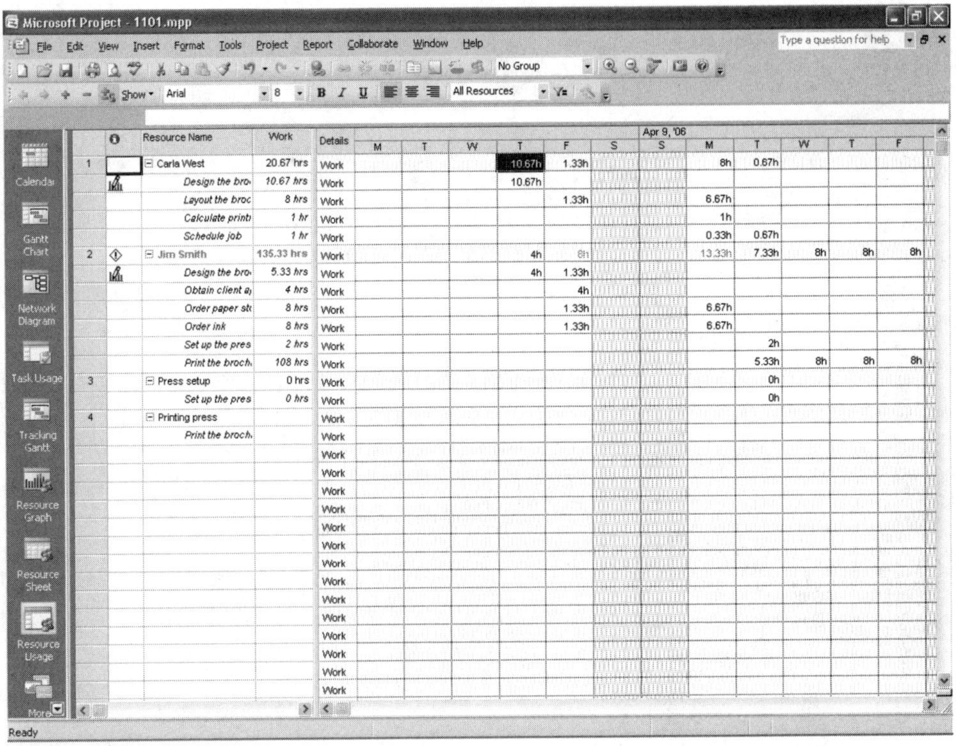

**FIGURE 11-2** Overallocated resources appear in red, boldface type in resource views.

The Resource Graph view presents a vivid representation of resource allocation; the amount of an overallocation appears in red, and the total allocation for each day appears at the bottom of each bar. To display this view (see Figure 11-3), click Resource Graph in the View bar or choose View | Resource Graph.

The Resource Allocation view (see Figure 11-4) is a combination view that is useful when you are trying to resolve a resource conflict. The top pane of the view displays resources and the bottom pane displays a Gantt Chart of the tasks assigned to the resource selected in the top pane. Using this view, it's easy to identify tasks that start at the same time or overlap in the Gantt Chart pane to which you've assigned the same resource.

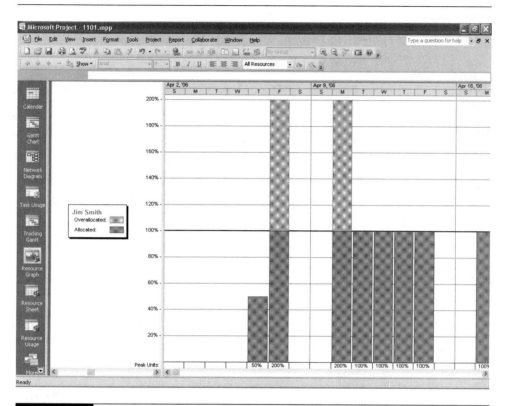

**FIGURE 11-3**   The Resource Graph view vividly displays overallocations.

To use to the Resource Allocation view, click the Resource Allocation button on the Resource Management toolbar.

You also can use filtering to identify resource conflict problems by displaying only overallocated resources. To filter a view, switch to it; in Figure 11-5, I used the Resource Usage view.

*To display the Resource Usage view, I took a shortcut: I removed the split provided with the Resource Allocation view by dragging the split bar to the bottom of the screen.*

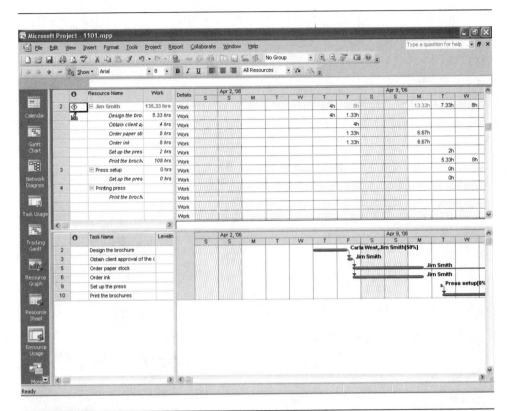

**FIGURE 11-4**    Use the Resource Allocation view to help you resolve a resource conflict.

Next, open the Filter drop-down list on the Formatting toolbar and click Overallocated Resources, or choose Project | Filtered | Overallocated Resources. Finally, add the Overallocation field to the view to identify the extent of the resource's overallocation. Choose Format | Details | Overallocation. Project adds a row to the timescale portion of the view to show you the number of hours that you need to eliminate to correct the overallocation.

Finally, you'll find a truly cool button on the Resource Management toolbar that helps you to spot resource conflicts; from any view, click the third button from the left edge of the toolbar—the Go To Next Overallocation button—and Project automatically selects either the overallocated resource or the task containing the overallocation.

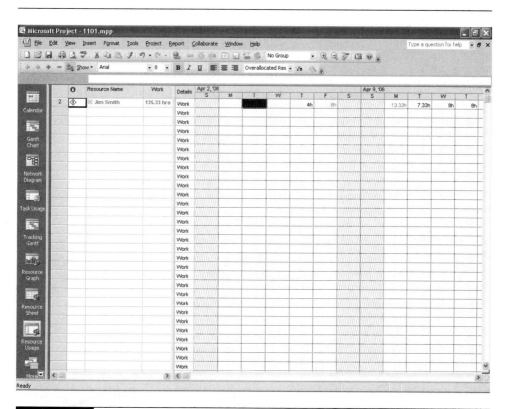

**FIGURE 11-5**   Filtering helps identify resource conflict problems.

# Adding a Resource to a Task

If the task assigned to an overallocated resource is effort-driven, you may be able to resolve the resource's conflict by adding another resource to the task. Suppose that Task 1, an effort-driven task, is running when Task 2 starts, and you need the same resource to work on both tasks. If you add another resource to Task 1, you'll reduce the amount of time that it takes to finish Task 1. If you can reduce the time sufficiently, you'll eliminate the resource conflict between the two tasks.

I suggest that you use a combination view; follow these steps:

1. Display the Gantt Chart view and choose Window | Split.

2. Click in the bottom pane of the view and then display the Resource Usage view by clicking Resource Usage in the View bar or by choosing View | Resource Usage.

3. In the upper pane, click the task to which you want to add a resource. In the bottom of the window, Project displays all the tasks assignments for each resource assigned to the selected task (see Figure 11-6).

4. Click the Assign Resources button on either the Resource Management toolbar or the Standard toolbar to open the Assign Resources window.

5. Highlight the resource you want to add, fill in the Units column, and click Close. Project adds the resource to the task.

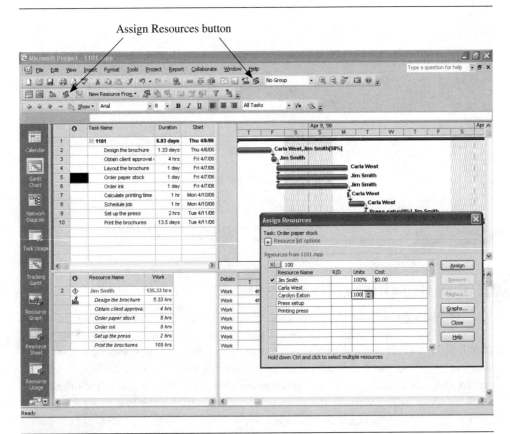

FIGURE 11-6    Add a resource to a task to help resolve a conflict.

# Selecting a Different Resource

You also can resolve resource conflicts by selecting a different resource for one of the tasks in conflict. Start in the Resource Usage view, where you can focus on resource conflicts and use the combination view (described in Steps 1 and 2 in the preceding section) that shows the Gantt Chart in the top of the view and the Resource Usage view in the bottom of the view. Then, follow these steps:

1. In the upper pane, click the task to which you want to assign a different resource. Project displays in the bottom of the window all the tasks assignments for each resource assigned to the selected task.

2. Click the Assign Resources button on the Resource Management toolbar or the Standard toolbar to open the Assign Resources window (refer to Figure 11-6).

3. Highlight the resource you want to remove from the task and click the Replace button. Project displays the Replace Resource dialog box (see Figure 11-7).

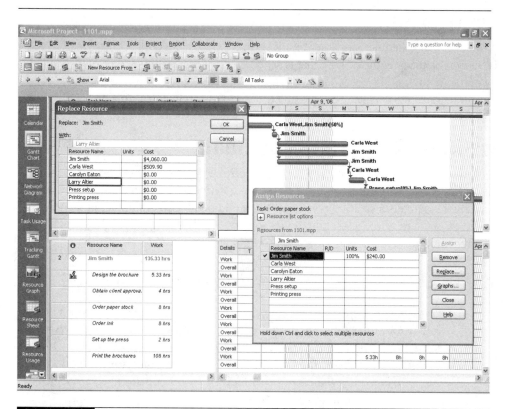

**FIGURE 11-7**   Replacing a resource.

4. Highlight the resource you want to use on the task, fill in the Units column, and click OK.

5. In the Assign Resources window, click Close. Project will change the assignment.

Using this technique, Project changes assignments without affecting historical actual data you recorded.

 *Although you can remove a resource assignment, you must be careful. If you remove a resource assignment for which you have recorded actual work, you may see misleading information about the task. For example, suppose that a resource assigned to a task completes the task, and then you delete the resource assignment. The actual work that had been applied for the resource will be lost and Project will adjust the Work field based on the other resources assigned and their units.*

## Using Overtime

You also can schedule overtime for a resource to resolve a conflict. Project defines overtime as the amount of work that is scheduled beyond an assigned resource's regular working hours, and Project charges overtime hours to the project using the resource's overtime rate. See Chapter 10 for detailed steps to assign overtime to a resource.

## Adjusting a Resource's Calendar

Salaried resources don't typically receive overtime pay for working beyond regularly scheduled hours. If the number of hours in conflict on a given day is low enough and the resource is a salaried resource, you might be able to eliminate the conflict by increasing the resource's working hours for that day. Project charges the extra hours the resource works at a regular rate instead of an overtime rate.

 *Although you can change non-working hours to working hours for any resource, you need to consider the effects on the cost of your project. Nonsalaried employees are typically paid using an overtime rate when they work more than the standard 40-hour work week. If you change non-working hours to working hours for a nonsalaried employee, you will understate the cost of your project, because your project won't take into consideration the extra pay received by the nonsalaried employee for working extra hours.*

To change a resource's working calendar, follow these steps:

1. In the Resource Usage view, note the number of hours in conflict for a resource.

2. Double-click the resource that has a conflict to open the Resource Information dialog box.

3. On the General tab, click the Change Working Time button to open the Change Working Time dialog box and view that resource's calendar.

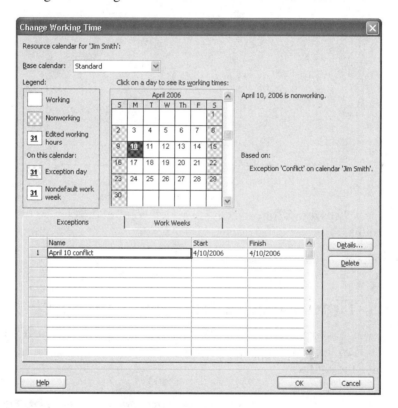

4. Click the date on which the conflict occurs.

5. On the Exceptions tab, type a name for this change; in the illustration, I called mine April 10 conflict.

6. Click the Details button.

7. In the Details dialog box, click the Working Times option button; in the From and To boxes, type the working times for the day.

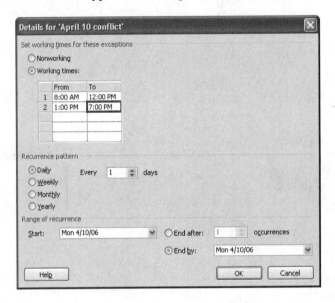

8. Click OK.

9. Repeat Steps 4 to 8 for each day for which you want to change the work schedule for a particular resource.

10. Click OK when you finish.

# Using Part-Time Work to Resolve a Conflict

When a resource is overallocated and you don't want to use any of the techniques I've described so far, you can assign the resource to work part-time on each of the tasks to solve the conflict.

*Using this technique may extend the project and increase its cost, because the tasks may take longer to complete. If the tasks to which the resource is assigned are effort-driven, you may want to use this method in conjunction with adding other resources to make sure that you can complete the task on time.*

To assign a resource to work part-time, you change the number of units of the resource that you apply to the task. By default, Project sets task types to Fixed Units and Effort Driven, so changing the amount of time that a resource works on a task also changes the duration of the task. But, you can preserve the task's duration by changing the task type to Fixed Duration.

NOTE
*You should understand the logic behind making this change. When you indicate that the task can be completed by the resource in the allotted amount of time, you are, in essence, shortening the amount of time that it takes to complete the task because you're applying less effort to complete the task in the same timeframe.*

To change the task type to Fixed Duration so that you can preserve the task's duration when you subsequently reduce a resource's assignment, follow these steps (remember, these steps are optional; complete them only to preserve the task's duration):

1.  Display the Resource Allocation view by choosing View | More Views | Resource Allocation | Apply.

2.  Click the task that you want to change in the upper pane. Project displays that task in Gantt format in the lower pane.

3.  In the lower pane, double-click the task that you want to change. When Project displays the Task Information dialog box, click the Advanced tab.

**11**

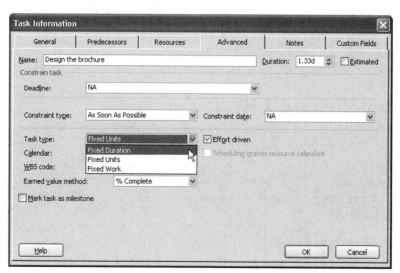

4. Open the Task Type drop-down list and select Fixed Duration.

5. Click OK.

Follow these steps to assign a resource to work part-time on a task:

1. In the top pane of the Resource Allocation view, click a task to which the overallocated resource is assigned.

2. Double-click the task to open the Assignment Information dialog box and then click the General tab.

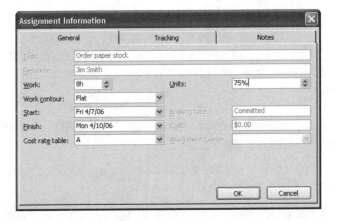

3. Change the value in the Units box to reflect the percentage of time that you want the resource to spend on the task; anything less than 100% qualifies as part-time work.

4. Click OK.

# Staggering Starting Times

On tasks to which you've assigned more than one resource, you might be able to resolve resource conflicts by staggering the times that the resources begin working on the task. When you delay a resource's start on a task, Project recalculates the start date and time for that resource's work on the task, which may eliminate the conflict. To stagger start times for resources, work in the Task Usage view and follow these steps:

CAUTION   *Using this technique might extend the duration of the task.*

1. Click Task Usage in the View bar or choose View | Task Usage.

2. In the Task Name column, select the resource whose work time you want to delay (see Figure 11-8).

3. Click the Assignment Information button or double-click the resource. When Project displays the Assignment Information dialog box, click the General tab.

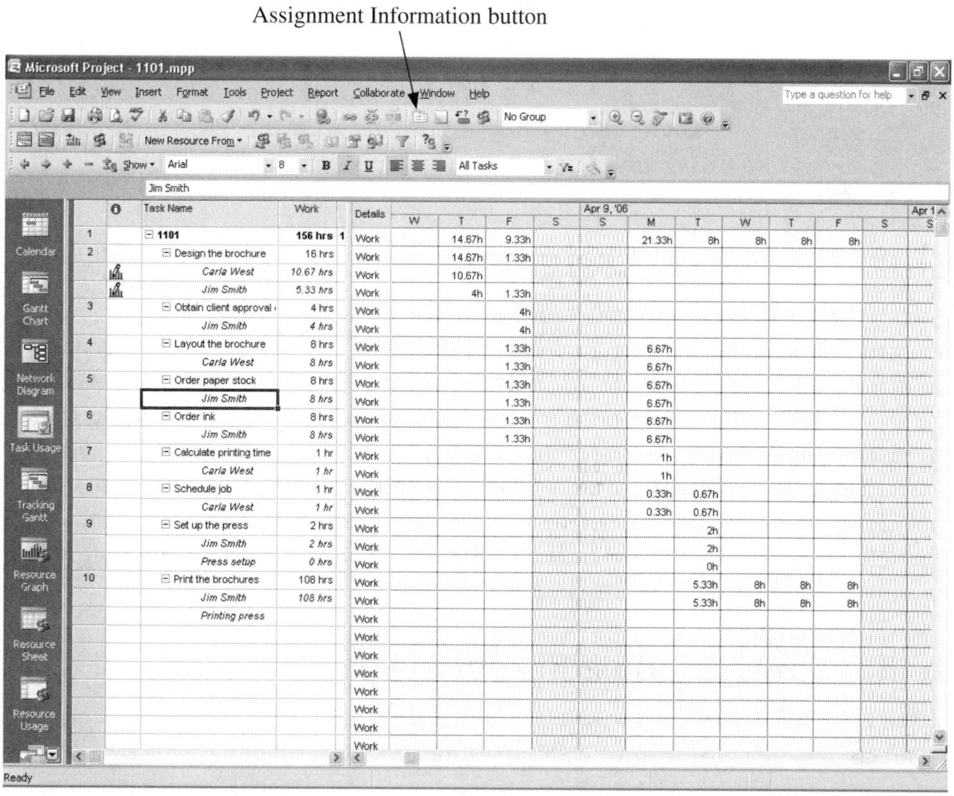

Assignment Information button

**FIGURE 11-8**   Select the task assigned to the resource whose work time you want to delay.

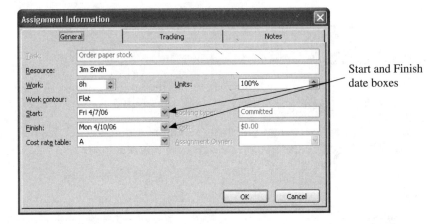

Start and Finish
date boxes

4.  Change the date in the Start or Finish box.

5.  Click OK.

*You also can change the assignment start and finish dates by typing directly in the Task Usage table.*

# Leveling Resource Assignments

Suppose that several concurrently running tasks in your project are causing resource conflicts. If you spread out—or *level*—the demand for your resources, you can resolve the conflicts. You spread out the demand for resources either by delaying a task until the resource is available to work on it or by splitting the task, performing some work on the task, and delaying the rest of the task until the resource is available to work on it. You can let Project select the tasks to delay or split; you can examine the project and identify tasks that you are willing to delay or split and then resolve the conflicts yourself; or, you can use a combination of the approaches and first let Project level resource loads and then make adjustments yourself.

## Letting Project Adjust Resource Loads

When Project automatically levels resource assignments in a project, it reschedules them, taking into consideration a variety of factors, including:

■  The resource's working capacity

■  The resource's assignment units

- The resource's calendar

- Available slack

- Task dependencies

- Scheduling dates

- The task's duration

- The task's constraints

- The task's priority

In earlier chapters in this book, you've read about all of these factors except a task's priority. You can set priority values for every task in your project; Project uses the priority values to determine the order in which to level resource assignments on tasks. If everything else is equal, Project delays tasks with lower priorities before delaying tasks with higher priorities. By default, Project assigns all tasks a priority of 500, but you can assign any value between 0 and 1000. If you assign a priority of 1000 to a task, Project will not delay the task.

To set a priority, display any task view; I tend to work in the Gantt Chart view. Then, double-click a task to display its Task Information dialog box. On the General tab, set the task's priority. After you prioritize tasks but before you level, you might want to sort tasks by priority; that way, you can quickly see the tasks that Project is most likely to level. To sort tasks, see Chapter 9.

**11**

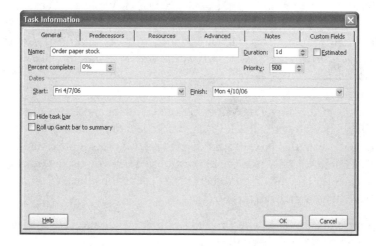

NOTE *You might prefer to add the Priority column to the table portion of the Gantt Chart view and then set priorities using the table; that way, you can easily see the priorities of each task. See Chapter 8 for help inserting a column.*

To level tasks automatically, follow these steps:

1. Choose Tools | Level Resources to open the Resource Leveling dialog box.

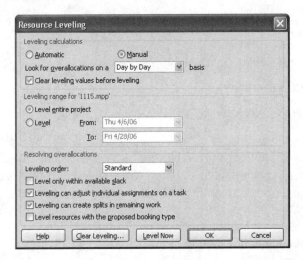

 *Click the Automatic option button; if necessary, Project will automatically level resources whenever you make a change to your schedule.*

2. Open the Look for Overallocations on a *x* Basis drop-down list and select a basis—a timeframe—such as Day by Day or Week by Week.

 *In the Resource Usage view, the Indicators column box beside an overallocated resource may contain a note that suggests the appropriate basis.*

3. Check the Clear Leveling Values Before Leveling check box to remove the delays created by previous leveling before leveling again. If you remove the check from this box, Project doesn't relevel tasks it previously leveled; instead, it levels only new overallocations. When you use automatic leveling, you can improve the time Project spends calculating the schedule if you remove the check from this box.

4. Either click Level Entire Project or click Level and select specific dates to level.

5. Use the Leveling Order list box to specify the order that you want Project to consider when leveling your project. The following are your options:

   ■ **ID Only**   Project delays or splits the task with the highest ID number.

   ■ **Standard**   Project looks at slack, dates, predecessor dependencies, and priorities when selecting the best task to split or delay.

   ■ **Priority, Standard**   Project looks first at task priority and then at all the factors listed for the Standard leveling order.

6. Check the Level Only Within Available Slack check box to avoid changing the end date of your project.

7. Check the Leveling Can Adjust Individual Assignments on a Task check box to adjust one resource's work schedule on a task independently of other resources that are working on the same task.

8. Check the Leveling Can Create Splits in Remaining Work check box to permit leveling to split tasks to resolve resource conflicts.

9. Check the Level Resources with the Proposed Booking Type check box to have Project include tasks containing proposed resources during the leveling process.

10. Click Level Now to apply leveling.

You can review the effects of leveling from the Leveling Gantt Chart view. Choose View | More Views | Leveling Gantt | Apply. Project adds green bars to your Gantt Chart, which represent the duration of tasks before leveling (see Figure 11-9). Depending on the nature of your project, Project may build more slack into your tasks.

To remove the effects of leveling, reopen the Resource Leveling dialog box and click the Clear Leveling button. A dialog box appears that lets you choose to clear leveling for the entire project or for selected tasks only.

## Making Adjustments to Leveling

When you have just a few resource conflicts to resolve or when automatic leveling doesn't provide acceptable results, you can make adjustments manually.

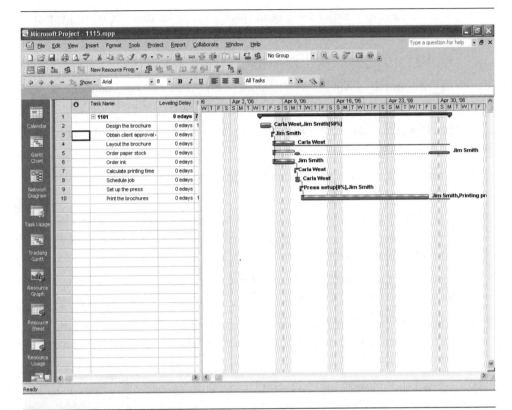

**FIGURE 11-9**　The Leveling Gantt Chart view shows you the effects of leveling.

To demonstrate, I've set up a very simple project—two tasks scheduled to start simultaneously, with the same resource assigned full-time to both. In Figure 11-10, you see the project in the Resource Allocation view before leveling.

*To display the Resource Allocation view, click the Resource Allocation View button on the Resource Management toolbar.*

To make leveling adjustments, identify the task that you want to delay in the top pane. Then, in the bottom pane, enter an amount in the Leveling Delay field for that task (see Figure 11-11). Project delays the task accordingly and reduces the resource's conflict.

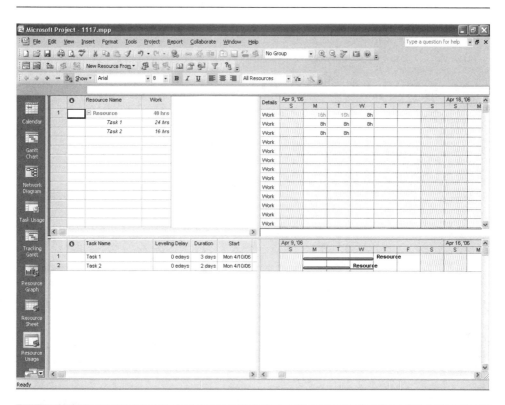

**FIGURE 11-10** A project before making leveling adjustments.

## Did you know?

# Leveling, Working Time, and Non-Working Time

Project considers both working and non-working time when leveling; that is, if the tasks involved in leveling run over a weekend, Project includes those weekend days in the leveling process. So, for example, if the project in the illustrations had started on a Friday, I would have needed to enter a Leveling Delay of 5 Days—two extra days to account for Saturday and Sunday—for Task 2 to resolve the conflict.

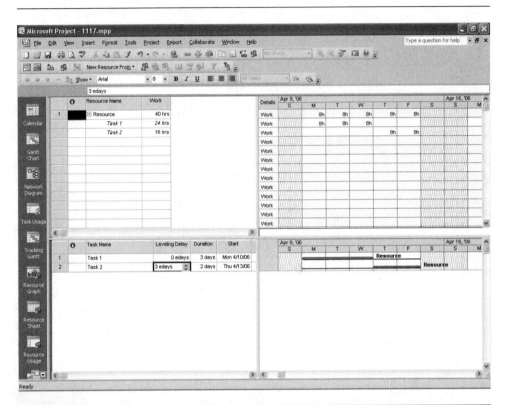

**FIGURE 11-11**  To manually level a task, enter an amount in the Leveling Delay field.

# Contouring Resource Work Patterns

A resource's work assignment over time can take a shape, which Project calls a *contour*. These contours vary; the most common ones in Project are Flat, Back Loaded, Front Loaded, and Bell. The default contour, Flat, means that a resource works on a task for the maximum number of hours that he or she is assigned to a task for the duration of the assignment. Contours can help you resolve a conflict by letting you control how much a resource is scheduled to work on a task at a particular time.

Contours help you to assign work to a task based on when the task requires the effort. For example, if a task requires less effort initially, consider using a Back

Loaded contour. If a task requires most effort in the middle of the task, consider using a Bell or Turtle contour.

 *Using a contour other than the default Flat contour can inadvertently cause a resource conflict, because the contour will shift work effort to a specific portion of a task's timeframe.*

To set a contour pattern, follow these steps:

**1.** Click Task Usage in the View bar or choose View | Task Usage.

**2.** In the Task Name column, double-click a resource or click the resource and then click the Assignment Information button on the Standard toolbar. In the Assignment Information dialog box, click the General tab.

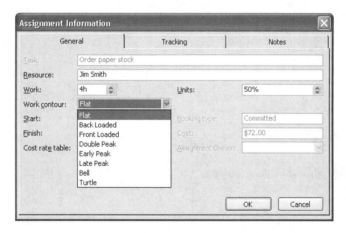

**3.** Open the Work Contour drop-down list and select a contour.

**4.** Click OK.

An indicator appears next to the resource if you select a contour other than Flat; pass the mouse pointer over the indicator to identify the contour applied to the resource (see Figure 11-12).

**NOTE** *Project adjusts contour patterns if you change the duration, start date, or total work values of a task or the start date of a resource's work on the task.*

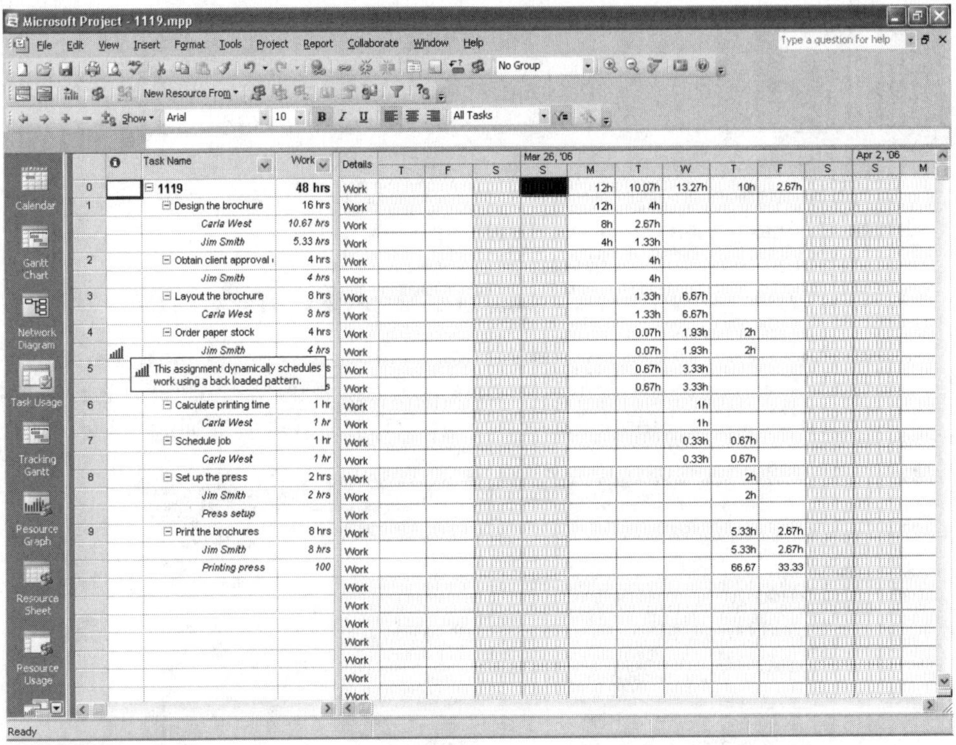

**FIGURE 11-12** Pass the mouse pointer over the indicator to identify the contour applied to the resource.

In addition to contouring work assignments, you can contour a resource's availability. For example, you can use this feature to indicate that a particular resource may be available to work on your project only part-time for a specified timeframe. In the Resource Availability portion of the General tab of the Resource Information dialog box, set Available From and Available To dates for the selected resource.

 *Open this dialog box by displaying the Resource Sheet and then double-click a resource.*

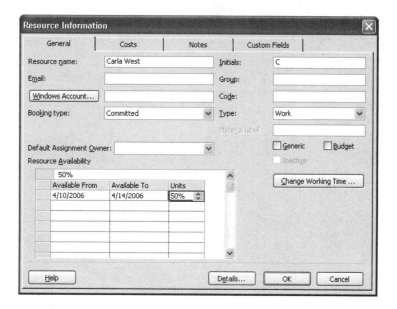

 **Pooling Resources**

In Project, a *resource pool* is the set of resources that is available to any project; typically, you and other project managers share the resources among several projects. You can try to solve resource conflicts by using a resource pool.

Resource pooling is useful only if you work with the same resources on multiple projects and you don't use Project Server. Resource pooling is closely tied to the topic of managing multiple projects, which I cover in Chapter 17.

If you're using Project Server, you don't need to use resource pooling. Instead, you'll be more interested in using Enterprise resources and the Resource Substitution Wizard to resolve resource conflicts. See Chapter 20 for information on Project Server.

11

In this chapter, you learned about the variety of techniques you can use to try to resolve resource conflicts. These techniques and the ones presented in Chapter 10 to resolve scheduling conflicts should help you produce a conflict-free schedule; once you reach that point, it's time to finalize your estimate and go forward to track progress.

# Part V  Tracking

# Chapter 12

# Establishing Baselines

## How to...

■ Set calculation options

■ Work with baselines

■ Work with interim plans

Up to this point in the book, you've been using Project as a planning tool. You've entered tasks and added resources. You've also made changes so that tasks relate properly to each other and so that resource assignments don't conflict. Now that you have a workable project schedule, you are ready to start the project. And, while planning is important, tracking what actually happens once you start your project and comparing actual events to your estimates of what would happen is the true source of power that Project can provide. By monitoring progress, you can anticipate challenges before they become problems, helping you to keep your project on schedule and within budget. Further, once you complete a project, comparing actual progress to estimated progress can help you make more accurate estimates on future projects. History is a powerful teacher.

To track progress, you need to set a *baseline* for your project; a baseline is a picture of your project schedule at the moment your planning is complete. But before we dive into setting baselines—you can set up to 11 baselines in a Project schedule—we'll review the principles of tracking and Project calculation options. To track effectively, you should understand the steps involved in tracking so that you can set up efficient procedures to handle tracking. And, Project's calculation options affect the bottom line of both the project's cost and the project's schedule.

# Reviewing the Principles of Tracking

Tracking in Project consists of entering information about actual information—called *actuals*—like the actual start date, the actual finish date, and the actual duration of a task. Resources report actual time worked and actual costs incurred, and you use the information to update the progress of your schedule.

On rare occasions, a project goes entirely according to plan. As the project manager, you need to be prepared to alter your schedule to adjust for the changes in timing and costs that are bound to occur in your project.

When you view the Tracking Gantt, you can see the revised schedule and how one delay affects your entire schedule. Suppose that you estimated five days to complete a task, and after seven days of effort, the task still isn't finished. Project not only tells you that you're running late but also adjusts the dates of future tasks that depend on the behind-schedule task. In Figure 12-1, the top bar of each task represents actual work, and the bottom bar represents estimated work.

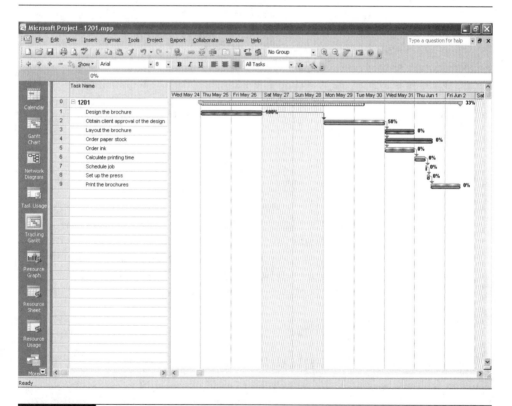

**FIGURE 12-1**    In the Tracking Gantt, you can compare actual work to estimated work.

*In Chapter 13, you'll find specific steps for updating a project to reflect actual progress.*

From resource views like the Resource Sheet and Resource Graph views, Project also shows any resource conflicts that result when resources have to put in more work than you estimated.

Using a "usage" view (the Task Usage view or the Resource Usage view), you can compare budgeted costs to actual costs. Project displays your projected total costs, based on a combination of actual costs and the remaining estimates; using this information, you can try to revise resource allocations to stay within your overall project budget.

Project managers usually track activity weekly or every two weeks, recording information about both completed tasks and tasks in progress. Tracking progress on a regular basis helps you to become aware of any deviation from your estimates quickly; the sooner you notice a delay, the more options you have to accommodate it.

By tracking actuals, you also can generate reports to show management where your project stands. Presenting actual data on your project's status can help persuade management that you need more time, more resources, or a shift in strategy if things aren't going as you expected.

*See Chapter 15 for information about the reports that Project can produce.*

To become a better project manager, take advantage of the tools in Project that let you quickly and easily compare your estimates with the actual outcome of the project. By evaluating this information, you can make changes in your strategy to keep you on track and meet your current project's goals. You also can use this data historically; by reviewing estimates versus actual data, you can make your next project plan more realistic.

# Setting Calculation Options

You can review and change the way Project calculates your project's schedule and cost on the Calculation tab of the Options dialog box. Choose Tools | Options to display the Options dialog box. Then, click the Calculation tab.

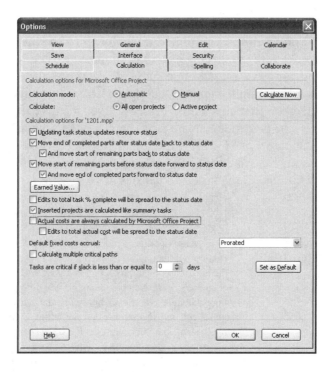

Use these options as described in Table 12-1.

Some of these options bear some further explanation and examples:

- **Updating task status updates resource status check box**   When you check this box and update the percentage of completion for a task, Project also updates the % Work Complete field for the resource and the assignment.

- **Move end of completed parts after status date back to status date, And move start of remaining parts back to status date check boxes**   To better understand Project's behavior and this pair of check boxes, suppose that the status date is May 9 and you have a task with a start date of May 14 and a duration of four days. Furthermore, suppose that the task actually starts on May 7. If you select the first check box, Project moves the task start date to May 7, sets the percent complete to 50 percent, and schedules the start of the remaining work for May 16, creating a split task. If you also select the second check box, Project makes the changes that I just described but moves the start of the remaining work to May 9.

**12**

■ **Move start of remaining parts before status date forward to status date, And move end of completed parts forward to status date check boxes**   As with the preceding example, suppose that the status date is May 9 and you have a task with a start date of May 1 and a duration of four days. Furthermore, suppose that the task actually starts on May 7. If you select the first check box, Project leaves the task start date at May 1, sets the percent complete to 50 percent, and schedules the start of the remaining work for May 9, once again creating a split task. If you also select the second check box, Project makes the changes that I just described but moves the task's actual start date to May 7.

| Option(s) | Purpose |
|---|---|
| Calculation Mode and Calculate option buttons | Using these options, you can control when Project calculates changes that you make to the project. Choose Automatic, the default, to make Project update your project as you make changes. Choose Manual to control when Project recalculates your schedule; when you choose manual calculation and you make a change that requires recalculation, Calculate appears in the status bar. You can press F9 to recalculate. For large projects, where calculating seems to take quite a while, switch to manual calculation to save time. You also can choose to apply the calculation mode to all open projects or only to the active project by choosing the corresponding button. |
| Updating task status updates resource status check box | Selected by default, this check box makes Project update resource status to correspond with any updated task status. This option works in reverse, too; if you update a resource's status, Project also updates task status accordingly. |
| Move end of completed parts after status date back to status date, And move start of remaining parts back to status date, Move start of remaining parts before status date forward to status date, and And move end of completed parts forward to status date check boxes | None of these check boxes is selected by default; when tasks begin late or early, Project doesn't change the task start dates or adjust the remaining portions of tasks. These check boxes enable you to change this default behavior so that Project updates the tasks in relation to the status date. You can find the project's status date in the Project Information dialog box (Project \| Project Information). If you haven't set the status date, Project uses the current date. These options only apply when you make total actual value edits, including task total actual work, task actual duration, total percent complete, and percent work complete. These options don't apply if you use timesheet information from Project Server to update your project or when you record actual information on summary tasks. |

**TABLE 12-1**    Calculation Options in Project

| Option(s) | Purpose |
|---|---|
| Earned Value button | Click this button to set earned value options for the project; see Chapter 16 for more information about earned value. |
| Edits to total task % complete will be spread to the status date check box | By default, this check box is not selected, making Project distribute changes to the task percentage of completion to the end of the actual duration of the task. If you select this check box, Project distributes the changes evenly across the schedule to the project status date. |
| Inserted projects are calculated like summary tasks check box | This box is selected by default, making Project treat inserted projects like summary tasks when calculating the project schedule, instead of treating inserted projects like separate projects. See Chapter 17 for more information about inserting projects. |
| Actual costs are always calculated by Microsoft Office Project check box, and Edits to total actual cost will be spread to the status date check box | By default, the first of these boxes is checked and the second is not checked. When you check this box, Project calculates actual costs. You can't enter actual costs until a task is 100 percent complete; if you do, Project will overwrite any costs that you enter prior to 100 percent completion as it recalculates costs. You also can't import actual cost values. The second check box makes Project distribute changes to a task's total actual cost evenly across the task's schedule to the status date. |
| Default fixed costs accrual list box | Use this drop-down list box to choose a method for Project to accrue fixed costs for new tasks. You can have Project accrue fixed costs at the start of a task or at the end of a task, or you can use the default Prorated setting to allocate the costs equally throughout the duration of the task. |
| Calculate multiple critical paths check box | When you select this check box, described in Chapter 10, Project calculates and displays separate critical paths in the project and sets the late finish date for tasks without successors or constraints to their early finish date. |
| Tasks are critical if slack is less than or equal to $x$ days list box | By default, Project sets this value to 0, so that only tasks with no slack appear on the critical path. This check box also was described in Chapter 10. |
| Set as Default button | Use this button to set the calculation options on this tab to apply to all projects. |

**TABLE 12-1**    Calculation Options in Project (*continued*)

# Setting or Changing a Baseline

A baseline is a snapshot of your project at a particular moment in time. Typically, you set a baseline when you complete the project's planning phase; in addition, you might set a baseline at the end of some critical phase of your project. You can set as many as 11 baselines, and each baseline that you save includes information about tasks, resources, and assignments. For tasks, Project saves duration, start and finish dates, work, timephased work, cost, and timephased cost. For resources, Project saves work, timephased work, cost, and timephased cost information with the baseline. For assignments, Project saves start and finish dates, work, timephased work, costs, and timephased costs.

During the planning phase of a project, you usually need to save the project file several times without saving a baseline. When you're ready to save a baseline, follow these steps:

1. Choose Tools | Tracking | Set Baseline to open the Set Baseline dialog box.

2. Select Set Baseline.

3. Open the Set Baseline drop-down list and select the baseline that you want to save.

4. Select Entire Project.

5. Click OK.

You can save a baseline for only some tasks; select those tasks before you perform Step 1. Then, in Step 4, choose Selected Tasks. When you save baselines for selected tasks, Project lets you choose to roll up baselines to all summary tasks and from subtasks into their parent summary task(s). To understand what happens when you save a baseline for selected tasks, suppose that you have a project set up like the one shown in Figure 12-2 and, before opening the Set Baseline dialog box, you select Task 6, a child of Task 1 and the parent of Tasks 7 and 8.

If you select only the To All Summary Tasks check box of the Set Baseline dialog box, Project rolls up baseline information from Task 6 to Task 1 without regard to the baseline information that is stored for Tasks 7 and 8. If you select only the From Subtasks into Selected Summary Task(s) check box, Project rolls up the information from Tasks 7 and 8 to Task 6. If you select both check boxes, Project rolls up baseline information from Tasks 7 and 8 to Task 6 and then rolls up that information to Task 1.

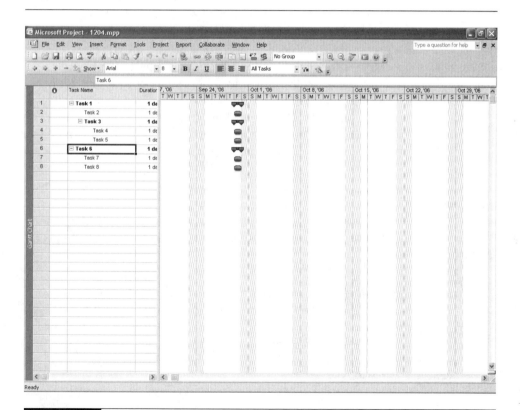

**FIGURE 12-2**   Saving a baseline for only some tasks

## Did you know?

# Costs Can Change a Baseline, Too

If cost-cutting measures hit your company after you save a baseline for a project with a $75,000 budget and you find that your budget is only $50,000, you should make the changes to your resources and costs and then reset your baseline so that you can accurately track cost information.

When you consider the purpose of a baseline—recording your project at a particular moment in time—you don't want to make changes to a baseline. But there are occasions when you need to modify a baseline and resave it, or to save a second or third baseline to document major changes to the project schedule. For example, it is fairly common to set the baseline for your plan and then realize that you left out a task or that you need to break one task into two tasks. Or, circumstances associated with your project may change. Suppose, for example, that your project is put on hold for three months. If this event occurs shortly after you complete the schedule, you'll be able to manage your project more effectively if you set a new baseline schedule before restarting. If, however, this event occurs six months into your project, you may want to modify the timing of future tasks and reset the baseline only for tasks going forward. That way, you retain the ability to accurately assess how well you estimated for all tasks in the project.

Under circumstances like these, make your schedule changes, select the affected tasks, and resave your baseline, using the preceding steps with the Selected Tasks option button and the appropriate Roll Up Baselines settings. Project will update the baseline for the changed tasks and then change all the summary levels to reflect the change.

NOTE *Add or change task information using the Gantt Chart view, but don't try to add baseline information using the Baseline Duration and Baseline Start or Finish columns in the Gantt table. Adding baseline data this way does not enable all baseline calculations. For example, adding a task at the end of the project with this method doesn't effect a change in the baseline finish date.*

# Saving an Interim Plan

The baseline may quickly become of more interest historically than practically, especially if the timing of your schedule changes significantly. The record of your original planning process is important to retain, so you should not change the initial baseline. However, if the timing of your project schedule shifts dramatically away from the baseline plan, you need to revise the schedule to better reflect reality. You can save another baseline, or you can save an interim plan to help you see how well you're meeting your revised goals.

Interim plans differ from baselines by the amount and type of information that Project saves. Interim plans contain a set of task start and finish dates that you can compare with another interim plan or with a baseline plan. A baseline includes more information—in addition to task start and finish dates, baselines also include duration, work, and cost information about tasks, resources, and assignments.

While you can set interim plans for all the tasks in the project, typically, you'll want to save an interim plan only for tasks going forward.

 *You also can use interim plans to copy baseline information from one baseline to another.*

You can save an interim plan by following these steps:

1. Select various tasks to include in the interim plan.

2. Choose Tools | Tracking | Set Baseline to open the Set Baseline dialog box.

3. Select the Set Interim Plan option button. Project makes the Copy and Into lists available.

**12**

4. Open the Copy list and select one of the Start/Finish dates.

5. From the Into list, select an item such as Start1/Finish1 to copy the dates into new fields; when you copy information from one set of Start and Finish date fields to another, you create an interim plan.

6. Select the Entire Project option button to create an interim plan for the whole project, or choose the Selected Tasks option button to create an interim plan that retains the original interim plan information for any tasks that you didn't select, yet saves new start and finish dates for the tasks that you have selected.

7. Click OK to save the interim plan.

You can use the various Start/Finish fields in the Copy and Into lists to save up to 11 interim plans.

## Clearing a Baseline or Interim Plan

Occasionally, you'll find a reason to clear a baseline or an interim plan. For example, suppose that you set a baseline because you considered the project plan complete. Then, you attend a meeting that changes the scope of your project by adding (or removing) tasks. The project hasn't yet started, but you now need to rework the project plan. In this case, there's little point to adjusting the baseline. Instead, you want to clear the baseline and set it again after you make your changes.

To clear a baseline or an interim plan, choose Tools | Tracking | Clear Baseline to display the Clear Baseline dialog box.

In this dialog box, you can choose to clear a baseline plan or an interim plan for the entire project or for selected tasks.

In this chapter, you've learned how to complete the planning stage of your project and prepare for the tracking stage. In the next chapter, we'll cover how to track schedule information.

# Chapter 13

## Tracking Schedule Information

## How to...

- ■ Enter tracking information

- ■ Use timephased fields to enter progress regularly

- ■ Modify the Tracking Table to make tracking easier

- ■ Reschedule remaining work

This chapter covers the methods you can use to record progress information—*actuals*—related to the tasks in your project schedule. In Chapter 14, you'll learn about similar techniques you can use to record actuals about project costs.

Recording actuals helps you provide management with a benchmark for your project's progress. In addition, you gain valuable information about your estimating skills that you can use as the project progresses and on future projects.

# Strategies for Tracking

Updating a project with actuals can become complicated regardless of the project's size. You can make the process run more smoothly if you establish efficient manual procedures for collecting the information you need, and your manual procedures should take into account the method you intend to use to enter the information and the frequency with which you intend to update. That way, you ensure that you have the information you need to update your project when you need it.

What do you need to know to enter progress information? You need to know if the task is on schedule, how much of the task is done, and whether revised estimates are available for the duration of the task and the work needed to complete the task.

You may want to create a form for team members to use. Or, check to determine if your organization has forms and processes in place to capture actuals and status information. Before you create a form, be sure to read the next section, "Entering Schedule Tracking Information," and decide on the method you intend to use to record progress. That way, you can ensure that you include the information you need on the form.

As the manager, you should decide how often to collect actual information for your project. You don't want your team members to spend more time reporting than working, but you need to receive actual information often enough that you'll be able to identify and resolve a problem before it becomes a major crisis.

*Don't forget to set a baseline before you enter actual information; see Chapter 12 for more information on setting baselines.*

To reduce the amount of work involved in tracking, delegate some of the updating to other people on your project. If a particular resource is in charge of one phase of the project, break that phase out into a separate project and let that resource update the activity. You can easily combine those smaller schedules into a master schedule that displays your entire project; see Chapter 17 for details.

You can set up a recurring task—one that occurs every week or two—in your project for tracking progress to help you remember to track.

**TIP** *Use task notes to record progress and changes that don't warrant changing the project baseline.*

Finally, if your organization sets and uses standards for measuring costs or determining when a task is complete, Project becomes a much more effective management tool, because each project manager will be using the same approach to measure progress and expenditures.

# Entering Schedule Tracking Information

Analyze progress information that you receive to identify unfinished tasks for which you need to adjust the planned duration, work, and costs. You'll find that these adjustments are easier to make before you record a task's actual dates or percentage of completion.

You can record actual information for a project by filling in various fields that track progress for each task. There are several combinations of fields that you can use; for example, some people update only the Actual Work and Remaining Work fields and then let Project update the other tracking-related fields. In this section, I'm going to describe the effects of updating the Actual Start and Finish Date fields, the Actual Duration field, the Percent Complete field, the Work Complete field, and the Remaining Duration field.

**13**

**NOTE** *If you use effort-driven scheduling, see the section "Using Timephased Fields" later in this chapter and use the method described there to update progress instead of the methods described in this section, because the duration of effort-driven tasks is affected by resource assignments.*

Be aware that Project calculates values for some fields when you enter information into other fields. For example, if you enter a percentage complete for a task, Project calculates and supplies a start date, an actual duration, a remaining duration, and an actual work value.

There is no "right way" to estimate the completeness of a task, but I suggest that you avoid using money or time spent as a gauge because it's too easy to find, after budgeting $12,000 for a task, that you've spent $15,000 on the task and it is only 25 percent complete. You may have to use gut instincts to estimate the progress. If your project has individual deliverables that you can track, use them consistently when you make your estimate.

## Recording Actual Start and Finish Dates

You can use a combination view of the Gantt Chart view and the Task Details view to enter and view actual start and finish dates and compare current, baseline, and actual dates.

Follow these steps to set up your screen:

1. Choose View | Gantt Chart.

2. Choose Window | Split to display the Task Form view (see Figure 13-1).

3. Click the bottom pane to select it.

*When you click a pane to select it, Project displays the pane name to the left but dims the pane name of the unselected pane.*

4. Choose View | More Views to open the More Views window.

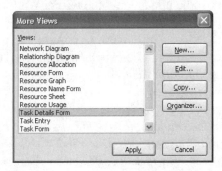

5. Select Task Details Form and click Apply.

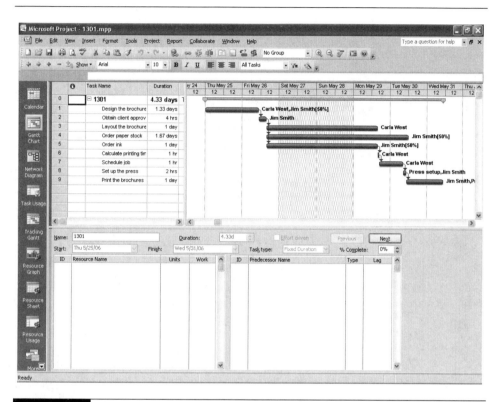

**FIGURE 13-1**   Setting up a combination view

**6.** In the top pane—the Gantt Chart view pane—select the task for which you
want to record actuals.

**7.** In the bottom pane, select the Actual option button (see Figure 13-2).

NOTE

*The three option buttons (Current, Baseline, and Actual) refer to the types
of dates that you can view and set.*

**8.** Record either a Start or a Finish date, and click OK.

How does setting an Actual Start Date and/or Actual Finish Date affect your
schedule? Project initially sets the Actual Start Date and Actual Finish Date fields

13

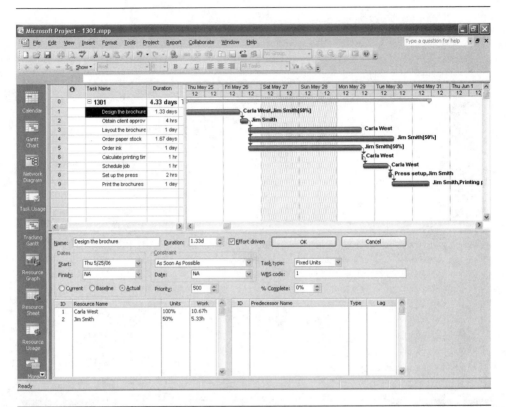

**FIGURE 13-2**    Select the task for which you want to record actual information.

to NA to indicate that you have not yet entered a date. When you update your project, Project makes the following changes:

- When you set an Actual Start Date and Finish Date, Project updates the projected start and finish dates to the actual dates that you enter.

- When you enter only an Actual Start Date, Project changes only one other field—the projected start date.

- When you enter only an Actual Finish Date, Project changes the Percent Complete field, the Actual Duration field, the Remaining Duration field, the Actual Work field, and the Actual Cost field. If you had not previously set an Actual Start Date, Project also changes that field.

TIP    *To return to a single view, choose Window | Remove Split.*

## Recording Actual Durations

You can record actual information by entering the actual duration, which is the amount of time that was needed to complete a task. You can use the Update Tasks dialog box to record an actual duration. To also update the work and cost figures for resources when you update a task's status, use the Calculation tab in the Options dialog box (choose Tools | Options; see Chapter 12 for details on the Calculation tab).

Follow these steps:

1. Choose View | Gantt Chart (or select any view that shows tasks).

2. Click the task for which you want to record an actual duration.

3. Choose Tools | Tracking | Update Tasks to display the Update Tasks dialog box.

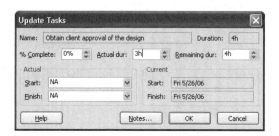

4. Type an amount in the Actual Dur box and click OK.

When you set an actual duration, Project makes the following changes:

- When you set an actual duration that is less than or equal to the planned duration, Project assumes that the task is progressing on schedule. When you click OK, Project sets the actual start date to the planned start date unless you previously set the actual start date. In that case, Project leaves the actual start date alone. Regardless of whether you previously set the actual start date, Project calculates the percentage complete and the remaining duration for the task.

*You can view the updated remaining duration and percentage complete if you reopen the Update Tasks dialog box.*

13

- When you set an actual duration that is greater than the planned duration, Project assumes that the task is finished but that it took longer than expected to complete. Project adjusts the planned duration to match the actual duration and changes the Percent Complete field to 100% and the Remaining Duration field to 0%.

- When you set an actual duration that equals the planned duration, Project assumes that the task finished on schedule and makes no changes to the planned duration, but changes the Percent Complete field to 100% and the Remaining Duration field to 0%.

## Setting the Percent Complete Value

You can assign a Percent Complete value to any task to record the task's progress. If you assign any value less than 100, you indicate that the task is not complete.

*Entering a Percent Complete value also affects the Actual Duration and Remaining Duration values. If you record any of these values, Project automatically updates the others.*

You can set a Percent Complete value in any of the following ways:

- From the Task Details form described earlier in this chapter, in the section "Recording Actual Start and Finish Dates"

- From the Update Tasks dialog box described in the preceding section, "Recording Actual Durations"

- From the Tracking Table described later in this chapter, in the section "Recording Remaining Durations"

- By selecting the task from any task view and using the percentage buttons on the Tracking toolbar

*To display the Tracking toolbar, right-click any toolbar and choose Tracking.*

Setting a Percent Complete value affects your schedule in the following way:

- Project assigns an Actual Start Date unless you had entered one previously.

- Project calculates the Actual Duration and Remaining Duration values.

- Project calculates the Actual Cost and Actual Work values if you set your options to update resources when you update tasks.

- Project assigns the planned finish date to the Actual Finish Date column if you enter 100 in the Percent Complete column. If the task didn't finish on the date you are using to enter actuals (status date or current date), don't enter a Percent Complete value; instead, enter an Actual Finish Date using the technique described in "Recording Actual Start and Finish Dates."

## Recording Remaining Durations

I find that it's easiest to enter all actual information into Project by using the Tracking Table view because it offers you the most in the way of options—you can enter any type of progress information using the Tracking Table.

In this section, I'll focus on entering remaining durations into the Rem. Dur. (Remaining Duration) field using the Tracking Table. The Rem. Dur. field shows how much more time you need to complete a task.

## Did you know?

# Customize the Tracking Table for Data Entry

13

To make data entry easy—and provide an easy way for someone else to enter the data—I suggest that you create your own version of the Tracking Table that displays the fields into which you will enter information in contiguous columns. See Chapter 8 for information on inserting and hiding columns in a table. You also might want to include the project's status date and the current date on your Tracking Table so that you can easily find any tasks not completed prior to the status date and identify work that needs to be rescheduled. To include these dates, you need to create custom fields; see Chapter 19 for details on creating custom fields.

To display the Tracking Table view, follow these steps:

1. Choose View | Gantt Chart.

2. Right-click the Select All button and click Tracking from the menu that appears. Project displays the Tracking Table view in the left portion of the Gantt Chart view (see Figure 13-3).

3. To see all the columns that are available on the Tracking Table view, narrow the chart portion of the window.

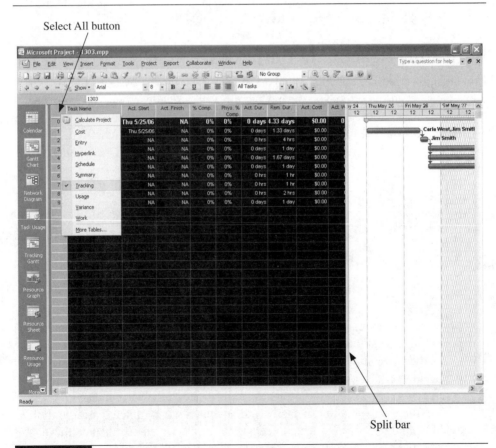

**FIGURE 13-3**    Displaying the Tracking Table view

Entering a Rem. Dur. (Remaining Duration) value has the following effects:

■ Project sets the % Comp. (Percent Complete) value using the Rem. Dur. value and the Act. Dur. value.

■ Project updates the work and cost figures for the resources on the task if you set Project's options to update the status of resources when you update a task's status.

# Recording Work Completed

When you schedule tasks based on the availability of certain resources, you'll find that tracking progress on a task is easiest if you update the work completed. When you update the Work Completed value, Project also updates the work that each resource is performing by subtracting the work performed from the total work scheduled.

Again, I like to use the Tracking Table view to enter information into the Act. Work (Actual Work) column, but I start in the Task Usage view to enter actual work performed for specific resources. Choose View | Task Usage. Then, right-click the Select All button and click Tracking from the shortcut menu that appears—see the preceding section for step-by-step instructions to display this view.

If you drag the split bar to the right, so that you can see the Act. Work column, you'll be able to see the effects of entering actual work (see Figure 13-4).

Click in the Act. Work column on the row of the individual who performed the work and enter the actual work value.

NOTE    *When you record actual work on the row of the task instead of the row of an individual resource, Project divides the actual and remaining work among all resources assigned to the task.*

13

Recording actual work has the following effects on your schedule:

■ Project updates the % Complete field, the Act. Dur. field, the Rem. Dur. field, and the Act. Cost field.

■ If you had not previously set an Actual Start Date, Project sets that date.

■ If the Actual Work value matches the planned work value, Project also sets the Actual Finish Date.

■ If the Actual Work value exceeds the planned work value, Project not only sets the Actual Finish Date but also sets the planned work value equal to the Actual Work value.

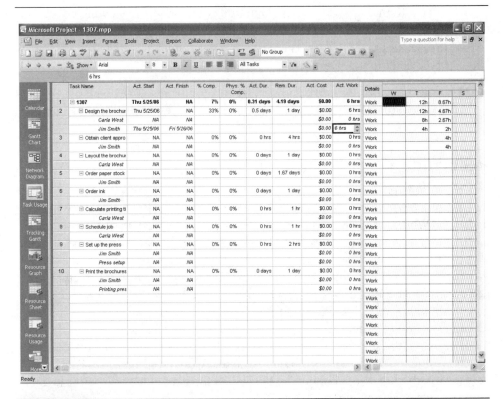

**FIGURE 13-4**  I use the Tracking Table in the Task Usage view to enter actual work performed.

*The right side of this view contains timephased fields that you can use to enter actual work on the day it was performed; see "Using Timephased Fields" later in this chapter for details.*

## Updating Tasks Simultaneously

Project provides you with a shortcut for updating actuals for several tasks that are on schedule or were completed on schedule. Follow these steps:

1. Select the Gantt Chart view.

2. In the Task Name column, select the tasks that you want to update. If you don't select any tasks, Project updates the entire project.

**NOTE**    *To select multiple contiguous tasks, click in the Task Name column of the first task, hold down SHIFT, and click in the Task Name column of the last task. To select multiple noncontiguous tasks, hold down CTRL instead of SHIFT as you click each task that you want to select.*

3. Choose Tools | Tracking | Update Project to display the Update Project dialog box (see Figure 13-5).

4. Check the date that appears in the Update Work as Complete Through list box to make sure that it is correct.

5. Select Set 0%–100% Complete to have Project calculate the percent complete for each task, or select Set 0% or 100% Complete Only to have Project mark completed tasks with 100% and leave incomplete tasks at 0%.

6. Select Entire Project or Selected Tasks, as appropriate.

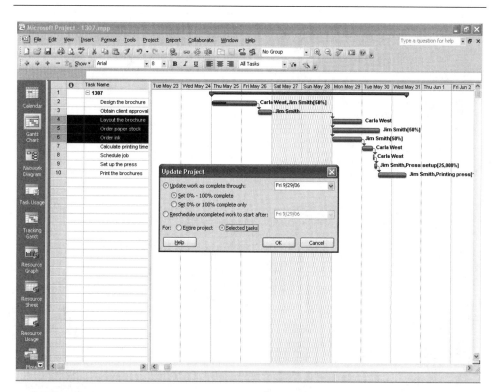

**FIGURE 13-5**  Update actuals for the selected tasks.

**NOTE**  *When you select Entire Project, Project sets the project status date to the date that you selected in Step 4.*

**7.** Click OK.

# Using Timephased Fields

Using Project's timephased fields, you can update the progress of your project by recording actuals on a daily or weekly basis. You record progress in timephased fields from a "usage" view—either the Resource Usage view, which organizes assignments by resource, listing the tasks to which the resource is assigned, or the Task Usage view, which organizes assignments by task, listing resources assigned to the task. Since you receive actuals typically from each resource, the Resource Usage view most closely matches the format of your data, so for this example, we'll work in the Resource Usage view (see Figure 13-6). Choose View | Resource Usage.

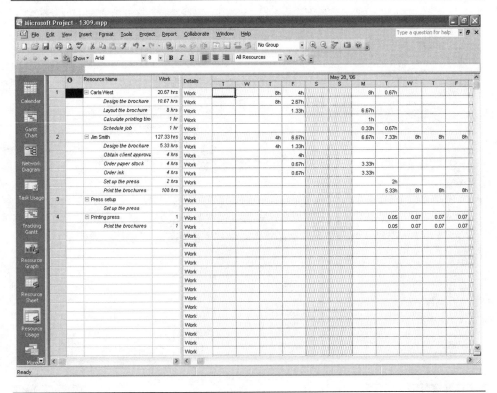

**FIGURE 13-6**    Use the Resource Usage view to record progress using timephased fields.

You enter actual data in the Details portion of the view, which is the right side of the view; right-click anywhere on the Details portion (the right-side) of the view and click Actual Work on the shortcut menu that appears to add a row for actual work to the Details portion of the view (see Figure 13-7).

*You remove a row in the Details portion of the view the same way that you add it.*

The frequency with which you intend to enter actual data dictates the appearance of the timescale in the Details section. In Figure 13-7, the timescale presents a daily view, enabling you to record actuals on the day they occurred.

Figure 13-8 shows a timescale that presents a weekly view, enabling you to record actuals for an entire week.

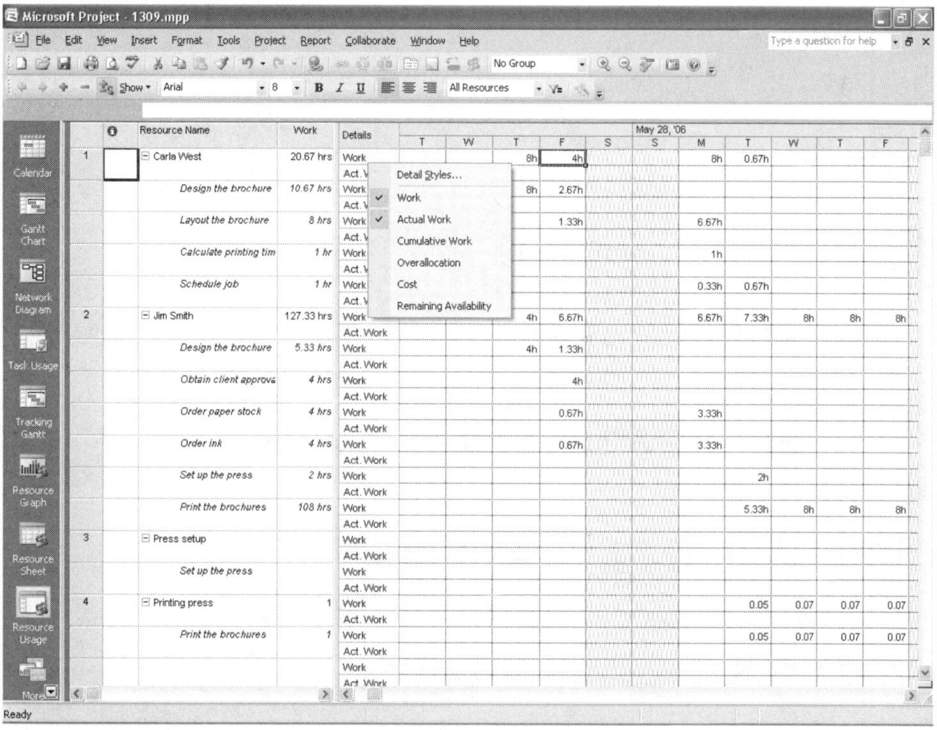

**13**

**FIGURE 13-7** You can add a row to the Details portion of the view.

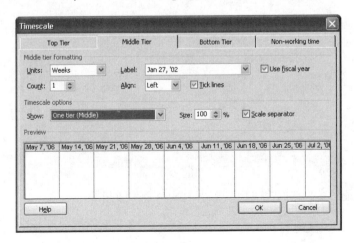

**FIGURE 13-8**    Recording actuals for an entire week

To change the timescale to match the frequency with which you want to update, choose Format | Timescale to display the Timescale dialog box.

By default, Project displays a daily timescale; to change the timescale to weekly, follow these steps:

**1.** Click the Middle Tier tab.

**2.** Open the Units drop-down list and select Weeks.

**3.** Open the Show drop-down list in the Timescale Options section and choose One Tier (Middle).

**4.** Click OK.

To enter hours worked, first focus on the table portion of the view; locate the resource and then the task for which you want to record actuals. Then, in the Details portion of the view, find the appropriate time period for which you want to record actuals and enter the actual data for the correct resource and task.

# Rescheduling Remaining Work

Suppose that, after you update your project, you have partially completed tasks. You may want to reschedule remaining work to start on the current date to ensure that all remaining work is scheduled for future dates.

When rescheduling work to start on the current date, Project doesn't remove constraints and reschedule tasks without progress. Because Project doesn't remove constraints, rescheduling remaining work may cause conflicts in your schedule, but don't worry; if conflicts arise, Project displays a message and enables you to manually make necessary changes.

Follow these steps to tell Project to reschedule remaining work for future dates:

**1.** Choose View | Gantt Chart.

**2.** In the Task Name column, select the tasks that you want to update.

**3.** Choose Tools | Tracking | Update Project to open the Update Project dialog box.

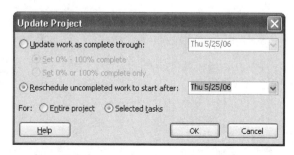

**13**

4. Click the Reschedule Uncompleted Work to Start After option button and choose the date from which you want to reschedule all unfinished work.

5. Click the Selected Tasks option button.

6. Click OK. Project reschedules uncompleted work for the selected tasks.

Project automatically splits partially completed tasks, displaying, on the Gantt Chart, a completed portion and the remaining portion of the task.

In this chapter, you learned a variety of ways to enter actual data for your schedule to enable you to track the progress of your project. In Chapter 14, we'll explore the techniques you use to enter cost-tracking information, and in Chapter 15, you'll learn how to view your project's progress using views and reports.

# Chapter 14

## Tracking Cost Information

## How to...

■ Entering costs for tasks

■ Entering costs for resources

■ Overriding resource cost valuations

In Chapter 13, you saw how to enter actual information regarding tasks into your project schedule so that you can track progress on your project. In this chapter, we're going to focus on entering actual cost data. Finally, in Chapter 15, we'll cover how you can view and report on project progress.

# Understanding How Project Calculates Actual Task Costs

Project calculates actual task costs by default. To calculate a task's cost, Project accrues the cost of the resources that are assigned to the task over the duration of the task and calculates total project costs by summing all resource and fixed costs. Therefore, if you set up resources and assigned a cost value to them and then assigned those resources to your tasks, Project has been calculating and accruing the costs for you. You only need to review and analyze the costs, as I'll describe in just a moment.

If you find that Project hasn't calculated costs for you, then one of three possibilities exists:

■ You didn't set up and assign resources to tasks.

■ You set up and assigned resources, but you didn't assign any cost to the resources.

■ You changed default options so that Project wouldn't calculate costs.

The first two possibilities are easy to understand; the third possibility took a little effort on your part that you may not remember doing. To check to make sure that Project is calculating costs, follow these steps:

1. Choose Tools | Options. Project displays the Options dialog box.

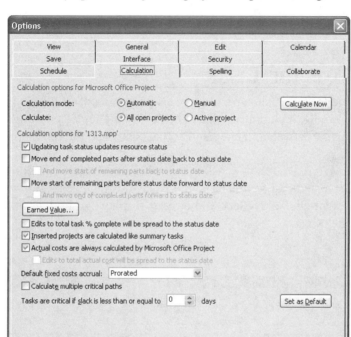

2. Click the Calculation tab.

3. Look at the Calculation options for your project. If the Updating Task Status Updates Resource Status check box is not checked, Project has not been calculating your project's costs.

*This check box is selected by default; if it is not selected in your project, you unchecked it at some point—not to worry; you can still calculate project costs.*

If you find that Project hasn't calculated costs for you for one of the reasons listed, you can correct the situation if you provide additional information after the

**14**

task is completed. You can review and update your project's costs from one of two cost tables: the Cost table for tasks or the Cost table for resources. You also can override the costs that Project assigns.

# Entering Costs for Tasks

The Cost table for tasks, shown in Figure 14-1, shows cost information for each task in your project, including the baseline cost (the planned cost), the actual cost, the variance between planned and actual costs, and the remaining cost of the task.

You can add a fixed cost to a task in this table, and Project will add the fixed cost to the calculated cost for the task. To display this table, choose View | Gantt Chart. Then, right-click the Select All button to display the shortcut menu of tables, and click Cost.

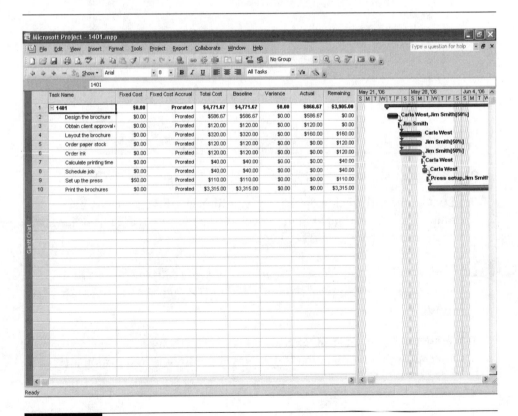

**FIGURE 14-1** The Cost table for tasks

  *You may also need to drag the split bar all the way to the right to see all the fields on the Cost table for tasks.*

This table provides really useful information if you saved a baseline view of your project, because you can use it to compare actual costs with baseline costs.

# Entering Costs for Resources

The Cost table for resources, shown in Figure 14-2, closely resembles the Cost table for tasks, but, as you'd expect, the Cost table for tasks breaks down costs by task and the Cost table for resources breaks down costs by resource.

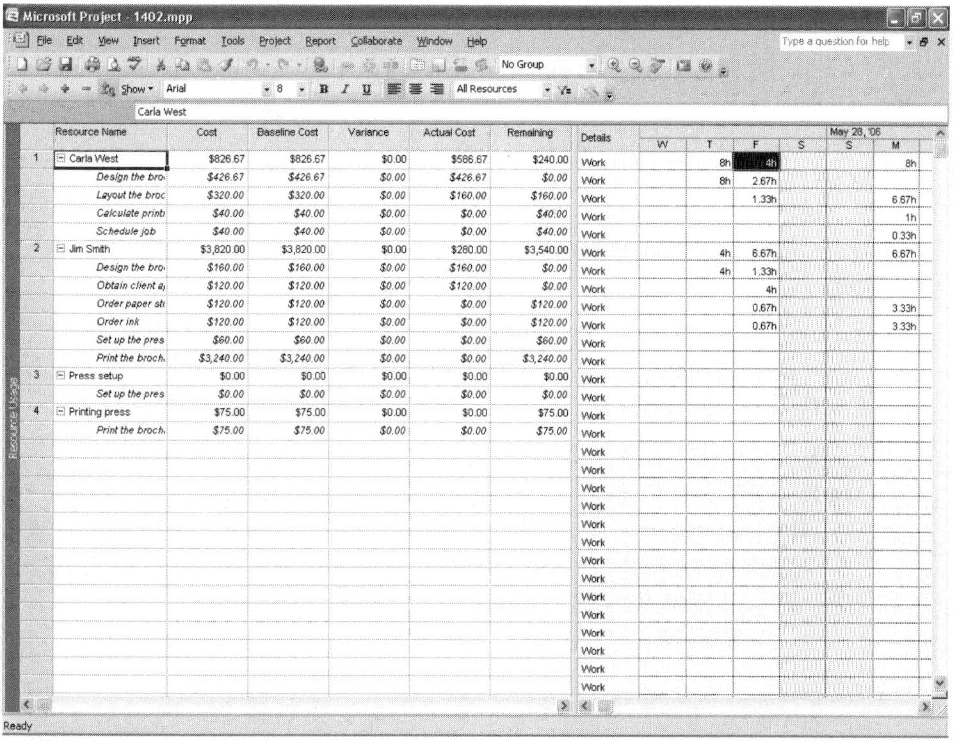

**FIGURE 14-2**   The Cost table for resources

14

You can display this table by first selecting a resource view like the Resource Sheet or the Resource Usage view. Then, right-click the Select All button and click Cost on the shortcut menu that appears.

Like the Cost table for tasks, the Cost table for resources is particularly useful if you saved a baseline view of your project, because you can compare actual costs with baseline costs.

# Overriding Resource Cost Valuations

If you didn't change Project's default settings on the Calculation tab of the Options dialog box shown earlier in this chapter, Project automatically updates costs as you record progress on a task. To allocate cost, Project uses the accrual method that you selected for the resource when you created the resource; you can double-check any resource's accrual method by viewing the Resource Sheet—choose View | Resource Sheet.

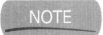

*For more information about setting a resource's accrual method, see Chapter 6.*

You can enter costs manually after a task is completed if you prefer to enter the actual costs for a resource assignment or to track actual costs separately from the actual work on a task. You must first turn off one of the Calculation options; follow these steps:

1. Choose Tools | Options to display the Options dialog box.

2. Click the Calculation tab.

3. Remove the check from the Actual Costs Are Always Calculated By Microsoft Office Project check box. The Edits to Total Actual Cost Will Be Spread to the Status Date check box becomes available. Check this box to make Project distribute the edits that you're going to make through the status date.

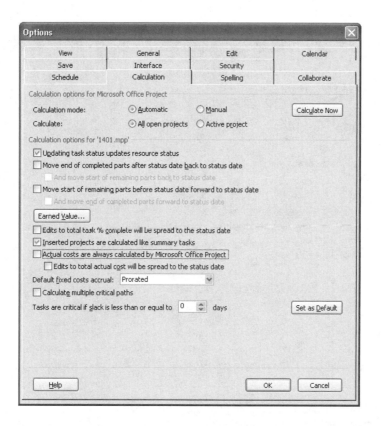

NOTE *When the Edits to Total Actual Cost Will Be Spread to the Status Date check box remains unchecked, Project distributes the edits to the end of the actual duration of the task.*

**4.** Click OK.

Now, you can enter costs manually using the Task Usage view, shown in Figure 14-3.

Follow these steps:

**1.** Choose View | Task Usage.

**2.** Right-click the Select All button and click Tracking from the shortcut menu.

14

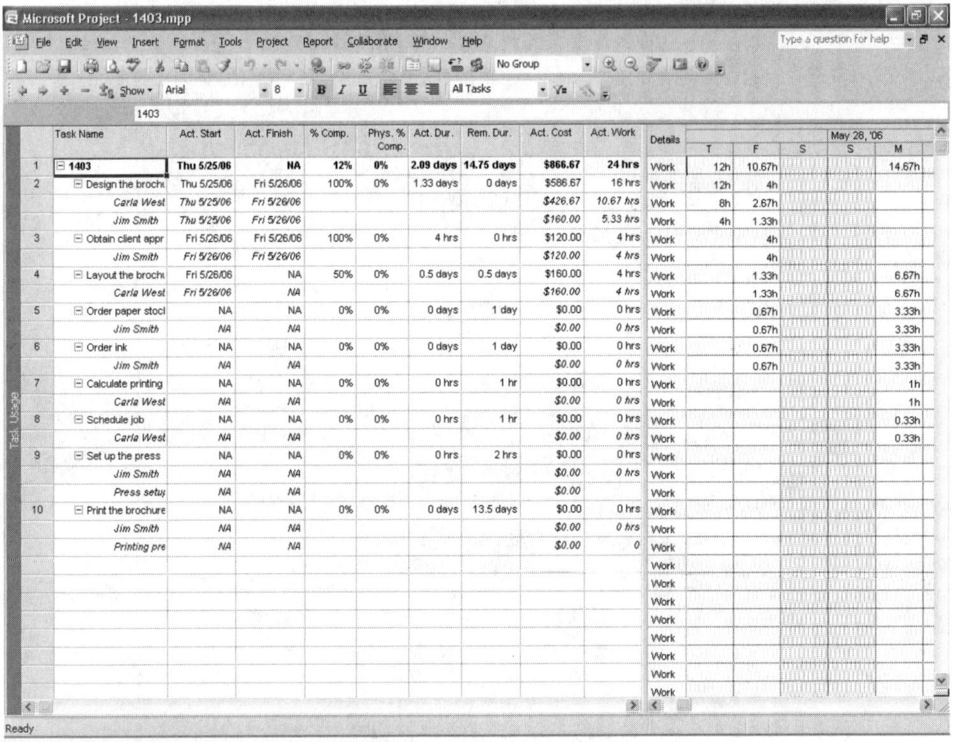

**FIGURE 14-3**    Entering costs manually

3. Drag the divider bar to the right so that you can see all the columns.

4. Select the task or resource to which you want to assign a cost.

5. Enter the cost in the Act. Cost (Actual Cost) column.

If you change your mind and want Project to calculate costs as it originally did, redisplay the Calculation tab of the Options dialog box and place a check in the Actual Costs Are Always Calculated by Microsoft Office Project check box to restore the default calculation method. Project warns you that it will overwrite any costs you entered when you click OK.

In this chapter, you learned how to view or enter costs in a project. In the next chapter, you'll learn how to view and report on progress.

# Chapter 15

# Reporting in Microsoft Project

## How to...

- View progress

- Print a report

- Customize a report

- Work with visual reports

In Chapter 12, you learned how to set a baseline after you set up estimates for your project; then, in Chapters 13 and 14, you learned how to enter actual information. In this chapter, we'll look at ways that you can compare your estimates with actual data.

You'll find fairly robust reporting in Project, using the traditional reports that come with Project as well as using Project's visual reporting capabilities that rely on Excel and Visio. But, printing reports isn't the only way to obtain information about a project; you can use some of the many views in Project to look at your project in varying perspectives, and you can print reports of those views.

# Viewing Progress

Now that you've set up a project, stored a baseline for it, and recorded some actual information, you can use a variety of tools to review your project's progress. The Tracking Gantt view is particularly useful when you want to compare baseline estimates with actual information. Using the Tracking Gantt, you can view the comparison both graphically, with baseline and actual task bars, and through data that appears in various tables you can assign to the Tracking Gantt view.

 *You can print any view by choosing File | Print. Project prints both the table and the chart portion of the view.*

## Using the Tracking Gantt

To display the Tracking Gantt view, click its icon in the View bar or choose View | Tracking Gantt. The Tracking Gantt bars indicate progress on tasks in the project.

At the top of the Tracking Gantt, you see the summary task for the project, and below it, you see a black-and-white hatched bar, which represents progress on the summary task.

Two bars appear on all tasks that aren't summary tasks. The top bar represents expected or actual duration—expected duration if the task has not yet begun, and actual duration if the task has begun. The bottom bar represents baseline duration. You can also use the formatting of the top bar of a task bar to determine a task's status:

- If a task has not yet started, the top bar appears as blue hatching or red hatching; the hatching is red if the task is on the critical path.

- If a task is complete, the top bar appears solid blue or solid red, depending on whether the task is on the critical path.

- If a task is partially complete, the completed portion appears as solid blue or red in the top bar, but the unfinished portion appears as blue or red hatching; again, red indicates a task on the critical path.

The percentage indicator at the edge of a task reflects the percentage complete for that task.

In Figure 15-1, Tasks 2 and 3 are complete, Tasks 4, 5, and 6 are partially complete, and none of the other tasks have begun yet.

You also can tell at a glance if a task began or finished earlier or later than estimated. In Figure 15-1, Task 3 took longer than planned; the top bar, which represents actual duration, extends beyond the bottom bar, which represents baseline duration. And, Task 5 began later than planned; the beginning of the top bar (actual duration) starts later than the bottom bar (baseline duration).

By default, the Tracking Gantt view shows the Entry table; you can add or remove fields (columns), or you can display other tables of information. In Figure 15-2, I displayed the Tracking table and added columns to include baseline information.

**15**

NOTE    *In Chapter 8, you'll find information about changing and modifying tables.*

I use the Baseline Duration and Baseline Cost fields that I added to the table and the Actual Duration and the Actual Cost fields that appear by default to

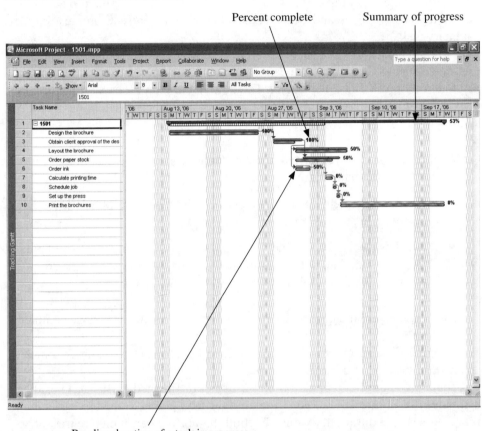

**FIGURE 15-1** Various task bar styles and colors help you to see, at a glance, the project's progress and variations from estimates.

compare estimated versus actual timing and costs. The default Tracking Gantt table also contains the information shown in Table 15-1.

## Changing Tables to View Different Information

Changing the table in a view changes the information you see, and different tables highlight different information. Project contains more than 20 tables—some for

| | Task Name | Act. Start | Act. Finish | % Comp. | Phys. % Comp. | Act. Dur. | Baseline Duration | Rem. Dur. | Act. Cost | Baseline Cost | Act. Work | Aug 20, '06 F S S M T W T |
|---|---|---|---|---|---|---|---|---|---|---|---|---|
| 1 | − 1501 | Mon 8/14/06 | NA | 53% | 0% | 4.25 days | 27 days | 12.75 days | $6,870.00 | $11,210.00 | 182 hrs | |
| 2 | Design the brochure | Mon 8/14/06 | Fri 8/25/06 | 100% | 0% | 10 days | 10 days | 0 days | $4,600.00 | $4,600.00 | 120 hrs | |
| 3 | Obtain client approval of the des | Mon 8/28/06 | Thu 8/31/06 | 100% | 0% | 4 days | 3 days | 0 days | $1,120.00 | $840.00 | 32 hrs | |
| 4 | Layout the brochure | Thu 8/31/06 | NA | 50% | 0% | 2.5 days | 5 days | 2.5 days | $800.00 | $1,600.00 | 20 hrs | |
| 5 | Order paper stock | Fri 9/1/06 | NA | 50% | 0% | 1.5 days | 3 days | 1.5 days | $210.00 | $420.00 | 6 hrs | |
| 6 | Order ink | Thu 8/31/06 | NA | 50% | 0% | 1 day | 2 days | 1 day | $140.00 | $280.00 | 4 hrs | |
| 7 | Calculate printing time | NA | NA | 0% | 0% | 0 days | 1 day | 1 day | $0.00 | $320.00 | 0 hrs | |
| 8 | Schedule job | NA | NA | 0% | 0% | 0 hrs | 4 hrs | 4 hrs | $0.00 | $160.00 | 0 hrs | |
| 9 | Set up the press | NA | NA | 0% | 0% | 0 hrs | 4 hrs | 4 hrs | $0.00 | $190.00 | 0 hrs | |
| 10 | Print the brochures | NA | NA | 0% | 0% | 0 days | 10 days | 10 days | $0.00 | $2,800.00 | 0 hrs | |

**FIGURE 15-2** You can modify tables in Project to display a wealth of information.

tasks and some for resources—that help you focus on a variety of factors in your project. In this section, I'll review the following tables, which are only the tip of the iceberg:

- Variance table
- Cost table for tasks
- Work table for tasks
- Work table for resources

15

| Field | Function |
|---|---|
| % Complete | This field shows the progress of various tasks in the schedule. Project calculates the % Complete field for you based on Total Duration or Actual Duration values you enter. |
| Physical % Complete | You can enter a value into this field and use the field to calculate Budgeted Cost of Work Performed (BCWP). Use this field to calculate BCWP when the % Complete value would not accurately represent the real work performed on a task. |
| Remaining Duration | This field displays the amount of time needed to complete an unfinished task. You can enter a value into this field or you can allow Project to calculate it for you by entering a value into either the Actual Duration field or the % Complete field. If you enter a Remaining Duration value, Project calculates a new % Complete value and a new Duration value; Project changes the Duration value to equal the sum of Actual Duration and Remaining Duration, leaving Actual Duration untouched. |
| Actual Work | In this field, you see the amount of work that resources have performed. There are Actual Work fields for tasks, resources, and assignments, as well as timephased Actual Work fields for tasks, resources, and assignments. |

**TABLE 15-1**    Default Fields in the Tracking Table

## Using the Variance Table

The Variance table, for example, focuses on the difference in task timing between baselines and actuals. To display this table, shown in Figure 15-3, start in any task view, right-click the Select All button, and click Variance in the list of tables that appears.

The Start Variance field shows you how many days late or early a task started, and the Finish Variance field shows you how many days late or early a task ended.

## Using the Cost Table for Tasks

The Cost table for tasks is most useful for pointing out variations in money spent on the project. In Figure 15-4, Task 2 cost as much as expected, but the positive number that appears in the Variance column for Task 3 indicates that the actual cost exceeded the baseline cost. If a task's actual cost is less than the baseline cost, you'll see a negative number in the Variance column. Be aware

Select All button

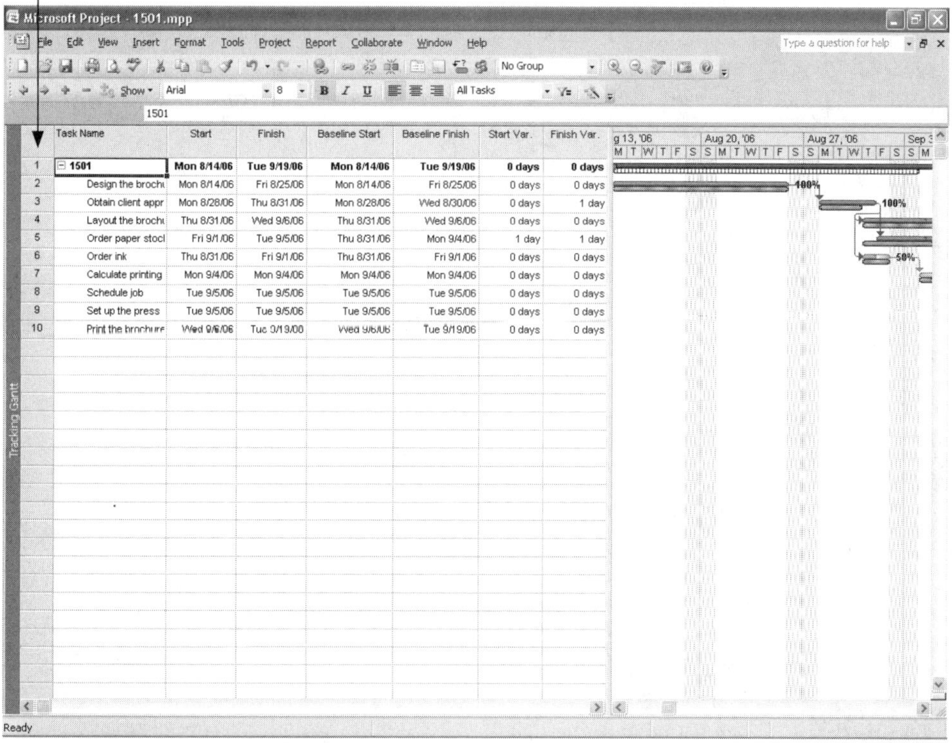

FIGURE 15-3    The Start Variance and Finish Variance columns quickly identify tasks that didn't start or finish on time.

that you can't assume that your costs are on track if you see $0 in the Variance column; the Variance is also $0 when you haven't yet started a task.

Project takes the following factors into account when calculating cost variations:

- Actual resource time worked

- The estimate of days of resource time still to be expended to complete the task

- Fixed costs (such as fees and permits) assigned to the task

**15**

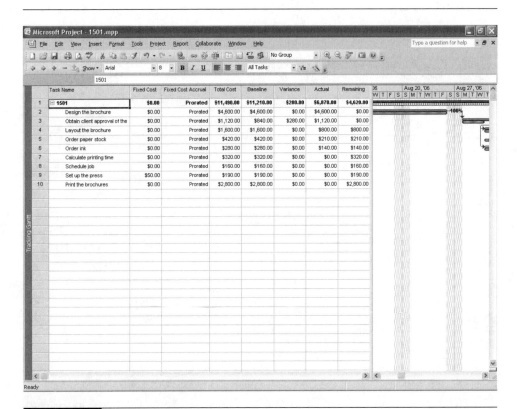

**FIGURE 15-4**  The Cost table for tasks helps you identify variations from planned costs.

## Using the Work Table for Tasks

You can use the Work table for tasks to help you focus on the variation in the number of hours actually worked compared to the expected number of hours of work. Start in any task view, right-click the Select All button, and choose Work.

In Figure 15-5, the baseline work for Task 3 was 24 hours. But, the task actually took 32 hours. The Variance column displays the difference between the baseline hours of work and the actual hours spent; in this case, it shows

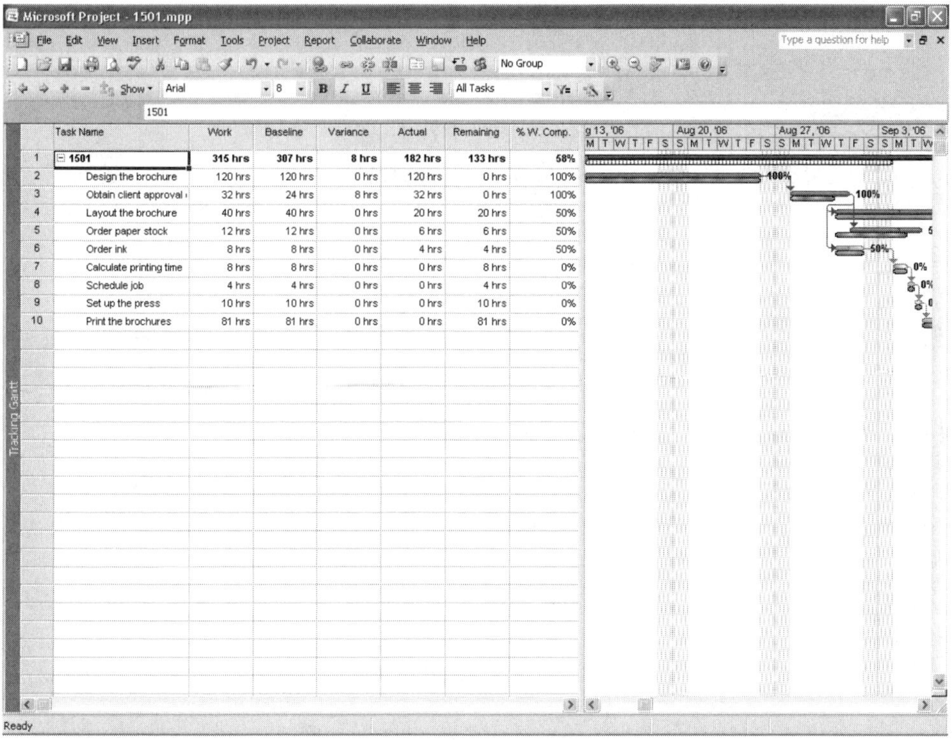

FIGURE 15-5   Use the Work table for tasks to help identify tasks that are taking more effort than you estimated.

a loss of 8 hours. If fewer hours are used than estimated, you'll see a negative value in the Variance column.

## Using the Work Table for Resources

You can use the Work table for resources to help identify any variance between estimated work and actual work by any particular resource. You can apply the Work table for resources to any resource view. In Figure 15-6, for example, I selected the Resource Sheet view; then, I right-clicked the Select All button and chose Work from the shortcut menu that appeared.

15

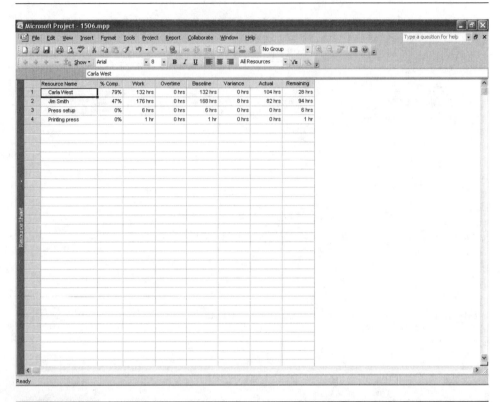

**FIGURE 15-6**    The Work table for resources helps you identify variations between estimated and actual work for any particular resource.

# Printing a Report

In addition to the many views and tables in Project, you can print traditional row and column reports. Project organizes text reports into six categories of information.

To open the Reports dialog box, choose Report | Reports. To view the reports in a particular category, click that category and then click Select.

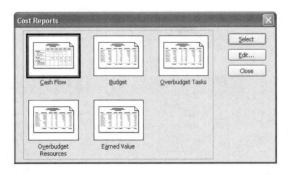

When you click a report and select it, Project displays it onscreen. For multipage reports, you can use the scroll arrows on the toolbar at the top of the screen to move around the report. The Zoom button enlarges the image so that you can read the report's content onscreen. Or, you can click the portion of the report that you want to enlarge; when you move the mouse pointer over the report, the pointer shape looks like a magnifying glass. To zoom out again, click the Full Page button or click again on the report. To display more than one page at a time, click the Multiple Pages button.

Microsoft Project - 1501.mpp

Page Setup... | Print... | Close | Help

Cash Flowas of Sat 9/2/06
1501.mpp

|  | 8/13/06 | 8/20/06 | 8/27/06 | 9/3/06 | 9/10/06 | 9/17/06 | 9/24/06 | Total |
|---|---|---|---|---|---|---|---|---|
| 1501 |  |  |  |  |  |  |  |  |
| Design the brochure | $2,300.00 | $2,300.00 |  |  |  |  |  | $4,600.00 |
| Obtain client approval of the design |  |  | $1,120.00 |  |  |  |  | $1,120.00 |
| Layout the brochure |  |  | $640.00 | $960.00 |  |  |  | $1,600.00 |
| Order paper stock |  |  | $140.00 | $280.00 |  |  |  | $420.00 |
| Order ink |  |  | $280.00 |  |  |  |  | $280.00 |
| Calculate printing time |  |  |  | $320.00 |  |  |  | $320.00 |
| Schedule job |  |  |  | $160.00 |  |  |  | $160.00 |
| Set up the press |  |  |  | $190.00 |  |  |  | $190.00 |
| Print the brochures |  |  |  | $840.00 | $1,400.00 | $560.00 |  | $2,800.00 |
| Total | $2,300.00 | $2,300.00 | $2,180.00 | $2,750.00 | $1,400.00 | $560.00 |  | $11,490.00 |

Page: 1 of 1

15

From the Page Setup dialog box, you can set the orientation and page scaling information; you also can use the Margins, Header, and Footer tabs to make changes to those settings.

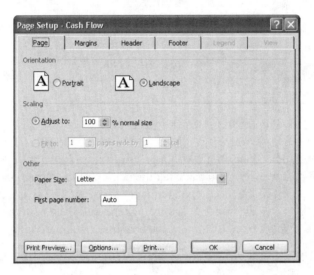

> **NOTE**  *The Legend and View tabs are available only when you are printing a view.*

From the Print dialog box, you can select a printer and, if appropriate, specify a print range and the number of copies.

I don't have enough space to show you each report, but Table 15-2 describes each of them and lists the Reports dialog box category in which you can find them.

| Report Category | Report Name | Description |
|---|---|---|
| Overview Reports | | |
| | Project Summary | Presents summarized information about dates, duration, work, costs, task status, and resource status. |
| | Top Level Tasks | For summary tasks at the highest level in your project, shows, as of today's date, the scheduled start and finish dates, the percentage complete for each task, the cost, and the work required to complete the task. |
| | Critical Tasks | Shows the status of the tasks on the critical path of your project, displaying each task's planned duration, start and finish dates, the resources that are assigned to the task, and the predecessors and successors of the task. |

**TABLE 15-2**     Text Reports Available in Project

| Report Category | Report Name | Description |
|---|---|---|
| | Milestones | For each milestone, displays the planned duration, start and finish dates, predecessors, and the resources that are assigned to the milestone. If you marked summary tasks to appear as milestones in the Task Information dialog box, summary tasks also appear as milestones on this report. |
| | Working Days | Shows the name of the base calendar for the project and the working hours that are established for each day of the week, along with any exceptions that you defined. |
| Cost Reports | | |
| | Cash Flow | Shows, by task, the costs for weekly time increments in tabular form. |
| | Earned Value | Shows the status of each task's costs when you compare planned to actual costs. |
| | Budget | Shows the budgeted costs as well as the variance between budgeted and actual costs for all tasks. |
| | Overbudget Tasks | Shows cost, baseline, variance, and actual information about tasks that exceed their budgeted amounts. |
| | Overbudget Resources | Displays resources whose costs are going to exceed baseline estimates, based on the current progress of the project. |
| Current Activities Reports | | |
| | Unstarted Tasks | Sorted by the scheduled start date, displays the duration, predecessor, and resource information (if you assigned resources) for each unstarted task. |
| | Tasks Starting Soon | Displays the duration, start and finish dates, predecessors, and resource information (if you assigned resources) for tasks that start or finish between two dates that you specify. Completed tasks also appear on this report; the check mark that appears in the Indicators column on the report identifies them. |
| | Tasks in Progress | Lists duration, start and planned finish dates, predecessors, and resource information (if you assigned resources) for tasks that have started but not yet finished. |
| | Completed Tasks | Lists the actual duration, the actual start and finish dates, the percent complete (always 100 percent—if a task is only partially complete, it won't appear on this report), the cost, and the work hours for tasks that have completed. |

**15**

**TABLE 15-2**    Text Reports Available in Project (*continued*)

| Report Category | Report Name | Description |
|---|---|---|
| | Should Have Started Tasks | Displays planned start and finish dates, baseline start and finish dates, and variances for start and finish dates and successor task information when available for tasks that should have started by a date you supply. |
| | Slipping Tasks | Lists planned start and finish dates, baseline start and finish dates, and variances for start and finish dates and successor task information when available for tasks that have been rescheduled from their baseline start dates. |
| Assignment Reports | | |
| | Who Does What | Lists resources and the tasks to which they are assigned, the amount of work planned for each task, the planned start and finish dates, and any resource notes. |
| | Who Does What When | Lists the same information that appears on the Who Does What report, but focuses your attention on the daily work that is scheduled for each resource on each task. |
| | To Do List | Lists, on a weekly basis, the tasks that are assigned to a resource that you select. Shows the task ID number, duration, start and finish dates, predecessors, and a list of all of the resources that are assigned to each task. |
| | Overallocated Resources | Shows the overallocated resources, the tasks to which they are assigned, and the total hours of work that are assigned to them as well as details of each task, such as the allocation, the amount of work, any delay, and the start and finish dates. |
| Workload Reports | | |
| | Task Usage | Lists tasks and the resources that are assigned to each task along with the amount of work assigned to each resource in weekly time increments. |
| | Resource Usage | Lists resources and the tasks to which they are assigned, along with the amount of work assigned to each resource for each task in weekly time increments. Two variations of this report display information limited to specific resource types: the Resource Usage (material) and Resource Usage (work) reports. |

**TABLE 15-2**    Text Reports Available in Project (*continued*)

# Customizing a Report

When you click the Custom category in the Reports dialog box and choose Select, Project opens the Custom Reports dialog box.

The Custom Reports dialog box lists all of the reports described in Table 15-2, along with three additional reports:

- Task report

- Resource report

- Crosstab report

You can display and print each report listed in Table 15-2 from its own report category, as I described previously, or you can print it from the Custom Reports dialog box; Project displays these reports in the Custom Reports dialog box because you can customize them. To print any of the three additional custom reports, you must use the Custom Reports dialog box.

The Task report shows task information, such as the ID number, task name, indicator icons, task duration, planned start and finish dates, predecessors, and (if resources have been assigned) resource names.

The Resource report shows resource information: resource ID numbers; indicator icons; resource names, initials, and groups; maximum units; rate information; accrual information; base calendar information; and code information.

The Crosstab report is a tabular report that shows task and resource information in rows and time increments in columns.

As I mentioned, you can customize almost every one of Project's reports. For a few reports, such as the Working Days report, the only item that you can change is the font information that Project uses to print the report. For other reports, however, you can change the table or the task or resource filter to change the content of the report.

**15**

To customize any report, click the Edit button when preparing the report to make any of these changes. When you click the Edit button, Project opens the dialog box that relates to the report that you selected. For example, if you select the Project Summary report in the Overview Reports dialog box or the Custom Reports dialog box and then click Edit, Project opens the Report Text dialog box, where you can control font settings.

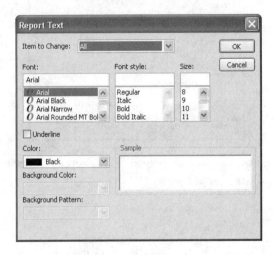

Similarly, if you select the Top-Level Tasks report from the Overview Reports dialog box and then click Edit, Project opens the Definition tab of the Task Report dialog box, where you can change the report's table or filter.

From the Details tab, select the information that you want to include on the report. You may want to display predecessors for tasks or place a gridline between details. The options on the Details tab change from report to report.

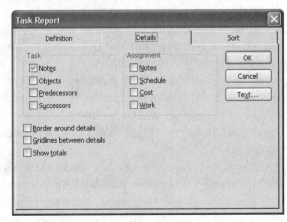

From the Sort tab, select the sort order for the report.

Remember that the type of report that you select initially determines the dialog box that you see when you click the Edit button. Depending on the report you select, you may also see the Resource Report dialog box or the Crosstab Report dialog box, both of which contain slightly different options (primarily on the Definition tab) than the Task Report dialog box. For example, on the Definition tab of the Resource Report dialog box, you can select filters that are related to resources, whereas the filters in the Task Report dialog box pertain to tasks.

# Working with Visual Reports

Visual reporting is a new kind of reporting available in Project 2007; visual reports use Project data to build PivotTables in Excel and PivotDiagrams in Visio. Once you produce a report, you can manipulate it in Excel or Visio using the techniques in those programs that you use to manipulate any Excel PivotTable or Visio PivotDiagram.

To create visual reports, you must install .NET Framework 2.0, Excel 2007, and Visio 2007.

NOTE
*If you install .NET Framework 2.0 after you install Project, you may need to update your Project installation. In the Windows Control Panel, open the Add or Remove Programs window, select Project 2007, and click Change. Select Add or Remove Features and click Continue. Then, expand the Office Project node and set Visual Reports to Run From My Computer. When you click Continue, your Project installation is updated.*

You produce visual reports from the Visual Reports - Create Report window (see Figure 15-7). You can open this window by choosing Report | Visual Reports.

On the All tab, you see all of the predefined visual reports; the other tabs in the window break the reports into six categories:

■ Task Usage

■ Resource Usage

■ Assignment Usage

15

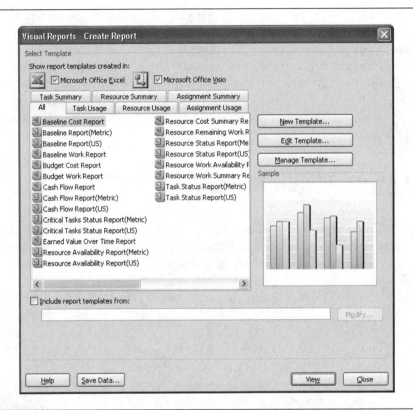

FIGURE 15-7    Use this window to create visual reports.

■ Task Summary

■ Resource Summary

■ Assignment Summary

Figure 15-8 shows you the Resource Work Summary Report, which creates an Excel PivotTable using your project data. Figure 15-9 shows you the Resource Status Report, an example of a Visio PivotDiagram based on your project data.

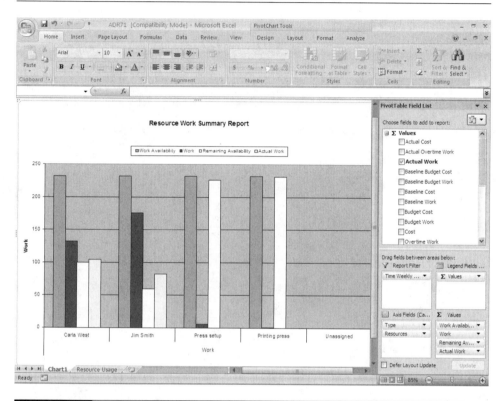

**FIGURE 15-8**    The Resource Work Summary Report, an Excel PivotTable based on
your project's data.

The reports that appear in the Visual Reports - Create Report window are the
templates that come with Project, but you also can create your own reports if
you don't find a report that suits your needs. Since Project comes with so many
visual reports and since my space is limited, I'm not going to cover creating your
own visual report templates. Table 15-3 describes the predefined visual reports
that come with Project.

15

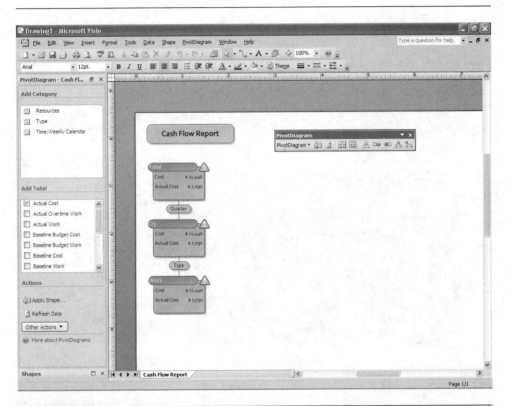

**FIGURE 15-9** The Resource Status Report, a Visio PivotDiagram based on your project's data.

| Visual Report Category | Visual Report Name | Visual Report Type | Description |
|---|---|---|---|
| Task Usage | | | |
| | Cash Flow | Excel PivotTable | Uses timephased data to produce a bar graph. |
| Resource Usage | | | |
| | Cash Flow | Visio PivotDiagram | Produces a diagram that shows planned and actual costs for your project over time and breaks the information down by resource type, showing work, material, and cost information. You'll find a Metric and a US version of the report. |

**TABLE 15-3** Visual Reports Available in Project

| Visual Report Category | Visual Report Name | Visual Report Type | Description |
|---|---|---|---|
| | Resource Availability | Visio PivotDiagram | Produces a diagram that shows total capacity, work, and remaining availability for work resources. You'll find a Metric and a US version. |
| | Resource Cost Summary | Excel PivotTable | Produces a pie chart that divides resource costs between resource types. |
| | Resource Work Availability | Excel PivotTable | Produces a column chart showing work and remaining availability over time. |
| | Resource Work Summary | Excel PivotTable | Produces a column chart showing work, remaining availability, and actual work for each work resource in your project. |
| Assignment Usage | | | |
| | Baseline Cost | Excel PivotTable | Produces a column chart that compares baseline cost, planned cost, and actual cost. |
| | Baseline | Visio PivotDiagram | Produces a diagram that shows baseline and actual work and costs for your project over time and identifies instances where planned work exceeds baseline work and where planned cost exceeds baseline cost. You'll find a Metric and a US version of the report. |
| | Baseline Work | Excel PivotTable | Produces a column chart that compares baseline work, planned work, and actual work. |
| | Budget Cost | Excel PivotTable | Produces a column chart that compares budget cost, baseline cost, planned cost, and actual cost. |
| | Budget Work | Excel PivotTable | Produces a column chart that compares budget work, baseline work, planned work, and actual work. |
| | Earned Value Over Time | Excel PivotTable | Uses timephased data to produce a chart that plots Actual Cost of Work Performed (ACWP), Planned Value–PV (BCWS), and Earned Value–EV (BCWP) over time. |

**TABLE 15-3**   Visual Reports Available in Project (*continued*)

15

| Visual Report Category | Visual Report Name | Visual Report Type | Description |
|---|---|---|---|
| Task Summary | | | |
| | Critical Tasks Status | Visio PivotDiagram | Shows the work and remaining work for both critical and noncritical tasks, along with the percent of work complete. This report comes in a Metric version and a US version. |
| | Task Status | Visio PivotDiagram | Shows work and percent of work complete for tasks at the highest level in your project outline. This report comes in a Metric version and a US version. |
| Resource Summary | | | |
| | Resource Remaining Work | Excel PivotTable | Produces a column chart that shows work, remaining work, and total work for each work resource on your project. |
| Assignment Summary | | | |
| | Resource Status | Visio PivotDiagram | Shows work and cost values for each of your project's resources. This report comes in a Metric version and a US version. |
| | Task Status Report | | Shows work and cost values for each of your project's tasks. This report comes in a Metric version and a US version. |

**TABLE 15-3** Visual Reports Available in Project (*continued*)

In this chapter, you learned about ways you can view and report on your project; in the next chapter, you'll read about analyzing financial progress in Project.

# Chapter 16

# Establishing Baselines

## How to...

- ■ Calculate and evaluate earned value information in Project
- ■ Use Excel to evaluate earned value information

In addition to measuring and monitoring the progress of your project's schedule, you'll also want to evaluate your project's progress based on the costs that you incur. In Microsoft Office Project, when you evaluate the financial progress of your project, you measure your project's earned value.

# Getting Started with Earned Value

In Project, you use a series of earned value fields to evaluate the progress of a project based on the cost of work performed up to the project status date. When Project calculates earned value, by default it compares your original cost estimates to the actual work performed to show whether your project is on budget. Project automatically calculates the values of these earned value fields when you:

- ■ Save a baseline for your project.
- ■ Assign resources with costs to tasks in your project.
- ■ Complete some work on your project.

## Selecting an Earned Value Calculation Method

When you record work performed on a task, you can enter your actual information in a variety of ways. For example, you can enter task start and end dates, record actual durations, or enter the % Complete value.

 *For a complete list of the ways you can record actual information, see Chapter 13.*

When you enter actual information, the % Complete field is updated, either by you or by Project. If you don't enter the % Complete value, Project calculates it by dividing actual task duration by total duration. By default, the % Complete field forms the foundation of the several earned value field calculations. If you prefer, you can have Project use the Physical % Complete field to calculate earned value.

 *You can have Project use the % Complete field to calculate earned value for some tasks and the Physical % Complete field to calculate earned value for other tasks.*

Although similarly named, the Physical % Complete field has no connection to duration like the % Complete field does. Instead, you enter your estimate of where a task stands into the Physical % Complete field.

If you prefer to use the Physical % Complete field as the foundation for earned value calculations for your project, follow these steps to set the default for all new tasks that you enter in your project:

**1.** Choose Tools | Options.

**2.** Click the Calculation tab.

**3.** Click the Earned Value button. The Earned Value dialog box appears.

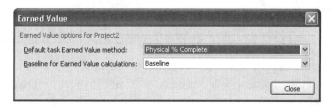

**4.** From the Default Task Earned Value Method list box, choose Physical % Complete.

**5.** From the Baseline for Earned Value Calculations list box, choose a baseline (Project stores 11 baselines).

 *Clearing a baseline after entering Physical % Complete values does not clear those values.*

**6.** Click OK twice to save the settings.

If your project already contains tasks or if you want to use the Physical % Complete method for some but not all tasks, set the earned value calculation method on a task-by-task basis:

**1.** Select the task(s) for which you want to set the earned value calculation method to Physical % Complete.

**2.** Click the Task Information button on the Standard toolbar.

16

**3.** Click the Advanced tab of the Multiple Task Information dialog box.

**4.** From the Earned Value Method list box, choose Physical % Complete.

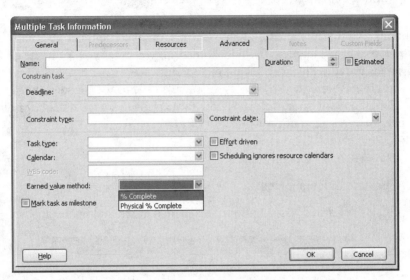

Now, when you record actual information in, say, the Tracking table, you can enter values into the Physical % Complete field, and Project will use them when calculating earned value.

## Understanding Basic Earned Value Calculations

The earned value fields in Project are currency fields that measure various aspects of earned value. Project uses a series of acronyms for the earned value fields, and the first three fields listed next are really at the heart of earned value analysis:

- The Planned Value (PV)—the Budgeted Cost of Work Scheduled (BCWS)—measures the budgeted cost of individual tasks based on the resources and fixed costs that are assigned to the tasks when you schedule them.

- The Earned Value (EV)—the Budgeted Cost of Work Performed (BCWP)—indicates how much of a task's budget should have been spent given the actual duration of the task. For example, after performing work for one day on a task budgeted at $100, you find that 40 percent of the work has been completed. You would expect that 40 percent of the cost of the task, or $40, would also be incurred. Therefore, the EV for the task is $40.

■ The Actual Cost of Work Performed (ACWP) measures the actual cost that is incurred to complete a task. During the completion process, ACWP represents the actual costs for work performed through the project's status date.

■ The Scheduled Variance (SV) represents the cost difference between current progress and the baseline plan, and Project calculates this value as EV minus PV.

■ The Cost Variance (CV) represents the cost difference between actual costs and planned costs at the current level of completion, and Project calculates this value as EV minus ACWP.

■ The Estimate at Completion (EAC) value shows the planned costs based on costs that are already incurred plus additional planned costs. EAC improved in Project 2003. In Project 2000, EAC was simply the cost of the task, retitled to "EAC." Starting in Project 2003, Project calculates this field using the following formula: $ACWP+(BAC-EV) / CPI$. This field appears by default in the Earned Value for Tasks and the Earned Value Cost Indicators tables and is not a timephased field.

■ The Variance at Completion (VAC) value represents the variance between the baseline cost (BAC) and the combination of actual costs plus planned costs for a task (EAC).

■ Cost Performance Index (CPI) is the result of dividing EV by ACWP. This field appears by default in the Earned Value Cost Indicators table and is a timephased field.

■ Schedule Performance Index (SPI) is the result of dividing EV by PV. This field appears by default in the Earned Value Schedule Indicators table and is a timephased field.

■ Project calculates Cost Variance % (CV%) by dividing CV by EV and multiplying the result by 100. This field appears by default in the Earned Value Cost Indicators table and is a timephased field.

■ Project calculates Schedule Variance % (SV%) by dividing SV by PV and multiplying the result by 100. This field appears by default in the Earned Value Schedule Indicators table and is a timephased field.

■ Project calculates the To Complete Performance Index (TCPI) using the following formula: $(BAC-EV) / (EAC-ACWP)$. This field appears by default in the Earned Value Cost Indicators table and is not a timephased field.

**16**

PV, EV, ACWP, SV, and CV are all calculated through today or through the project status date. Project calculates EV at the task level differently from the way it calculates EV at the assignment level. Because Project rolls the task-level EV values into summary tasks and the project summary task, I suggest that you use the task-level EV values.

Project contains task field, resource field, and assignment field versions of PV, EV, ACWP, SV, and CV along with timephased versions of each field. BAC, EAC, and VAC, however, are task fields only.

# Comparing Expected and Actual Costs

Using four earned value tables in Project, you can compare your expected costs with your actual costs, evaluate the relationship between work and costs, and forecast whether a task will finish within the budget based on the comparison of the actual costs incurred for the task to date and the baseline cost of the task.

## Using the Earned Value Table for Tasks

Using the Earned Value table for tasks, you can compare the relationship between work and costs for tasks, helping you evaluate your budget to estimate future budget needs and prepare an accounting statement of your project. The information in the Earned Value for tasks table helps you assess whether the money that you're spending on a task is enough money, too much money, too little money, or perhaps wasted money.

To display the Earned Value table for tasks, follow these steps:

1. Start in any task view, such as the Task Usage view.

2. Right-click the Select All button and choose More Tables from the shortcut menu that appears.

3. In the More Tables dialog box that appears, select Earned Value.

4. Click Apply. Project applies the Earned Value table for tasks to the view (see Figure 16-1).

All the fields on this sheet are calculated, but you can type a value into the BAC field, and Project will update both the fields dependent on BAC using the information you supply.

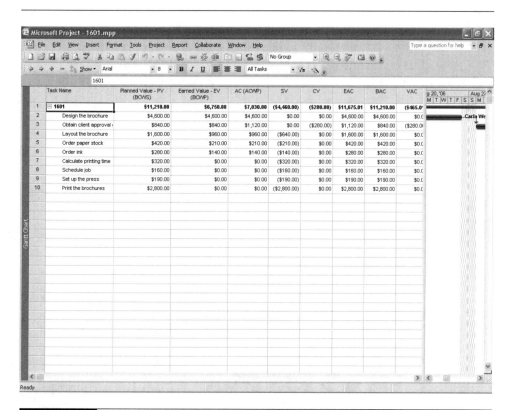

**FIGURE 16-1**    The Earned Value table for tasks.

## Using the Earned Value Table for Resources

When you use the Earned Value table for resources, you can compare the relationship between work and costs for resources and determine whether the work is getting done for the money that you're paying or whether you need more or less of a particular resource. You can use the information in this table to estimate future budget needs and prepare an accounting statement of your project.

To display the Earned Value table for resources (see Figure 16-2), follow the same steps you used in the preceding section to display the Earned Value table for tasks, but start in any resource view, such as the Resource Sheet view.

16

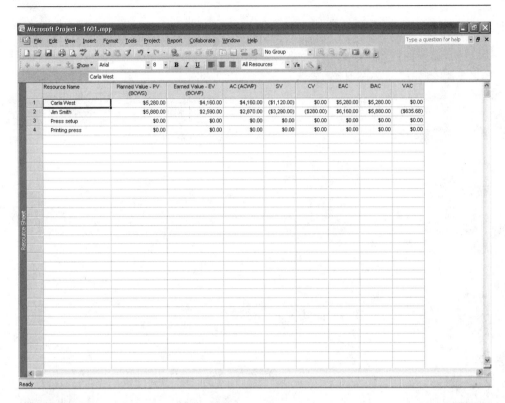

**FIGURE 16-2** The Earned Value table for resources.

All the fields in this sheet are calculated, but you can type a value into the BAC field, and Project will update the fields dependent on BAC using the information you supply.

## Using the Earned Value Schedule Indicators and Earned Value Cost Indicators Tables

These two tables are similar to the Earned Value table for tasks. The Earned Value Schedule Indicators table for tasks enables you to focus on the effects of scheduling variances on the cost of your project (see Figure 16-3). The Earned

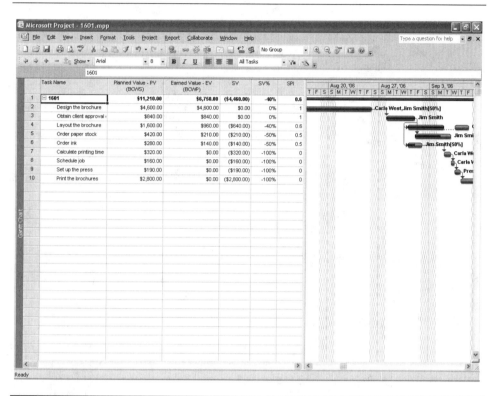

**FIGURE 16-3**   The Earned Value Schedule Indicators table.

Value Cost Indicators table enables you to compare the various cost factors related to tasks in your project (see Figure 16-4).

To display either table, start in any task view that contains a table. Then, right-click the Select All button and choose More Tables from the shortcut menu that appears. In the More Tables dialog box, select either Earned Value Cost Indicators or Earned Value Schedule Indicators and click Apply.

16

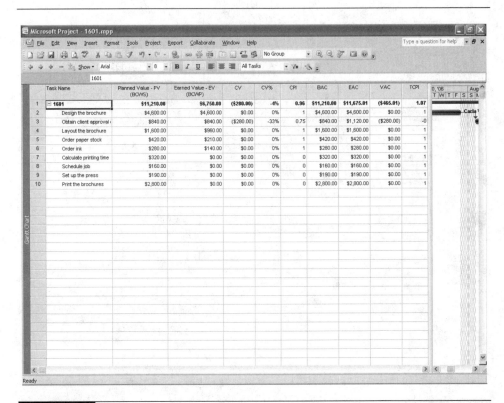

**FIGURE 16-4**    The Earned Value Cost Indicators table.

# Using Excel to Evaluate Earned Value Information

You can use Microsoft Excel to assist you in evaluating cost information. You can export project information to Excel, where you can chart earned value or create PivotTables.

## Exporting the Project

They say that 70 percent of the world learns visually, using pictures. You may better understand the earned value information Project produces if you use a picture. You can easily export the earned value information to Microsoft Excel (you must be using Excel version 5.0 or later) and then create charts of earned value information.

When you export earned values from Project to Excel, you create an Excel workbook that contains a task ID, a name, and the various earned values for each task (see Figure 16-5).

To create an Excel workbook like the one shown in Figure 16-5, follow these steps:

**1.** In the Project file containing the information that you want to use in Excel, choose File | Save As to open the Save As dialog box.

**2.** Type a name for the Excel workbook in the File Name list box. Don't worry about the extension; Project supplies it.

**3.** Open the Save as Type list box and select Microsoft Excel Workbook.

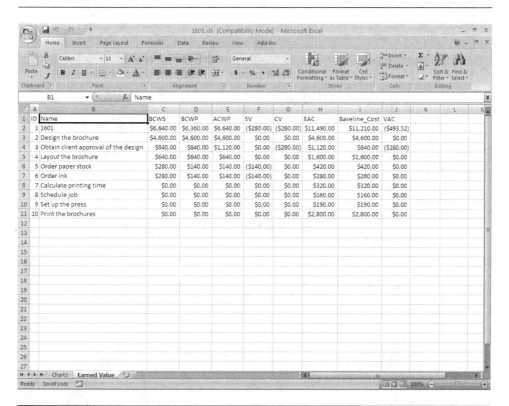

| | ID | Name | BCWS | BCWP | ACWP | SV | CV | EAC | Baseline_Cost | VAC |
|---|---|---|---|---|---|---|---|---|---|---|
| 1 | ID | Name | BCWS | BCWP | ACWP | SV | CV | EAC | Baseline_Cost | VAC |
| 2 | 1 | 1601 | $6,640.00 | $6,360.00 | $6,640.00 | ($280.00) | ($280.00) | $11,490.00 | $11,210.00 | ($493.52) |
| 3 | 2 | Design the brochure | $4,600.00 | $4,600.00 | $4,600.00 | $0.00 | $0.00 | $4,600.00 | $4,600.00 | $0.00 |
| 4 | 3 | Obtain client approval of the design | $840.00 | $840.00 | $1,120.00 | $0.00 | ($280.00) | $1,120.00 | $840.00 | ($280.00) |
| 5 | 4 | Layout the brochure | $640.00 | $640.00 | $640.00 | $0.00 | $0.00 | $1,600.00 | $1,600.00 | $0.00 |
| 6 | 5 | Order paper stock | $280.00 | $140.00 | $140.00 | ($140.00) | $0.00 | $420.00 | $420.00 | $0.00 |
| 7 | 6 | Order ink | $280.00 | $140.00 | $140.00 | ($140.00) | $0.00 | $280.00 | $280.00 | $0.00 |
| 8 | 7 | Calculate printing time | $0.00 | $0.00 | $0.00 | $0.00 | $0.00 | $320.00 | $320.00 | $0.00 |
| 9 | 8 | Schedule job | $0.00 | $0.00 | $0.00 | $0.00 | $0.00 | $160.00 | $160.00 | $0.00 |
| 10 | 9 | Set up the press | $0.00 | $0.00 | $0.00 | $0.00 | $0.00 | $190.00 | $190.00 | $0.00 |
| 11 | 10 | Print the brochures | $0.00 | $0.00 | $0.00 | $0.00 | $0.00 | $2,800.00 | $2,800.00 | $0.00 |

**FIGURE 16-5**   An Excel workbook created as a result of exporting earned value information from Project to Excel.

**16**

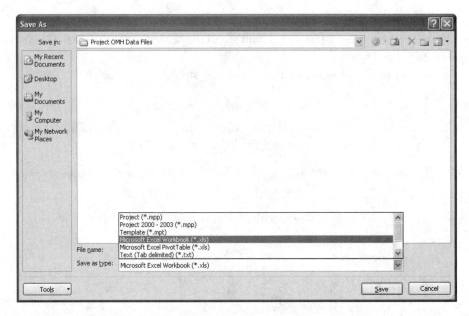

**4.** Click Save to start the Export Mapping Wizard.

**5.** Click Next in the first wizard dialog box.

**6.** Choose Selected Data in the next box of the wizard, and then click Next.

**7.** Choose Use Existing Map in the next box of the wizard, and then click Next.

**8.** Choose Earned Value Information from the list of available maps in the Export Wizard dialog box and click Finish.

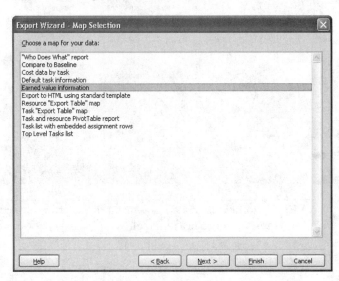

  *To chart earned value in Excel, you usually don't need to make any*
*changes in the remaining dialog boxes that the wizard presents.*

## Using Excel to Chart Project Information

Once you've exported your project's earned value information to an Excel workbook,
you can chart it in Excel. Open Microsoft Excel, click the Microsoft Office button
and then click Open. In the Open dialog box that appears, navigate to and open the
workbook that you just created. You can create as many charts from this data as
you want. For example, the chart in Figure 16-6 compares budgeted cost of work
performed with actual cost of work performed.

To create a chart like the one shown in Figure 16-6, follow these steps:

1. Select the cells you want to chart.

2. Click Insert and then click Column to open the Column gallery
(see Figure 16-7).

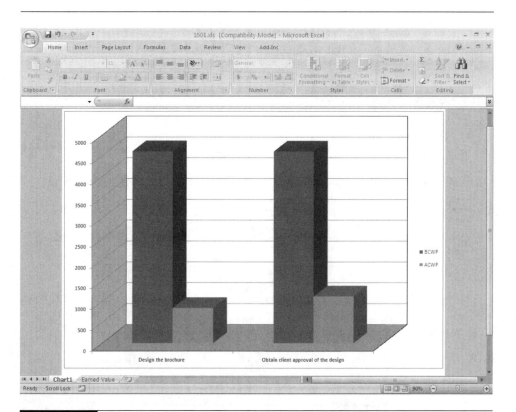

**FIGURE 16-6**    An Excel chart comparing two earned values for selected tasks.

16

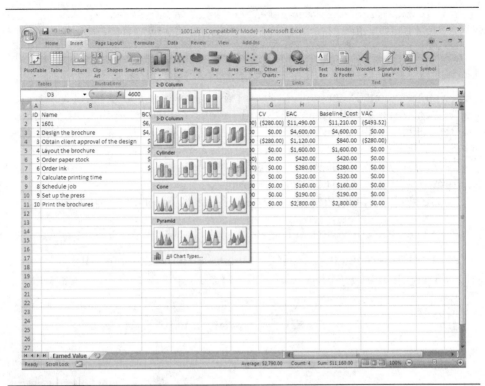

**FIGURE 16-7**  Select a column chart style for the selected data.

**3.** Select a column style. Excel inserts the chart in your spreadsheet; the chart is selected. Chart Tools appear on the Ribbon.

**4.** Click Select Data on the Ribbon to display the Select Data Source dialog box and assign meaningful labels to the data in the chart.

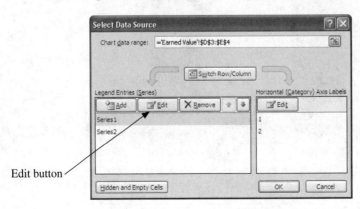

5.  Click an entry in the Legend Entries list; in the example, I clicked Series1.

6.  Click Edit. Excel displays the Edit Series dialog box, from which you can select a legend label.

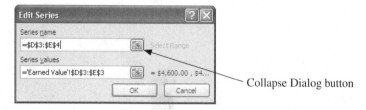

Collapse Dialog button

7.  Click the Collapse Dialog button at the right edge of the Series Name box. Excel collapses the dialog box so that you can select a cell in the spreadsheet.

8.  Click the cell containing the column heading for the value represented by the leftmost bar; in the example, I clicked D1, which contains the label for EV. Excel changes the information in the collapsed Edit Series dialog box to match your selection.

9.  Click the Collapse Dialog button to redisplay the Edit Series dialog box, and click OK to redisplay the Select Data Source dialog box. Excel shows the name change in the Legend Entries list in the dialog box (see Figure 16-8).

10.  Repeat Steps 5 to 9 for Series2.

11.  For the entries in the Horizontal Axis Labels list on the right side of the Select Data Source dialog box, repeat Steps 5 to 9 to select row headings to use as X-axis labels with one exception: select all row labels simultaneously. In the example, when I repeated Step 8, I selected cells B2.B3 to replace the numbers 1 and 2 that Excel assigned to the X-axis of the chart. You only complete Step 11 once; this step assigns labels to all entries in the Horizontal Axis Labels list simultaneously.

**16**

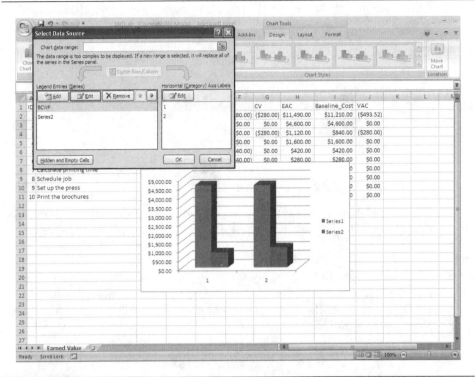

**FIGURE 16-8** The legend for the first set of values now displays a name instead of the generic title that Excel assigns.

When you complete this step, the Select Data Source dialog box will resemble the one shown in the illustration.

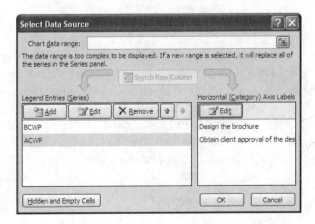

**12.** Click OK.

In the chart shown previously in Figure 16-6, I placed the chart in its own sheet by making sure that the chart was selected and clicking Move Chart Location at the right edge of the Design tab on the Ribbon. In the Move Chart dialog box that appeared, I clicked the New Sheet option. You can switch between the chart and the data using the tabs at the bottom of the workbook.

## Using PivotTables for Earned Value Analysis

The Excel PivotTable, an interactive table that summarizes large amounts of data in a cross-tabular format, can be useful and interesting in analyzing Project earned value data. When you export Project data to Excel to create a PivotTable, you get two PivotTables and two worksheets in the same workbook:

- A Task PivotTable

- A Resource PivotTable

- A Tasks worksheet

- A Resources worksheet

The Task PivotTable shows resources, tasks to which the resources are assigned, and costs for the resource per task. The Resource PivotTable summarizes resources by showing work that is assigned to each resource and the total cost of each resource. Excel uses the Tasks and Resources worksheets to create the two PivotTables.

To export Project information to create PivotTables in Excel, follow these steps:

1. Start in any view of your project.

2. Choose File | Save As to open the Save As dialog box.

3. Type a name for the Excel workbook that you want to create in the File Name box. Don't worry about the extension, because Project supplies it.

4. Open the Save as Type list box and select Microsoft Excel PivotTable.

5. Click Save to start the Export Mapping Wizard.

16

6. Click Next in the first dialog box the wizard displays.

7. Choose Use Existing Map, and click Next.

8. Click Task and Resource PivotTable Report and click Finish. The hourglass icon for the mouse pointer appears, indicating that you should wait while action takes place.

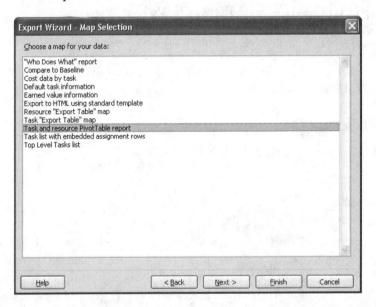

 *To create earned value PivotTables in Excel, you usually don't need to make any changes in the remaining dialog boxes that the wizard presents.*

To view the PivotTables and their source data, start Excel and open the file that you just created. The workbook contains four sheets; in Figure 16-9, you see the sheet containing the Resource PivotTable. Use the tabs at the bottom of the workbook to switch to the other worksheets.

NOTE *You also can use the visual report Earned Value Over Time to help you analyze earned value information. See Chapter 15 for more information on producing visual reports.*

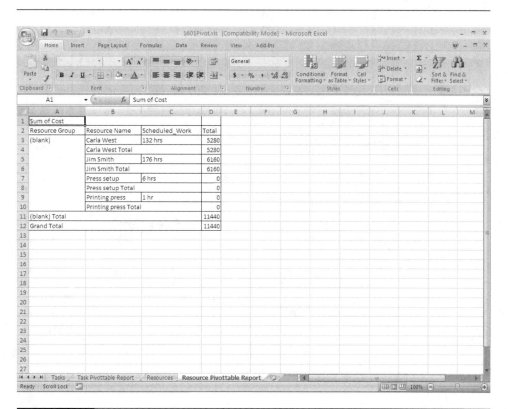

**FIGURE 16-9**   The Resource PivotTable.

In this chapter, you learned how to evaluate your project's financial progress. Chapter 17 begins Part VI of this book, which focuses on advanced tools in Project. Chapter 17 shows you how to consolidate projects—a useful tool for managing a large project, because it enables you to break the large project into smaller projects without losing the integrity of the larger project's dependencies.

**16**

# Part VI

# Advanced Project Management

# Chapter 17

## Consolidating Projects and Sharing Resources

## How to...

- Understand consolidation
- Create subprojects
- Create a consolidated project
- Update links in a consolidated project
- Reorganize a consolidated project
- Work with dependencies in consolidated projects
- View the critical path across consolidated projects
- Share resources across projects

Organization is a cornerstone to good project management, and in a large project, the sheer number of tasks makes the job more difficult than usual. If you use Microsoft Office Project without using Project Server (discussed in Chapter 18), you may want to use the consolidation techniques described in this chapter. When you consolidate projects, you create smaller projects that let you focus on a portion of the large project; when you need to see the bigger picture, you combine the smaller projects into one consolidated project.

In addition to using consolidation to more easily manage large projects, you also can set up a resource pool so that you can share resources across projects. If several project managers use the same set of resources on various projects, consider using a resource pool to schedule resources and resolve resource conflicts.

# Understanding Consolidation

You may find managing a complex project with many tasks easier if you create a series of subprojects instead of trying to create one large project. Each subproject file contains the tasks that constitute a subset of your large project; in this way, you can focus on a limited number of tasks at one time.

You can assign resources and set up each subproject with links and constraints, just as if it were the entire project. When you need to view the bigger picture, you can consolidate the subprojects into one large project. When you consolidate, you insert one project into another project; therefore, subprojects are also called *inserted projects*. In a consolidated project, subprojects appear as summary tasks; you can use Project's outlining tools to hide all tasks that are associated with any subproject, and you can view, print, and change information for any subproject.

NOTE    *While Project Professional users often use Project Server to manage large projects, a project manager who uses Project and Project Server may want to use consolidation techniques to see one critical path across all consolidated projects.*

Consolidation is also useful when sets of tasks in a project are managed by different people. Using consolidation techniques, you can allow each project manager to create the correct dependencies and assign the necessary resources for his or her portion of the project while accurately displaying the project's schedule.

Last, if you pool resources for several projects, you can consolidate the projects so that you can level the resources. Pooling resources is discussed at the end of this chapter.

# Creating Subprojects

It doesn't really matter when you decide to use consolidation. You may realize right away that a project is large enough that you need to break it down to focus on individual aspects of it, or you may discover that the project is bigger than you originally thought as you work on it. Suppose, for example, that the two-day conference for physicists from three local universities that you are planning expands to a five-day conference for physicists from all universities in your state. You've just been handed an opportunity to use consolidation to manage the tasks that result from expanding the number of seminars and the number of attendees.

If you decide to use consolidation before you start your project, simply create separate Microsoft Office Project files for various portions of the project. These files will be the subproject files that you will consolidate. Set up each subproject file so that it is independently complete and create task dependency links for the tasks within each subproject file, as necessary. Ultimately, you'll link the subprojects to form the consolidated project.

17

If you decide that you want to use consolidation after you've already started a project, you can create subprojects by following these steps:

1. Save your large project file.

2. Select all the tasks that you want to save in your first subproject file, and click the Copy button.

3. Click the New button to start a new project, and use the Project Information dialog box to set basic project information, such as the project's start date and scheduling method. If the Project Information dialog box doesn't appear automatically when you start a new project, choose Project | Project Information to display it.

*To make the Project Information dialog box appear each time you start a new project, choose Tools | Options. In the Options dialog box, click the General tab and check the Prompt for Project Info for New Projects check box.*

4. Click the Paste button.

5. Save the subproject, and close it.

6. Repeat Steps 2 through 5 until you have saved several separate files that contain portions of your larger project.

# Creating a Consolidated Project

To consolidate project files into one large project, you insert several individual project files into one project file, which I'll call the consolidated project file. Each project that you insert appears as a summary task in the consolidated project file, and Project calculates inserted projects like summary tasks. An icon in the Indicators field identifies an inserted project (see Figure 17-1).

Although you see three inserted projects in Figure 17-1, you can include more than just inserted projects in a consolidated project file. You can include tasks as well; the point here is that a consolidated project file behaves just like a regular Microsoft Office Project file, and you can store tasks in it as well as inserted projects.

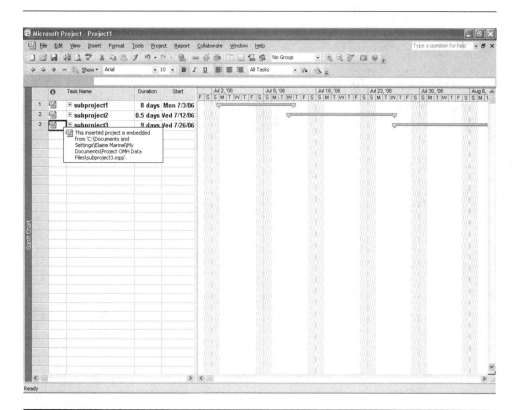

**FIGURE 17-1**   An icon in the Indicators field identifies an inserted project.

When you insert a project, Project places the inserted project immediately above the selected row in the consolidated project file. To insert a project, follow these steps:

1. Open the project in which you want to store the consolidated project.

2. Switch to the Gantt Chart view.

3. Click in the row of the Task Name column where you want the inserted project to begin. If your consolidated project already contains tasks, click the task in the Task Name column that you want to appear below the subproject.

17

**4.** Choose Insert | Project to open the Insert Project dialog box.

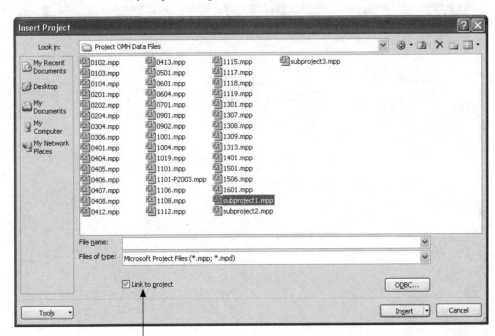

This box controls how Project updates inserted projects.

**5.** Use the Look In list box to navigate to the folder that contains the project that you want to insert.

**6.** Highlight the file that you want to insert. If you remove the check from the Link to Project check box or choose Insert Read-Only from the Insert drop-down menu, Project doesn't update the subproject file when you change the inserted project in the consolidated project file.

**7.** Click Insert. Project inserts the selected file into the open project. The inserted file appears as a summary task, with its subordinate tasks hidden.

The level at which an inserted project appears depends on the outline level that appears at the location where you intend to insert a project. Typically, an inserted project appears at the same level as the selected task. However, if the task that is above the selected task is indented farther than the selected task, the inserted project appears at the same level as that indented task. To produce a consolidated project in which the inserted projects line up at the highest outline level, like the project that appears in Figure 17-1, make sure that you collapse the preceding inserted project so that you can't see its tasks when you insert the next subproject.

*To hide or show tasks after you insert a project, click the summary task's outline symbol—the plus or minus sign next to the task name.*

# A Quick Way to Consolidate

You can use a shortcut to consolidate several projects. Open all the subprojects that you want to consolidate using the Open command—the same way you'd open any project. Then, choose Window | New Window. Project displays the New Window dialog box.

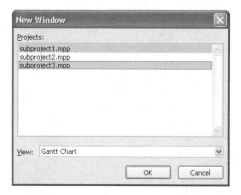

Press and hold down the CTRL key on your keyboard and click each project that you want to consolidate. When you click OK, Project creates a new consolidated project that contains the projects that you selected in the New Window dialog box. Project inserts the subprojects into the consolidated project in the order in which the subprojects appear in the New Window dialog box.

# Updating Links

Linking inserted project files to their source files makes updating easier. When you link subprojects to their source files, any changes that you make in the consolidated project affects the subproject file, and any changes you make in the subproject file affects the consolidated project file.

When you insert a project and link it to its source file, the link you create works like any link that you create between any two files in the Windows environment.

17

For example, if you rename the subproject file or move it to a different folder than the one in which you originally saved it, you need to update the link to the consolidated project; otherwise, the link does not work.

You can use two approaches to update the link. When you click the plus sign next to the subproject, Project automatically displays a dialog box that looks like the Open dialog box; navigate to the new location of the file, and click OK to re-establish the link between the files.

Or, you can update the link on the Advanced tab of the Inserted Project Information dialog box for the inserted project. Double-click the summary task of any inserted project to display the Inserted Project Information dialog box; then click the Advanced tab and use the Browse button beside the Link to Project box to navigate to the current location of the inserted project.

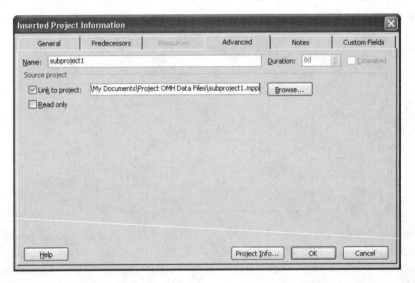

*You also can unlink subprojects from their source files from the Advanced tab of the Inserted Project Information dialog box; remove the check from the Link to Project check box.*

# Reorganizing a Consolidated Project

You can move subprojects around in the consolidated project by cutting a subproject row to delete it and then pasting the row where you want it to appear. When you select a summary row that represents a subproject and click the Cut button on the Standard toolbar, Project opens a Planning Wizard dialog box that asks you to confirm that you want to delete the subproject.

Select the Continue option button, and click OK. Project removes the summary task that represents the subproject and all its subordinate tasks. When you paste the subproject, Project places the subproject immediately above the selected row. Therefore, in the Task Name column, you must click the task that you want to appear below the subproject and then click the Paste button on the Standard toolbar.

*If you're going to be moving a lot of tasks, you may want to select the Don't Tell Me About This Again check box in the Planning Wizard dialog box to avoid viewing the Planning Wizard each time you cut a subproject.*

# Consolidation and Dependencies

Consolidation wouldn't work well if you had no way of linking a task in the consolidated project or in one subproject with a task in another subproject. After all, you'd have a difficult time truly managing that large project you broke down if you couldn't link it together the way it should be linked.

You can create links between subprojects in a consolidated file and, if necessary, change the links that you create.

## Creating Dependencies in Consolidated Projects

You can create the same four types of dependencies in a consolidated project that you can create in any Project file: finish-to-start, start-to-start, finish-to-finish, and start-to finish. In addition, these dependency types support lead and lag time. The process of linking tasks with dependencies across projects is very similar to creating dependencies for tasks within the same project. Starting in the consolidated project file, follow these steps:

1.  Click the Gantt Chart on the View bar.

2.  Select the tasks that you want to link. To select noncontiguous tasks, press and hold down CTRL as you click each task name.

3.  Click the Link Tasks button on the Standard toolbar. Project creates a finish-to-start link between the two tasks.

You also can link tasks by typing in the Predecessors field, using the format *project name\ID#*. The project name should include the path to the location of the

**17**

file as well as the filename, and the ID# should be the ID number of the task in that file. In Figure 17-2, the Buy Room Decorations task, Task 3 in a Project file called subproject2.MPP, is linked to the Site task, which is Task 8 in a Project file called subproject1.MPP. You can see the complete pathname of a linked task in the Entry bar (just below the toolbars) when you highlight the task.

When you link tasks between projects, the task links look like standard links in the consolidated project. However, when you open a subproject file, you can easily identify external links. The name and the Gantt Chart bar of each externally linked task appear gray; in Figure 17-3, tasks 9 and 10 are externally linked. If you point at the Gantt Chart bar, Project displays information about the task, including the fact that it is an external task.

Path of the linked task

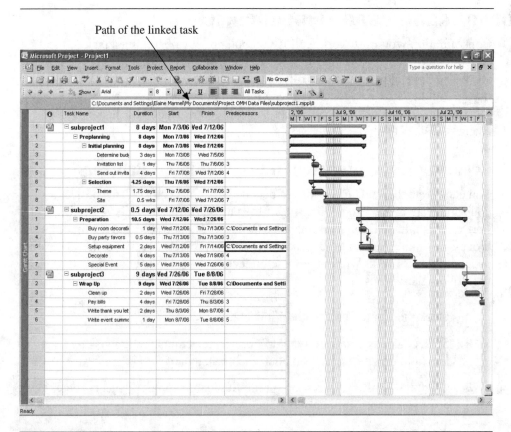

**FIGURE 17-2**    You can type in the Predecessors field to create a link between tasks across Project files.

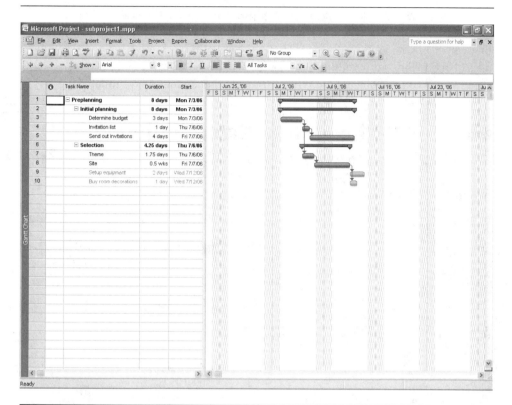

**FIGURE 17-3**   External tasks and their task bars appear light gray.

# Changing Dependencies in Consolidated Projects

You can modify a link between tasks in different subprojects from the subproject
or from the consolidated project. In the subproject, double-click the line that links
an internal task to the external task. In the consolidated project, double-click the
line that links the two tasks. In both cases, Project displays the Task Dependency
dialog box, where you can change the dependency information about tasks that are
linked across projects.

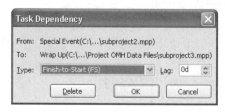

The two versions of the dialog boxes differ slightly. If you work from within the subproject, you can update the path of the link and use the Type list box to change the type of link and the Lag box to change the amount of lag time between the linked tasks. If you work from within the consolidated project, you can't update the path of the link, but you can change the type of link and the amount of lag time.

# Viewing and Saving Consolidated Projects

Creating a consolidated project makes your work easier because you can display and hide selected portions of your project. The consolidated project that appears in Figure 17-4 contains three inserted projects. As you can tell from the outline

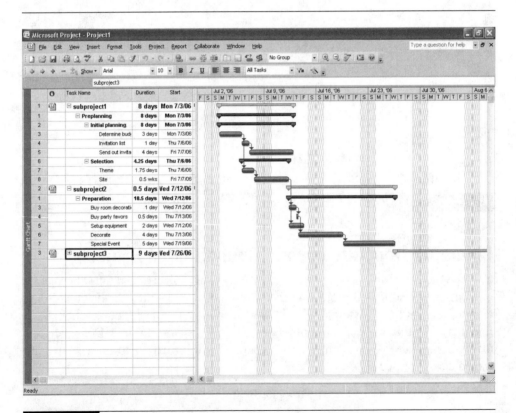

**FIGURE 17-4**    This consolidated project contains three inserted projects.

symbols, you can't see all the tasks in this consolidated project in the figure; the tasks for subproject 3 are hidden.

To focus on the middle portion of the project, click the outline symbols to the left of each summary task to expand only the portion of the project that you want to view.

You don't need to save consolidated project files. You can use the consolidated project to create links and even reports, and then close the consolidated project file without saving it. When you close the consolidated project, Project first asks if you want to save the consolidated project. Whether you choose to save the consolidated project doesn't change Project's behavior; Project next asks if you want to save changes that you made to inserted projects.

If you save the changes to the subprojects, even if you don't save the consolidated project, external tasks like the ones shown previously in Figure 17-3 appear in the subproject files when you open them.

# Viewing the Critical Path
# Across Consolidated Projects

When you consolidate projects, by default Project calculates inserted projects like summary tasks, effectively showing you the overall critical path across all the projects by using the late finish date of the consolidated project to make calculations. This behavior can make subprojects within the master project look like they don't have critical paths of their own (see Figure 17-5).

To see each subproject's critical path while viewing the consolidated project, tell Project to stop treating subprojects as summary tasks. In this case, Project uses the late finish dates that the subprojects pass along to the consolidated project to determine the critical path, and you're likely to see each subproject's critical

**17**

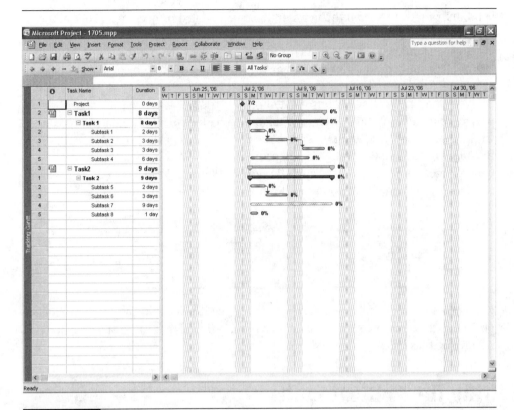

**FIGURE 17-5**     By default, you don't see critical paths for individual inserted projects.

path (see Figure 17-6). When you turn off this setting, you see critical paths in the consolidated project as they appear in each subproject.

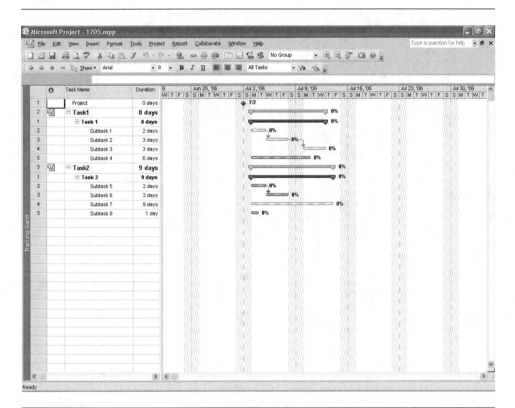

**FIGURE 17-6** When Project doesn't treat inserted projects like summary tasks, you're likely to see multiple critical paths in a master project.

To change Project's behavior in the master project, choose Tools | Options. On the Calculation tab of the Options dialog box, remove the check from the Inserted Projects Are Calculated Like Summary Tasks check box.

17

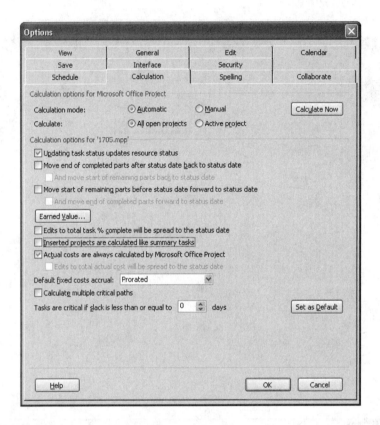

# Sharing Resources Across Projects

A resource pool is a set of resources that you make available to any project, enabling you to share the resources among several projects. If several project managers use the same set of resources on various projects, consider using a resource pool to schedule resources and resolve resource conflicts.

*Project Professional users using Project Server can use the Enterprise Resource Pool in Project Server instead of the technique I describe in this section.*

## Creating a Resource Pool

Creating a resource pool is very easy. You simply set up a Project file that contains only resource information. If you have already set up a project that contains all the resources that are available, you can use that project as a model; you don't need to delete all the tasks in the project that will serve as the model for the resource pool. I saved a copy of the project that contains the resources I want available; I cleverly named it "resource pool.mpp" to avoid confusion.

After you identify a project that can serve as the resource pool, you designate it as the resource pool project by using the following steps:

1.  Open the project that contains the resources and that will serve as the resource pool file.

2.  Open the project that is to use the resource pool (that is, the project on which you want to work).

3.  Choose Tools | Resource Sharing | Share Resources. Project displays the Share Resources dialog box.

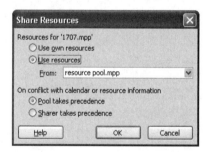

4.  Click the Use Resources option button, and then use the From list box to select the resource pool project. This indicates that you want to use the resources that are defined in that project. If you have any other projects open, they appear as candidates for the resource pool project when you open the From drop-down list.

5.  Select an option to tell Project how to handle calendar conflicts. If you select the Pool Takes Precedence option button, the resource calendars in the resource pool file take precedence when conflicts arise. If, however, you select the Sharer Takes Precedence option button, the resource calendars in the file that you're updating take precedence over the resource calendars in the resource pool file when conflicts arise.

6.  Click OK.

If you switch to the Resource Sheet view of the file that you want to update, Project displays all the resources that are contained in the resource pool file, along with any resources that you may have set up in your project file.

You can now continue working in your project, making resource assignments. The resources to whom you assign work will continue to appear on the Resource Sheet of your project after you save and close both your project and the resource pool file.

## Opening a Project that Uses a Resource Pool

When you next open your project file that shares resources, you don't need to open the resource pool file. When you open your file after you have set it up to share resources, the Open Resource Pool Information dialog box appears.

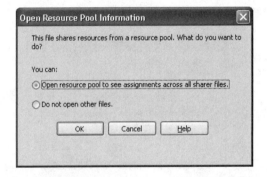

If you select the first option, Project opens the resource pool as a read-only file in addition to your file, enabling you to make changes to your project without tying up the resource pool file; therefore, multiple users can use the resource pool simultaneously.

If you select the second option, Project opens only your file. If you make changes to resources in your project, Project does not update the resource pool file with those changes because the resource pool file isn't open.

## Updating Information in the Resource Pool

You must update the resource pool file if you make changes to resource information while you're working on your project. To update the resource pool, make sure that the resource pool file is open, even in read-only mode. Then choose Tools | Resource Sharing | Update Resource Pool.

If you forget to update the resource pool after you make a change in your project that affects the resource pool, Project displays a message when you save your project, asking if you want to update the resource pool. Click OK to update the pool with your changes.

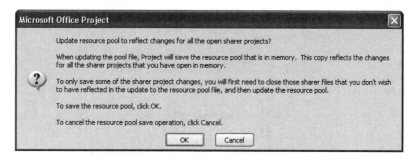

# Stop Using Shared Resources

You don't have to use the resource pool forever; if you have a good reason to disconnect a project from the resource pool, open that project. Then, choose Tools | Resource Sharing | Share Resources. In the Share Resource dialog box, select the Use Own Resources option button. Project displays a warning message that asks you if you're sure you want to remove the connection between your file and the resource pool. Click Yes to complete the action.

You also can disable the resource pool in general for all files that are sharing the resources of one resource pool without opening each file. Follow these steps to disable the resource pool file in general:

1. Open the resource pool file in read-write mode by using the Open dialog box, the same way that you would open any file. Project displays the Open Resource Pool dialog box.

2. Choose the middle option or the last option in this dialog box; either option enables you to disable the pool. Click OK.

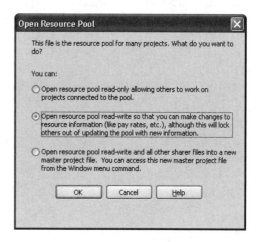

17

**3.** Choose Tools | Resource Sharing, | Share Resources. Project displays the Share Resources dialog box.

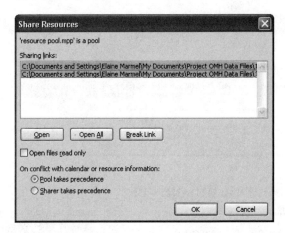

**4.** Select the project(s) that you want to exclude from the resource pool. You can select multiple noncontiguous projects by pressing and holding down the CTRL key when you click the mouse, or you can select contiguous projects by pressing and holding down the SHIFT key when you click the mouse.

**5.** Click the Break Link button.

**6.** When you finish, click OK. Project breaks the link between the resource pool and the selected files.

In this chapter, you learned how to use consolidation to make large projects more manageable, and you learned how to create a resource pool so that you can share resources across projects. In the next chapter, you read about Project Server, which allows you to manage projects across an enterprise.

# Chapter 18

## Using Project Server

## How to...

- Describe Project Server and Project Web Access
- Understand the role of the Project Server administrator
- Approach using Project Server and Project Professional as a project manager
- Handle Project Web Access as a team member
- Use Project Web Access as an executive
- Describe the Project Server working environment

For many organizations, project management involves managing projects and resources that are widely dispersed, not only throughout the organization but geographically as well. Since managing projects effectively affects the bottom line, managing far-flung projects well presents a challenge. Project Server helps you meet this challenge.

Project Server integrates a web-based interface called Project Web Access with Project Professional. Project managers can build projects using the familiar tools found in Project Professional and upload those projects to Project Server, which resides in a secured network environment. Using the Enterprise Resource Pool available in Project Server, project and resource managers can find appropriate resources to assign to tasks. Team members with proper security permissions use Internet Explorer to provide updates to work assignments on the projects to which they are assigned. Executives can view and report on the organization's portfolio of projects to evaluate project status and identify projects that have the potential to miss deadlines and exceed costs. Project Server can help you provide strong coordination and standardization between projects and project managers and utilize centralized resource management to complete your projects on time and within budget.

In this chapter, I'm going to provide you with an overview of the way Project Server works and how Project Professional interfaces with Project Web Access. I'm not trying to teach you how to do any of the tasks you'll read about; instead, I'm trying to give you an idea of how the products work. Since different people within the organization use Project Server differently, I'll present this overview from the perspective of the following role players, describing tasks these role players typically use when working in Project Server and Project Web Access:

- The Project Server administrator
- The project/resource manager

■ Team members

■ Executives

 *Project Server works only with Project Professional. If you're using Project Standard, you cannot connect to Project Server.*

# Understanding Project Server and Project Web Access

As your organization manages an increasing number of projects, you hire more resources to complete those projects. Increased workload and increased resources requires a corresponding need to increase management. That is, you need to manage the management of projects.

Project Server enables you to store all projects and all resources for the organization in one central database on your company's local-area network (LAN) or intranet. In this network environment, you can use the Enterprise Resource Pool feature of Project Server to match limited resources to projects. I'll describe the Enterprise Resource Pool in greater detail later in this chapter, but you can think of it as a network-based holding tank that contains information about all resources in your company. Because the Enterprise Resource Pool is on the network, all project and resource managers can use it to find the resources they need to complete their projects.

Project managers install and use Project Professional to create projects that they subsequently upload to the Project Server database. Using the Enterprise Global template, each project that you create contains all the same fields, maps, views, tables, reports, filters, forms, toolbars, groups, and calendars that are stored in the global template file that's included in Project Professional, along with additional enterprise-only fields. Because the settings are stored in the Enterprise Global template, they can be used repeatedly without having to re-create information.

Anyone with Internet Explorer 6.0 (or a later version), knowledge of the Project Server web address, and proper viewing rights can use Project Web Access, the browser-based client side of Project Server, to view project information as it appears in Project Professional. Using Project Web Access, team members, managers, and executives can, for example, enter and view timesheet information, view a project's Gantt Chart, update assignments with progress and completion information, and send status reports.

Project Server is built on a scaled-down version of Windows SharePoint Services, which aims at making collaboration easy. Using Windows SharePoint Services features, Project Web Access users can attach documents to tasks

**18**

and record issues and risks associated with tasks, which can then be viewed by all team members. This increased communication helps ensure that things don't fall through the cracks during a project, which helps increase the quality of the product or service you provide to your client.

# The Project Server Administrator

The Project Server administrator is typically the person responsible for setting up and customizing the Project Server database to meet your organization's needs. To do the job effectively, you need the skills of both an information technology (IT) person with background in hardware, networking, and connectivity and a project management person with extensive knowledge of your organization's needs while managing projects.

Once you have Project Server up and running, the role of the Project Server administrator becomes more of a maintenance job and is best filled by someone with project management background.

The Project Server administrator uses Project Web Access and makes changes to Project Server's behavior working primarily from the Server Settings page (see Figure 18-1).

As you can see in Figure 18-1, the Server Settings page organizes the kinds of changes the Project Server administrator can make. The following list describes what you can do as Project Server administrator from each of the page's sections:

- **Security** Define the users who are allowed to have access to Project Web Access and assign those users to predefined groups or groups created especially for your organization. The predefined groups are associated with the roles of the people who will use Project Web Access; for example, you'll find an Administrators group, a Project Managers group, and a Team Members group. Project Server provides these groups to make setting up security profiles easier; the Project Server administrator creates users, assigns the users to groups, and assigns groups to security templates, which are sets of permissions that define the actions you can and cannot take in Project Web Access. Similarly, Project Server uses categories to let the Project Server administrator define the projects, resources, and views that can be seen by users and groups.

- **Enterprise Data** Create enterprise custom fields, make changes to the Enterprise Global template, and create Enterprise calendars.

- **Database Administration** Maintain the Project Server database, by deleting old information and backing up and, if necessary, restoring the database.

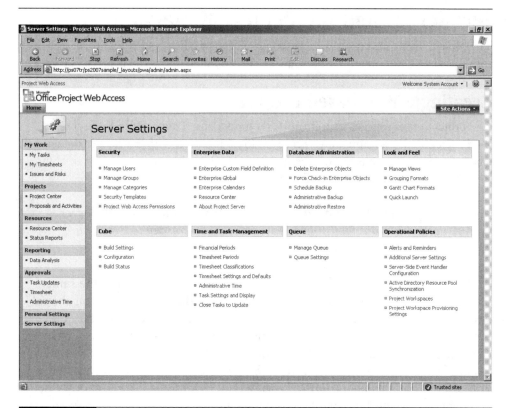

**FIGURE 18-1** The Project Server administrator makes changes to Project Server's behavior from this page.

■ **Look and Feel** Manage the way Project Web Access appears to users.

■ **Cube** Manage the OLAP cube needed to produce reports in Project Web Access.

■ **Time and Task Management** Set up financial and timesheet time periods, manage the appearance of timesheet information and task tracking and display settings.

■ **Queue** Manage the queue that Project Server uses when updating Project Web Access.

■ **Operational Policies** Determine the conditions under which users receive alerts and reminders and set up Windows SharePoint Services workspaces for projects.

18

# Project Server and the Project Manager

The project manager creates web-based projects using Project Professional, assigns resources using the Enterprise Resource Pool, and then tracks the project's progress.

## Creating a Web-based Project

The project manager creates a Project Server account from within Project once the Project Server administrator provides the URL to the Project Server database. Then, the project manager uses the Login dialog box that appears while opening Project Professional to log onto Project Server.

 *Project Server uses Windows account authentication or SQL Server authentication; the Project Server administrator can tell you your username and password.*

Project Professional opens, and you can create a project using the same techniques you've been reading about throughout this book. And, you should save a copy of the project to your local hard disk. To create a web-based project, you save the project to the Project Server database; when you first save the project to the Project Server database, Project Server saves a draft version on the database. Other Project Server users won't have access to the draft project. You can continue to work with the draft project and modify it, and the project won't be visible to other users.

When you are ready for other users to see your project, you use Project Professional to publish it, creating two versions of your project in the Project Server database—the draft version and the published version. You can continue to work with your project in Project Professional; typically, you'll work with the draft version and ultimately republish it to update the version that everyone else sees.

To save a draft version of a project to the Project Server database, open Project Professional and log onto Project Server. Open the project that you want to store in the Project Server database and choose File | Save As. The Save to Project Server dialog box appears; type the name you want to assign to the project in the Project Server database. Any custom fields stored in the Enterprise Global template appear at the bottom of the box. As appropriate, you can select values for the custom fields. When you finish, click Save, and Project uploads the project to the Project Server database as a draft project.

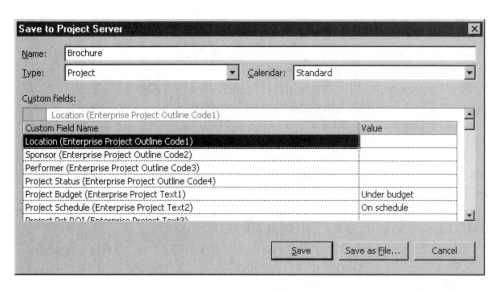

You can continue to work on the project in Project Professional until things are the way you want them to be; at that point, you publish the project to make it visible to all concerned parties. With the project open in Project Professional, choose File | Publish to open the Publish Project dialog box.

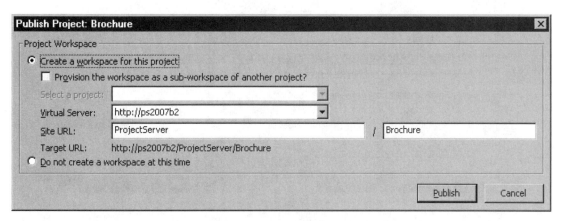

By default, no Windows SharePoint Services workspace is created when you publish the project, but you can choose to create the workspace if you want to use the Windows SharePoint Services features that help manage documents, issues, and risks associated with projects. If you don't create the workspace now, you can create it later. Project fills in all the information for you, and there really isn't any reason to change any of it.

18

# Managing Resource Assignments

If you use Project Server, your organization will probably use the Enterprise Resource Pool, which provides a list of all resources in your organization. Typically, the Project Server administrator builds the initial Enterprise Resource Pool, and, if you have appropriate permissions, you can add resources to the Enterprise Resource Pool.

You can use the Enterprise Resource Pool to select resources for a project. You also can assign generic resources to your project and then use the Enterprise Resource Pool to replace the generic resources with real resources. And, if appropriate, you can take advantage of the Resource Substitution Wizard to identify the best possible utilization of limited resources.

## Viewing and Assigning Enterprise Resources

To view the resources in the Enterprise Resource Pool and assign them to your project, choose Tools | Build Team from Enterprise. Project displays the Build Team dialog box (see Figure 18-2).

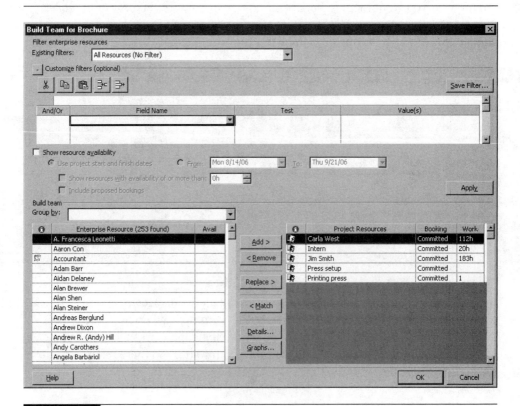

**FIGURE 18-2**   You can limit the resources that you see by applying filters.

After you select resources and click OK, the resources appear on the Resource Sheet of your project, and you can assign tasks to them. When you republish your project, the Enterprise Resource Pool is updated to reflect the assignments. In addition, team members to whom you assigned work see notification of the assignment on their Home page when they log into Project Web Access.

If you're a resource manager and you don't have access to Project Professional, you can use Project Web Access to assign resources. From the Project Center, you'll see links for each project you're authorized to view. When you click any project's link, you see the Gantt Chart view of that project—very much the way it would appear in Project Professional. On that page, you can click the Build Team button to display the Build Team page (see Figure 18-3).

*You can view assignments and availability for any resource you select in either list and you can replace generic resources by matching them.*

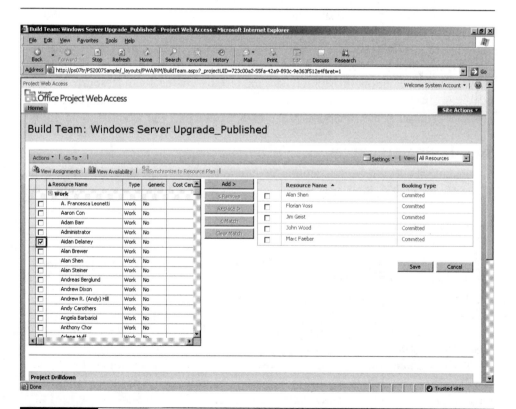

**FIGURE 18-3**   From this page, you can identify resources already assigned to the project and select new resources to add to the project.

18

## Working with Generic Resources

Generic resources are not people, but job descriptions. To use generic resources, your organization takes two actions:

■ Creates an enterprise resource custom outline code with a value list; each value in the list represents a job description.

■ Assigns a value for the enterprise resource custom outline code to each resource in the Enterprise Resource Pool.

To take advantage of generic resources, you assign a generic resource to a task in your project. Project can then use the code to match the skills you need, which are represented by the generic resource you assigned to your project, with skills that are possessed by resources in your organization. While working in the Build Team dialog box, click the generic resource for which you want to search for a replacement in the list on the right side of the dialog box. Then, click the Match button. Project displays, in the left side of the dialog box, those resources with skills that match the selected generic resource. To replace a generic resource with a real resource, click the resource that you want to use in your project from the list on the left and click the Replace button. Project replaces the resource in the Team Resource list with the Enterprise Resource that you selected. When you click OK, Project updates the project by replacing the generic resource with the one that you selected.

## Substituting Resources

You can use the Resource Substitution Wizard to help you smooth work assignments and reduce overallocations across one or more projects. The Resource Substitution Wizard can be particularly useful if you are managing multiple projects with the same set of resources.

The Resource Substitution Wizard can consider the resources in the projects that you select and reallocate them to better utilize their time. Or, the wizard can use the enterprise custom outline code that is assigned to resources to match skills required by resources that are already assigned to tasks and then substitute other resources with the same code.

To run the Resource Substitution Wizard, open the project(s) for which you want to substitute resources. Then, choose Tools | Substitute Resources.

The first screen of the Resource Substitution Wizard appears and explains that it will help you substitute resources. As you walk through the wizard, you have the opportunity to select the project(s) and resources that you want the wizard to consider while substituting resources.

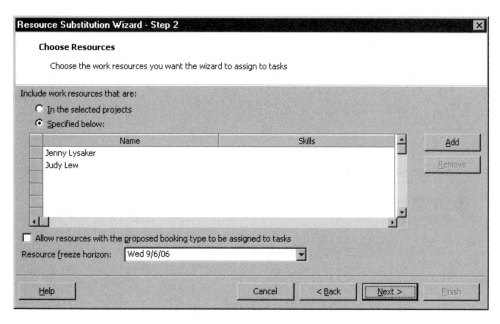

The wizard also gives you the opportunity to select related projects to consider when rescheduling, and you can set scheduling options that indicate whether to use resources from the pool or from the project. Before you actually substitute, you see a summary of the options that you've selected.

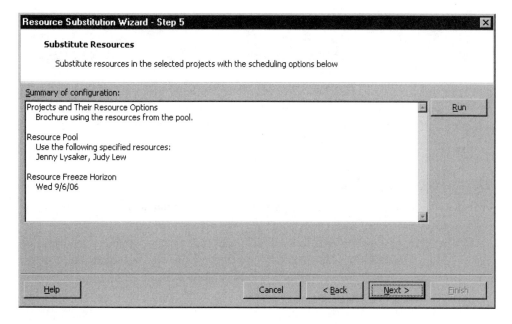

Click the Run button, and the wizard runs; while the wizard runs, the Run button changes to the Stop button. When the Run button reappears, click next to display the proposed assignment changes. You can review the results and, if you want, click the Back button to change options and try again. If you click Next, the wizard displays the Update Options screen, where you can choose to have Project update the projects considered by the wizard based on the results of the wizard. If you aren't satisfied with the results of the wizard, simply close the affected projects without saving them.

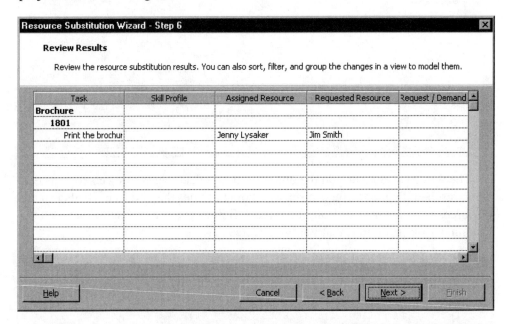

After the wizard has finished, I suggest that you level the projects to see how the wizard's resource assignments change project finish dates and resource utilization. If you aren't satisfied with the results of the wizard, simply close the affected projects without saving them.

## Tracking Progress

Project offers three tracking methods when recording actual work:

- **Percent of Work Complete** Resources enter the percentage amount. Using this method, resources can record time quickly, but this method is the least accurate of the three methods because it is based on the resource's estimate of the total amount of work to be done, along with the amount that is actually completed.

■ **Actual Work Done and Work Remaining**    Resources enter the hours, days, weeks, and so on of the amount of work done and the amount of work remaining to be completed. This method is both moderately accurate and moderately fast.

■ **Hours of Work Done per Time Period**    Resources enter the actual hours worked on each task for a specified time. This the most accurate and the most time-consuming of the three methods.

If your organization hasn't selected a tracking method for you, you can select a tracking method from the Collaborate tab of the Options dialog box in Project Professional.

As a project manager, you can use Project Web Access to set up a status report that you want to receive from team members. You specify how often you want status reports, when reporting should begin, which resources should report, and the sections you want included in the report. At the bottom of the page (see Figure 18-4),

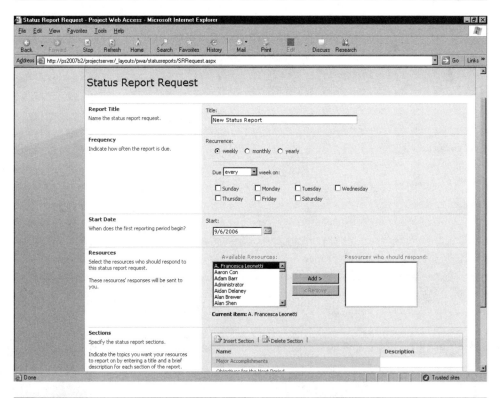

**FIGURE 18-4**    You specify the section that should appear in the status report team members will submit to you.

identify the sections that you want included in the report. When you finish, Project Web Access creates the status report and sends a skeleton of the status report to the selected team members, requesting a status report. The team members can then use the skeleton to fill in the information that you want to see.

When team members record task updates, the project manager sees a notification on the Home page in Project Web Access and in Project Professional when s/he opens the project. Using the Task Updates link in the Quick Launch pane that runs down the left side of the Project Web Access window, you can view and accept or reject the task update in Project Web Access (see Figure 18-5).

If you open the project in Project Professional and choose to review the updates, you see the same window in Project Professional as appears in Figure 18-5.

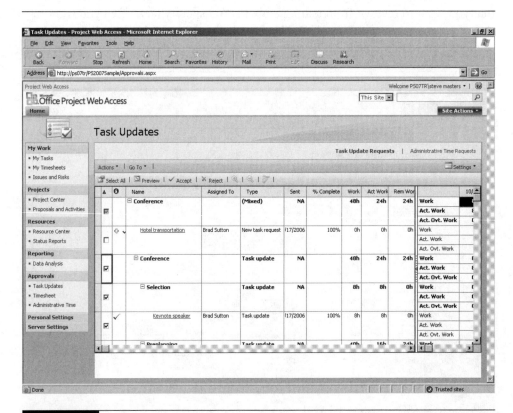

**FIGURE 18-5**   You can view and accept or reject task updates in Project Web Access.

# Project Server and the Team Member

Team members use Project Web Access and typically focus on reporting work on tasks and completing status reports. If your organization uses Windows SharePoint Services features, team members can report issues and risks that arise as they work, and they can attach documents to task work.

*Due to space considerations in the book, I'm not going to cover the collaboration features offered by Windows SharePoint Services.*

When a team member logs onto Project Web Access, the Home page indicates whether any new assignments exist (see Figure 18-6).

Team members can record work using either the My Tasks page or the My Timesheets page.

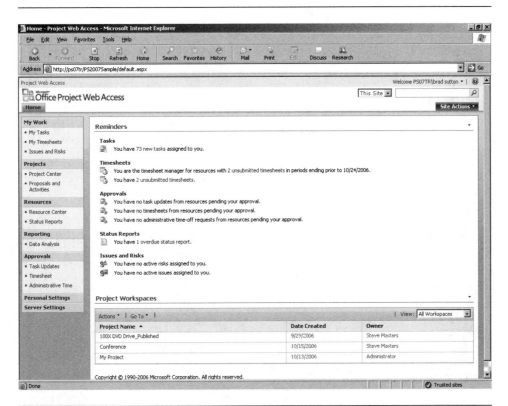

**FIGURE 18-6**   The center portion of the Home page in Project Web Access provides a quick overview of your workload.

18

## Working with Tasks

As a team member, you can view all assignments from the My Tasks page; click the My Tasks link in the Quick Launch pane that runs down the left side of Project Web Access.

You can click any task to record time worked on the task; Project Web Access displays the Assignment Details page (see Figure 18-7). Simply fill in the hours you worked on the appropriate day and click Save.

Saving the work you recorded doesn't send that information to the project manager—and that's deliberate. When Project Web Access redisplays the My Tasks page, you can select another task and record work, repeating this process until you've accounted for all of the work you want to report. At that point, you can, from the My Tasks page, select the appropriate tasks and send the updates to the project manager (see Figure 18-8).

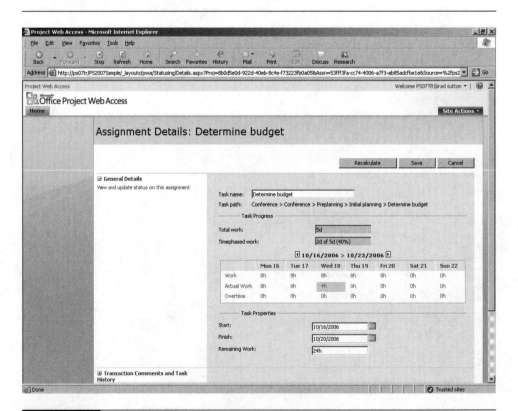

**FIGURE 18-7**   You can record work on a task using the Assignment Details page.

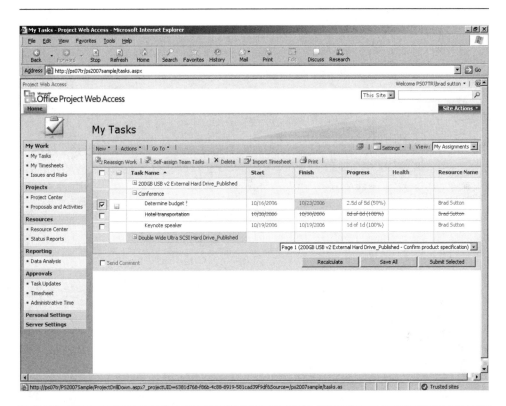

**FIGURE 18-8**   After you record work on assignments, use the My Tasks page to send the updates to the project manager(s).

*Are you used to tracking work in Outlook? Using the Outlook add-in that's available in Project Web Access, resources can import tasks from Project Server and export work information from Outlook to Project Server.*

## Using the Timesheet

Project Web Access also enables you to record the time you work on tasks using a timesheet. Timesheets for appropriate periods appear on the My Timesheets page. If you don't have any timesheets in progress, click the Click to Create link beside the appropriate timesheet period. Project Web Access displays the timesheet for the period you selected (see Figure 18-9). If you click the task name, you see the Assignment Details page shown earlier in Figure 18-7.

**18**

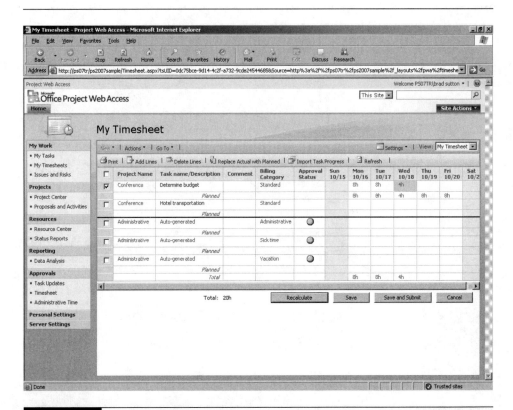

**FIGURE 18-9** A typical timesheet contains tasks for which work is due during the timesheet period.

*If your organization has set up administrative time for you, lines for each administrative time category appear on the timesheet.*

You can enter time manually, by replacing actual with planned time, or by importing progress you reported on tasks. And, if you record time worked using the timesheet, you can display the My Tasks page and import the time, so there's no "double data entry" going on.

To record time manually, click in the box that represents the intersection of the date for which you want to record work and the task on which you want to record work. Then, type the number of hours you want to record. If tasks on which you need to report don't appear on your timesheet, click the Add Lines button. Project Web Access displays a dialog box that you can use to create a new line for your timesheet. You can choose from among tasks assigned to you or you can type a title for the line.

*The numbers that you can enter depend on the tracking method that your project manager or your organization has selected. You may be able to fill in the % work complete, actual work done and work remaining, or the hours of work done per day.*

You don't typically finish recording all information on a timesheet at one time. If you click the Save button on the Timesheet page, Project Web Access saves your entries and the timesheet remains available so that you can add to it.

When the timesheet period no longer covers your working period, click the Save and Submit button to save your work and submit your timesheet for approval.

## Reporting Status

Your project manager will probably expect you to submit a status report from time to time; typically, your project manager will create a status report layout that contains the information on which you need to report. You can view the Status Report Response page by first clicking the Status Reports link in the Quick Launch pane on the left side of the Project Web Access window. Then, click the link to the status report.

You don't need to do much more than fill in the form; at the bottom of the page, you can add sections to the report if necessary and click Send to submit the status report.

If the need arises, you also can submit an unsolicited status report. On the Status Reports page, click the Submit Unrequested Report button.

# Project Server and the Executive

Executives can use Project Web Access to keep their finger on the pulse of the projects within the organization. They also can make use of the Project and Resource Centers to gain high-level views of the organization's work and, if appropriate, drill down to get details. The Project Center provides a high-level picture of all the projects that you have security permissions to view. Your organization can create custom views for the Project Center, each providing you with different kinds of detail. The Resource Center lists all resources stored in the Enterprise Resource Pool; executives can view resource assignments and availability.

18

Using the OLAP cube and a variety of views that the Project Server administrator builds, executives can use the reporting feature to analyze data about the organization's portfolio of projects.

# Considering the Project Server Working Environment

Project Server works in a network environment—either a local-area network or a wide-area network. The total number of users, the number of concurrent users updating the Project Server databases, and the number of projects that you store in the Project Server databases relate directly to the amount of traffic that you can expect on your network. Therefore, the hardware and software configuration that you select will directly affect the overall performance of Project Server.

On any Project Server machine, you must install Windows 2003 Server, Standard or Enterprise edition, Internet Information Services (IIS), SQL Server, and Windows SharePoint Services. Optionally, you can install SQL Analysis Services and SQL Reporting Services. And, of course, you load Project Server. You're loading a lot of software.

You can load all of the software on a single server or, because of the architecture of Windows SharePoint Services, the foundation of Project Server 2007, you can use a server farm. In the server farm, you place various components and services on several networked computers. The server farm also improves your ability to gracefully meet organizational growth needs. And, when you use a server farm, you limit the impact created when a single component or service misbehaves.

You can set up Project Server 2007 in a small farm, a medium farm, or a large farm, and you can arrange the configuration of each server farm size in many different ways. When you're ready to set up Project Server, review the guidelines that Microsoft will be publishing to help you decide whether to use a server farm and, if so (the likely case for Project Server installations), determine the size of the server farm to set up based on the number of tasks, resources, and assignments in your projects, the number of projects you have, and whether most of your projects are small, medium, or large in nature.

To give you a sense of how you might arrange each server farm size, I'll review the recommendations that Microsoft makes about the various server farm configurations. These configurations focus primarily on the web front-end servers, application servers, and SQL servers.

In the Project Server environment, you typically find software arranged in the following way:

- On web front-end servers, you find Windows SharePoint Services and Project Web Access.

- On application servers, you install applications such as the Project Server Interface (used by developers to customize Project Server), Project Server business objects, and Project Server reporting and queuing services.

- SQL servers usually house Project Server SQL databases, SQL Analysis Services, and SQL Reporting Services.

The structure of Windows SharePoint Services enables you to configure server farms in tiers so that you can improve performance by balancing loads. Using a server farm also makes it easy to expand any tier within the farm to improve performance.

## The Small Server Farm

A small server farm usually uses two servers, but before I describe the two-tier configuration, we should consider the single-server setup.

Microsoft refers to the single-server setup as "stand-alone installation mode." As you would expect, you load everything onto one server. This approach can work in a very small company, or if you simply want to evaluate Project Server, but it has limitations. Using a single server, any failure (hardware or software) will bring down your system. In addition, you have no way to balance the load on the server, and expanding to meet growth demands is difficult.

In the two-tier configuration, you separate database processing from other processing to improve performance. You install SQL Server 2000 or SQL Server 2005 and SQL Analysis Services and SQL Reporting Services on one computer. On the other computer, you install Project Server and Windows SharePoint Services, using this computer as both a web front-end server and an application server.

## The Medium Server Farm

In a medium server farm, you use three tiers, installing each component—database server, web front-end server, and application server—in a separate tier. This approach balances the load well and makes it easy for you to accommodate more users and more data because you can add additional web front-end servers, application servers, and database servers to the appropriate tier.

18

## The Large Server Farm

The large server farm closely resembles the medium server farm, because you still use three tiers and install each component in a separate tier. In the large server farm configuration, you may also be using other services available through SharePoint Server 2007—such as Search, Index, or Excel Calculation Services. In this case, you set up each of these services on its own server.

In this chapter, I provided you with an overview of the way organizations use Project Server, the tool provided by Microsoft to manage projects in an enterprise environment. In the next chapter, I'll show you how to use custom fields in Project Professional; and information I'll provide in Chapter 19 also applies, conceptually, to Project Server.

# Chapter 19

# Working with Custom Fields

## How to...

- Take advantage of custom fields and codes
- Create a custom field
- Create a formula in a custom field
- Define custom outline codes
- Use work breakdown structure codes

Project contains a vast number of fields; you see them in the various tables and form views that you use as you enter and evaluate data in Project. But suppose that, even though there are tons of fields available, you need one that is not offered. That's when you can make use of custom fields to create the fields that you need.

Project contains a plethora of custom fields that you can define to use in any way you need. In this chapter, you'll learn how to create custom fields and you'll work with two special kinds of custom fields—work breakdown structure codes and outline codes.

# Understanding Custom Fields

The columns in every table in Project are nothing more than fields. The columns that appear in the default tables in Project are predefined fields. Custom fields are empty fields, waiting for you to define and use them as you need. Project contains tons of custom fields that you can define; you can define text, cost, date, duration, finish, flag, number outline code, start, and text fields—for both tasks and resources. You can create custom fields that include formulas, and you can attach lookup tables— tables that contain a selection of possible values for the field—to custom fields, making them powerful tools for data entry. In this chapter, I'm going to show you how to create custom fields—custom fields with formulas and custom fields with lookup tables—and show you how you can use them for data entry.

Project distinguishes work breakdown structure (WBS) codes from all the other custom fields, but, essentially, WBS codes are simply special custom fields; you'll learn more about them later in this chapter.

# Creating a Custom Field

I find it helpful to display the Status Date field on my Tracking table; having it appear provides me with a much-needed visual reminder to change the status date before updating a project. Custom fields serve my purpose perfectly, because they enable me to display a Project field that ordinarily appears in a dialog box. I'm going to show you how to add the Status Date field to the Tracking table. With the Status Date appearing on your Tracking table, you should easily remember to choose Project | Project Information to display the Project Information dialog box and set the Status Date there.

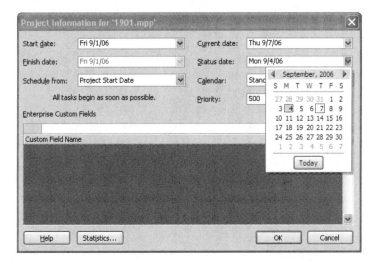

To add the Status Date field, we'll start by modifying the Tracking table to include a date field that will appear as a column in the Tracking table; then, we'll customize that date field to display the Status Date that appears in the Project Information dialog box.

To add the date field, insert a column. Project inserts columns into tables to the left of the selected column, and I like the Status Date to appear immediately next to the Task Name column. So, right-click the Act. Start column heading to select that column and then click Insert Column from the shortcut menu that appears. Project displays the Column Definition dialog box.

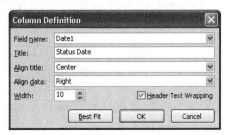

In the Field Name box, select Date1, and in the Title box, type **Status Date**. You don't need to change any of the other settings; when you click OK, Project inserts a column called Status Date into the Tracking table (see Figure 19-1).

At this point, you can open the list box for the Status Field column and select a date, but Project doesn't know that you want that date to represent the Status Field. So, let's set the custom field's definition using these steps:

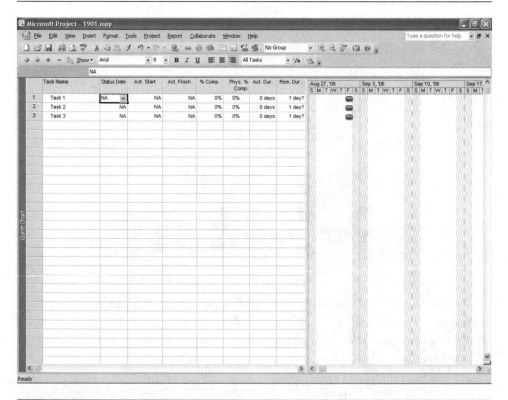

**FIGURE 19-1**    Project inserted a column called Status Date into the Tracking table of my project.

1. Click anywhere in the Status Date column.

2. Choose Tools | Customize | Fields. Project displays the Custom Fields dialog box.

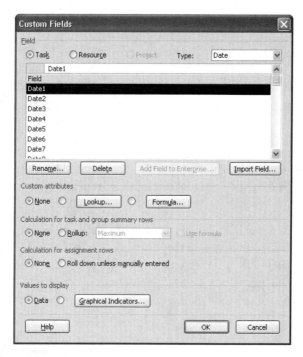

3. At the top of the dialog box, make sure that Task is selected and that Date appears in the Type list box.

4. Select Date1—the field you inserted into the Tracking table—and click the Formula button. Project displays the Formula dialog box.

5. Click the Field button and choose Project | Date | Status Date. Project inserts [Status Date] in the text box portion of the Formula dialog box.

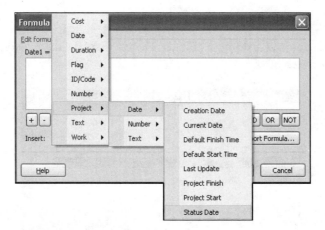

6. Click OK. Project warns that existing data in the Date1 field will be deleted to be replaced by the formula; click OK to redisplay the Custom Fields dialog box.

7. Click the Rename button and type **Status Date**. Renaming the Date1 field to Status Date allows you to find the field using the name Status Date instead of Date1 in any task view.

*If you don't rename the field, you may forget that you assigned a formula to it.*

8. Click OK. Project assigns the Status Date as it appears in the Project Information dialog box to the date field you added to the Tracking table and displays that date on the Tracking table (see Figure 19-2).

Technically, you just assigned a simple formula to a custom field; your formula told Project to make Date1 equal to the project status date. In the next section, we'll create a slightly more complicated formula for a custom field.

# Creating Formulas in Custom Fields

In the preceding section, we used a custom field to display a Project field. But custom fields are very powerful; you can also use them to calculate almost anything you want. Let's add a field for the current date to the Tracking table; although the calculation is a simple one, it will help you get the idea of creating custom fields to make calculations.

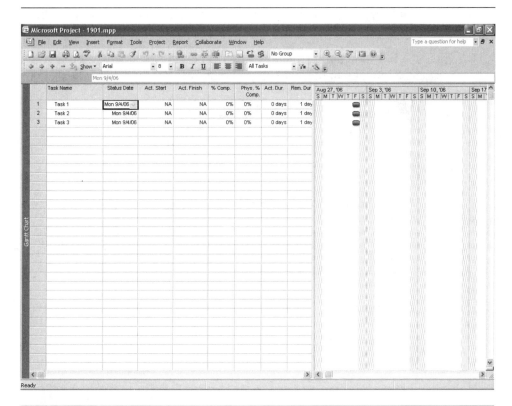

**FIGURE 19-2**   After you define the Date1 field to display the Status Date, Project updates the field on your Tracking table.

Once again, add a column to the Tracking table; this time, select Date2 from the Field Name list box and type **Current Date** in the Title text box. I added the Current Date column between the Act. Start column and the Status Date column.

Next, follow these steps to assign the formula for the current date to the custom field Date2:

**1.** Click anywhere in the Current Date column.

**2.** Click Tools | Customize | Fields. Project displays the Custom Fields dialog box.

**3.** At the top of the dialog box, make sure that Task is selected and that Date appears in the Type list box.

19

4. Highlight Date2—the field you inserted into the Tracking table—and click the Formula button. Project displays the Formula dialog box.

5. Click the Function button, point to Date/Time, and click Now(). Project inserts the function in the text box portion of the Formula dialog box.

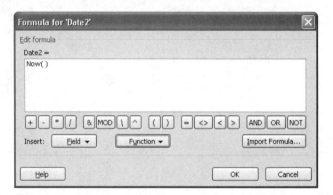

NOTE    *You can create almost any kind of a formula for a custom field by using the mathematical operators that appear below the Edit Formula text box or the functions that appear when you click the Function button. Use the Field button to assign the value of any available Project field to a custom field.*

6. Click OK. Project warns that existing data in the Date2 field will be deleted to be replaced by the formula; click OK to redisplay the Custom Fields dialog box.

7. Click the Rename button and type **Current Date**. Renaming the Date2 field to Current Date allows you to find the field using the name Current Date instead of Date2 in any task view.

8. Click OK. Project assigns the Current Date as it appears in the Project Information dialog box to the date field you added to the Tracking table and displays that date on the Tracking table.

# Numbering Tasks

Project provides three ways to assign numbers to tasks: you can use outline numbers, outline codes, or WBS codes. Both outline codes and WBS codes are basically custom fields; that's why I've included this information in this chapter.

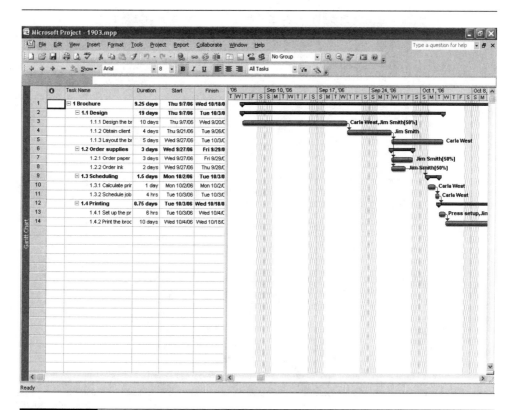

**FIGURE 19-3** A project where tasks display outline numbers

# Using Outline Numbers

Project automatically assigns an outline number to each task in your project; all you need to do is display the numbers. In Figure 19-3, I've displayed outline numbers.

To display outline numbers, choose Tools | Options. In the Options dialog box, click the View tab. Then, place a check in the Show Outline Number check box at the bottom of the tab.

19

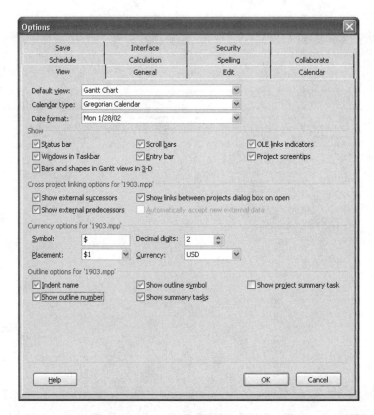

The outline number is assigned to the task based on its position in the project. If you move any of your tasks around, Project renumbers the tasks instead of permanently assigning the number to the task.

## Using Outline Codes

Suppose that you want to assign permanent outline numbers to tasks—numbers that won't change even if you move tasks around in the project. In this case, don't use outline numbers; instead, used custom outline codes. Outline codes are static.

*If you have a good reason, you certainly can use both outline numbers and outline codes. Just be sure to clarify the purpose of assigning two sets of numbers to your tasks.*

Outline codes are custom fields; although they provide outlining capabilities, they are not tied to the outline structure of your project. Many people commonly use outline codes to assign department codes or accounting cost center codes to tasks; that way, they can view their project organized by department code or cost code. And, there's nothing stopping you from assigning more than one outline code—for example, you can assign a department code *and* a cost center code.

Outline codes work as you would expect; you define codes at the highest level—we'll call that Level 1—and then additional codes at various subordinate levels—Level 2, Level 3, etc. Level 2 codes would appear subordinate to Level 1, Level 3 subordinate to Level 2, and so on.

To make your outline code work effectively, you create a list of valid outline codes for users to enter so that the outline codes assigned are meaningful and consistent. Project calls this valid list of codes a *lookup list*.

You set up outline codes in much the same way you set up any other custom field. You define the code and then you add a column to a table in your project to display and use the outline codes. The order in which you do these tasks doesn't matter, so we'll start by defining an outline code field and a lookup list for it. Follow these steps:

1. Choose Tools | Customize | Fields. Project displays the Custom Fields dialog box.

2. Open the Type drop-down list and choose Outline Code.

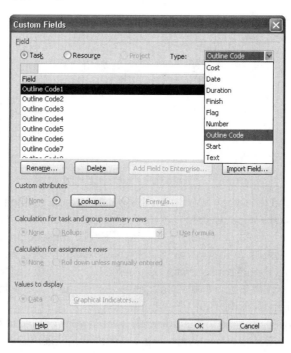

3. Choose an outline code to customize.

4. Click the Rename button and type the new name to provide a meaningful name for the code; I called mine Dept. Code. Then click OK to redisplay the Custom Fields dialog box.

5. Click the Lookup button; Project displays the Edit Lookup Table dialog box, where you establish the valid values for the outline code.

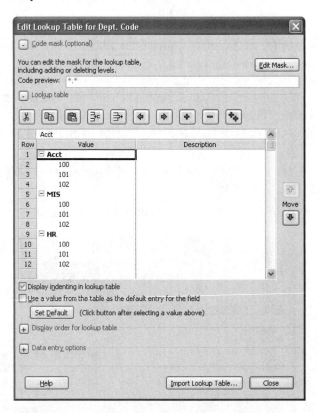

6. If you intend to create a lookup list that contains more than one level, you need to use the code mask to specify the format for all levels below the first level. For example, you specify whether the code must be numbers, characters, uppercase letters, or lowercase letters. You also can restrict the length of the code and incorporate a separator between the code mask and the code. Click the plus sign (+) beside Code Mask at the top of the Edit Lookup Table dialog box and then click the Edit Mask button to display the Code Mask Definition dialog box. Define the format for each level in your outline code. When you finish, click OK to redisplay the Edit Lookup Table dialog box.

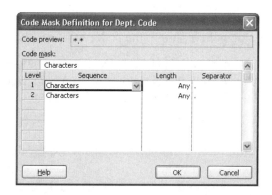

7. On Row 1 of the Value column, type a permissible outline code for the first level of your outline—we'll call it Level 1—and press ENTER.

   On Row 2 of the Value column, type an outline code for the second level that is permissible under Level 1 and press ENTER; after Project displays the code, move the pointer back into Row 2 and click the Indent button (the right arrow) at the top of the dialog box to indent the code.

*By default, Project assumes that you're creating a one-level lookup table. To create more than one level, you must update the code mask; you can identify undefined levels because they appear in red. See the notes immediately following these steps to learn how to update the code mask.*

8. On the third line, type another acceptable Level 2 outline code.

9. Click Close to redisplay the Custom Fields dialog box.

10. Click OK to save your outline code settings.

Some notes about outline codes:

■ You can supply a Level 3 outline code under a Level 2 outline code using the same technique described in Steps 6 and 7. To supply another Level 1 code, type the code, place the pointer on the code's row, and click the Outdent button (the left arrow) as many times as necessary, depending on the last code that you entered.

■ If you forget to include a code, highlight the code that you want to appear below the code that you'll add, and then click the Insert Row button at the top of the dialog box. And, if a code becomes invalid at some later date, reopen this dialog box, highlight the code, and click the Delete Row button.

■ You can click the plus sign (+) beside Data Entry Options at the bottom of the dialog box to check boxes to allow additions to the codes to the lookup table during data entry or to force entry of only the lowest-level code—the one with no subordinate values.

You're now ready to insert a column in a table to display the outline code. Right-click the column that you want to appear to the right of the Outline Code column. Then, from the shortcut menu that appears, click Insert Column. In the Column Definition dialog box, open the Field Name list box and select the outline code that you defined. Click OK, and Project displays the column, empty and waiting for you to assign outline codes to your project's tasks.

You enter codes by clicking in the Outline Code column; Project displays a drop-down arrow. When you click the arrow to open the list, the entries from the lookup table appear (see Figure 19-4). Simply select an entry to assign it to a task.

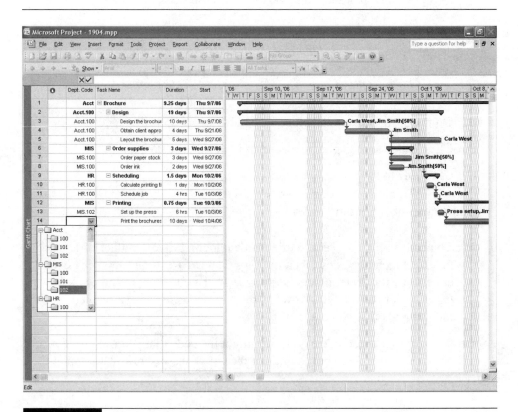

FIGURE 19-4    The lookup table entries appear in the outline code column.

# Working with Work Breakdown Structure Codes

The U.S. defense establishment initially developed the work breakdown structure (WBS) chart, which shows a list of numbered tasks that you must complete to finish a project; the WBS chart relates the tasks you need to accomplish to each other and to the end product of your project. Figure 19-5 shows a sample WBS chart.

Project doesn't contain a view that displays a WBS chart of your project, but you can assign WBS codes to each task. WBS codes can be letters, numbers, or combinations of letters and numbers. You also can use an add-on product, WBS Chart Pro, to create a WBS chart of your project; visit Critical Tools, Inc. at http://www.criticaltools.com.

You can use any numbering system that you want for your WBS code structure. Suppose that you assigned codes to the tasks in your project that are similar to the ones shown in Figure 19-5. Although Project doesn't produce the graphic representation, it assigns the numbers based on the task's level within the project outline.

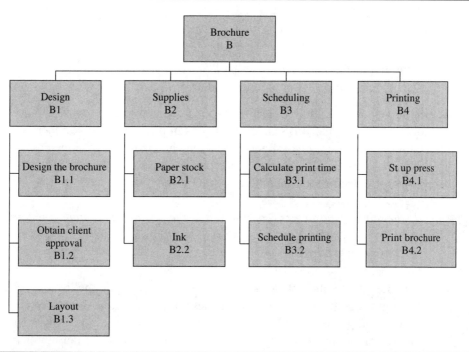

**FIGURE 19-5**    A typical WBS chart

To assign WBS numbers to tasks, we'll first create the layout of the code and then we'll insert the WBS field into the project to assign WBS codes to tasks. Follow these steps:

1. Choose Project | WBS | Define Code. Project displays the WBS Code Definition dialog box. The Code Preview box shows you the format of the WBS code that you're designing as you design it and therefore remains blank until you make selections in this dialog box.

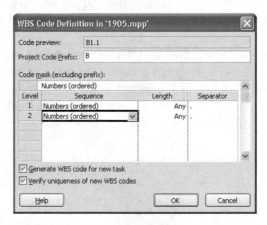

2. In the Project Code Prefix box, type a prefix that you want to include in all WBS codes. For my example, I used B.

3. In the Sequence column, select the type of character that you want to use for each level of the WBS code. For my example, I selected Numbers (Ordered) for both Levels 1 and 2, but you can also include Uppercase Letters or Lowercase Letters. If you choose Characters (Unordered), Project inserts an asterisk at that position of the code preview.

*If you choose Characters (Unordered) in the Sequence column, you can enter any characters that you want into that part of the WBS code when you assign the code to a task.*

4. In the Length column, click the drop-down arrow to open the list and select the length for the level of the WBS code. For this example, I allowed any number of digits for both Level 1 and Level 2. You can choose Any, select from the predefined list of numbers 1 to 10, or type in any other number.

 *For the technically curious, I tested the number 100, and Project accepted it, but using a 100-digit number in a WBS code isn't particularly practical.*

**5.** In the Separator column, use the drop-down list box to select period (.), dash (−), plus (+), or slash (/), or type in any character that is not a number or a letter (such as =).

**6.** Repeat the previous steps for each level that you want to define.

 *Checking the two check boxes at the bottom of the WBS Code Definition dialog box ensures that Project assigns WBS codes to all tasks and that the codes are unique.*

**7.** Click OK when you finish.

To view the WBS codes, you add the WBS column. To add the WBS column to the left of the Task Name column, right-click the Task Name column. From the shortcut menu that appears, click Insert Column, and Project displays the Column Definition dialog box. Open the Field Name drop-down list and select WBS. Click OK to add the column to the table (see Figure 19-6).

Project doesn't automatically renumber WBS codes in all cases when you change the structure of the project outline. Project does automatically renumber WBS codes if you do one of the following:

■ Promote or demote a task

■ Move a task so that it appears at a new level in the outline

■ Move a subtask to a new parent task

Project doesn't change the WBS code if you do either of the following:

■ Drag a Level 1 task to a new Level 1 location

■ Drag a subtask to a new location beneath its original parent task

At times, you'll want to renumber the WBS codes, even though Project didn't renumber them automatically. You can renumber the entire project or only selected portions of the project. If you choose to renumber selected portions, you must select the tasks before starting the renumbering process.

19

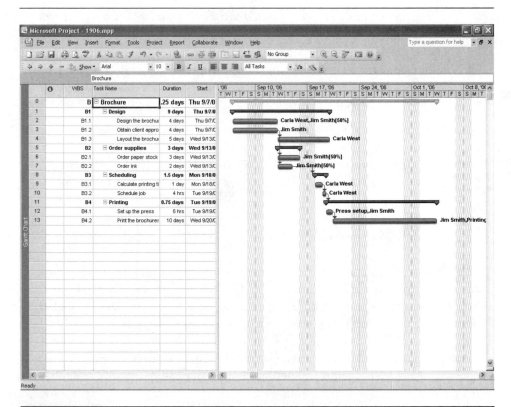

**FIGURE 19-6** Project displays the WBS codes for each task in your project.

To renumber all tasks in the project, choose Project | WBS | Renumber. Project displays the WBS Renumber dialog box. If you selected tasks before you started the renumbering process, you can choose between renumbering selected tasks or renumbering the entire project. If you didn't select tasks, you can renumber the entire project. Click OK, and Project reassigns all WBS numbers.

In this chapter, you got a taste of the power of custom fields; in the next chapter, you'll learn how to change the Project interface to work the way you want.

# Chapter 20

## Changing the Project Interface

## How to…

- Control Project's levels of Undo
- Control Project icons on the Windows taskbar
- Use Organizer to share elements between Project files
- Control toolbar and menu behavior
- Add and delete toolbar buttons
- Create a custom toolbar
- Customize Project menus

You can customize the Project working environment to support the way that you work. For example, you can change the way that you use Project's tools and commands and how various elements appear onscreen. Microsoft Project enables you to customize most of its elements. This chapter shows you how to make changes to the behavior of the Project interface, and create and modify toolbars and menus to make Project work the way that's best for you.

# Controlling the Levels of Undo

In versions of Project prior to Project 2007, you could undo the last action you took—and only the last action. In Project 2007, you can undo up to your last 99 actions since the last time you saved your project.

By default, Project automatically tracks 20 Undo levels—the last 20 actions you took. While you might be tempted to set the Undo level to 99, be aware that Project tracks all of your actions in memory, and some actions, like saving baselines, take more memory than others. Setting the Undo level to 99 could have performance repercussions.

To change the number of Undo levels Project tracks, choose Tools | Options. Then, click the General tab; you'll find the number of Undo levels toward the top of the tab.

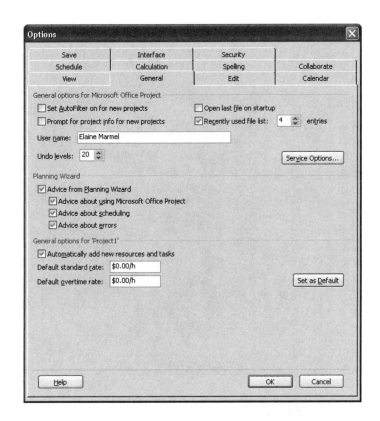

*Nearby, you'll also notice that you can control the number of files that appear at the bottom of the File menu, making it easier to open recently used files.*

# Controlling Project Files on the Windows Taskbar

By default, Project displays one taskbar icon on the Windows taskbar for each Project file you open. If you open enough files, you won't be able to identify the names of the open files. You can modify Project's behavior so that only one icon shows on the Windows taskbar, and you use the Window menu to switch between open files.

Choose Tools | Options. Then, click the View tab; in the Show section, remove the check from the Windows in Taskbar check box and click OK.

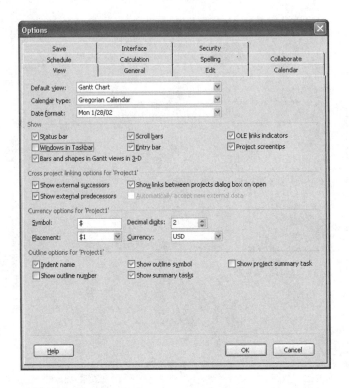

# Using the Organizer

You can share views, tables, forms, reports, and other elements among projects by using the Organizer window. To open the Organizer window, choose Tools | Organizer.

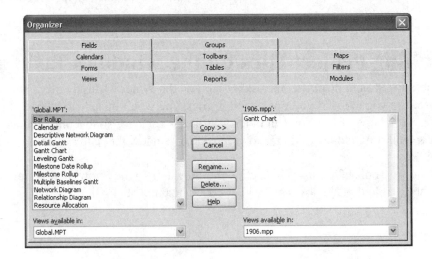

## Copying Elements Between Projects

All elements stored in the Global template (Global.mpt) file appear on the left side of the Organizer window. These elements are available to every project file you base on the Global.mpt file.

By default, the elements in the project you were viewing when you opened the Organizer window appear on the right side of the Organizer window. You can copy elements on the various tabs of the Organizer window from the Global template (Global.mpt) to the current project and from the current project to the Global template.

At the bottom of the Organizer window, two list boxes appear. The options in these list boxes will be the Project files you have open. So, you also can copy elements between projects if you open the projects between which you want to copy elements. Then, in the Organizer window, use the list boxes at the bottom of each tab to select the project file containing the information and the project file that should receive the information. Highlight an element and click the Copy button.

## Deleting an Element

To delete an element view in the current project, find the element on the appropriate tab of the Organizer window; make sure you are looking at the element in the *right* side of the window. Remember, your project name appears in the list box at the bottom of the right side of the window and the Global template appears in the list box at the bottom of the left side of the window. Because the Global template contains all the elements in Project and makes them available to all projects based on the Global template, be careful not to delete an element from the Global template; if you do, that element will no longer be available to *any* project.

On the right side of the tab, click the element you want to delete and then click the Delete button. Project deletes the view from the current project.

 *You rename an element in the same way; highlight it on the appropriate tab and side of the Organizer window and click the Rename button. In the Rename dialog box that appears, type the new name and click OK.*

# Controlling Toolbar and Menu Behavior

Project displays the Standard and Formatting toolbars on one row by default; in this arrangement, you can't see all of the tools on either toolbar and must use the More Tools button that appears at the end of the toolbar to view additional toolbar buttons.

Similarly, Project menus initially display a subset of commands and, after a few moments or if you click the arrow at the bottom of the menu, the rest of the commands appear.

You can control this behavior using the Options tab of the Customize dialog box; choose Tools | Customize| Toolbars. Then, click the Options tab.

You can display the Standard and Formatting toolbars on separate rows if you check the Show Standard and Formatting Toolbars on Two Rows check box.

If you prefer to view all the commands on a menu when you open the menu, check the Always Show Full Menus check box. If you leave the box unchecked but check Show Full Menus After a Short Delay, Project initially shows only a subset of commands and, after a few moments, displays the rest of the commands. If you don't check either box, Project displays a subset of commands when you open the menu, and you must click the small arrows that appear at the bottom of the menu to see the rest of the commands.

# Adding or Deleting Toolbar Buttons

You can add or delete buttons from any Project toolbar, customizing the toolbar to include the tools you use most often.

To add tools to any toolbar, display the toolbar by right-clicking any toolbar and then clicking the toolbar you want to display. Then, follow these steps:

1. Choose Tools | Customize| Toolbars to open the Customize dialog box.

2. Click the Commands tab.

**3.** Click the category of command that contains the tool that you want to add to a toolbar. For example, the Timescale tool, which opens the Timescale dialog box, appears in the Format category. If you don't know the category to which a tool command belongs, scroll down the Categories list on the left side of the Customize dialog box and select All Commands at the bottom of the list. The Commands list on the right side of the dialog box then displays every available command in alphabetical order.

**4.** Drag the item from the Commands list in the dialog box into any position on the toolbar of your choice (see Figure 20-1). The shape of the mouse pointer indicates where the new tool will appear.

You also can easily remove a tool from a toolbar. With the Customize dialog box open, display the toolbar that contains the tool that you want to remove and drag the tool off the toolbar. Releasing the mouse button removes the tool.

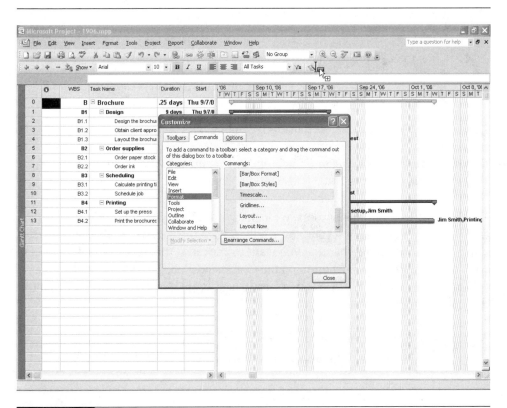

**FIGURE 20-1**    Adding a button to a toolbar.

 *You can restore a toolbar's original settings from the Customize dialog box. Click the Toolbars tab, click the name of the toolbar, and click Reset. Project restores the default tools.*

# Creating a Custom Toolbar

If you'd prefer not to make changes to the original toolbars, you can, instead, create a custom toolbar and place the tools on it that you use most often. Follow these steps:

1. Choose Tools | Customize| Toolbars. The Customize dialog box appears.

2. Click the Toolbars tab and then click the New button. The New Toolbar dialog box appears.

3. Type a toolbar name and click OK. A small toolbar, containing no tools at the moment, appears. You can drag this floating toolbar to any location on the screen that's convenient for you.

4. Click the Commands tab.

5. Click tools in any category, and drag them onto the new toolbar. Figure 20-2 shows the new toolbar that I created.

6. Click Close to close the Customize dialog box.

 *You can reorder the tools by simply dragging a tool to a different location on the toolbar.*

You can create groups of tools, typically with related functions, if you add dividers (thin gray lines) to your new toolbar. With the Customize dialog box open, select the tool on the toolbar that you want to appear to the right of the divider, and click the Modify Selection button on the Commands tab. The Modify Selection pop-up menu appears. Click Begin a Group, and Project inserts a thin gray line to the left of the selected tool.

 *To delete a divider, select the tool to the divider's right and, using the Modify Selection pop-up menu, select Begin a Group again.*

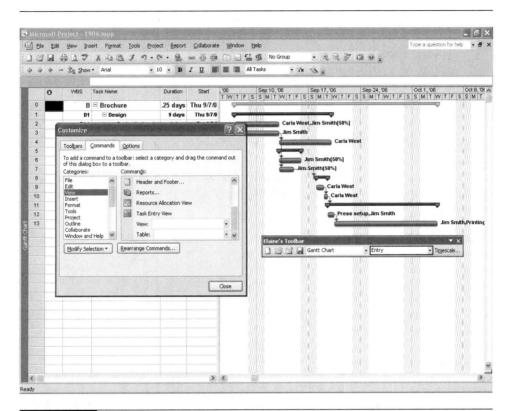

Creating a new toolbar.

# Customizing Project Menus

Like Project toolbars, you can customize Project menus. You can add commands to menus, remove commands from menus, and create a complete menu of your own. I'll make this an all-inclusive example by creating a new menu and adding commands to it. Follow these steps:

1. Choose Tools | Customize| Toolbars to open the Customize dialog box.

2. Click the Commands tab.

3. Scroll to the bottom of the list of Categories and click the New Menu category. The single selection, New Menu, appears in the list of commands.

4. Drag the New Menu item up to the location on the menu bar where you want the new menu to appear. When the dark vertical line of your mouse pointer appears where you want to place the new menu, release the mouse button. Project places the new menu on the menu bar.

Okay, you've got a new menu on the menu bar, but it isn't very useful, since it has no functional name and contains no commands. So, let's name the new menu and add commands to it by following these steps:

1. With the Customize dialog box still open and displaying the Commands tab, and the New Menu item selected on the menu bar, click the Modify Selection button.

2. From the Modify Selection pop-up menu, highlight New Menu and type a specific menu name (see Figure 20-3).

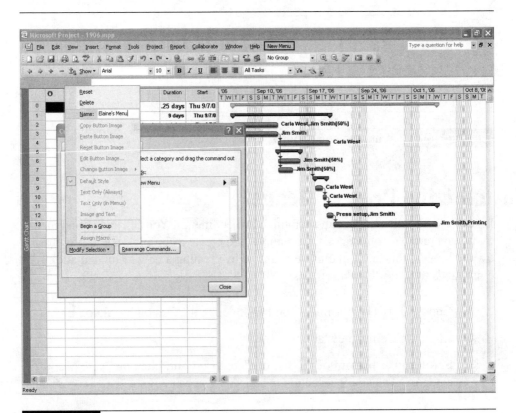

**FIGURE 20-3**    Assigning a name to the new menu.

**3.** Click outside the Modify Selection menu to close it. Project assigns the name to the menu.

**4.** In the Categories list, click a category containing commands that you want to place on the new menu.

**5.** Drag an item in the Commands list up to the new menu on the menu bar. A small, blank box appears under the menu heading.

**6.** Place the mouse pointer in that blank area, and release the mouse button to place the command on the menu (see Figure 20-4).

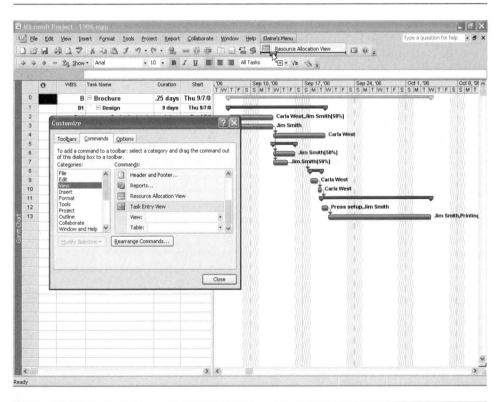

**FIGURE 20-4** Adding a command to a menu.

**7.** Repeat Steps 4 through 6 to add other commands to the new menu.

*To divide the menu into groups of commands, click Modify Selection and choose Begin a Group from the pop-up menu.*

**8.** Click Close to close the Customize dialog box.

In this chapter, you learned how to customize the Project interface to make it work the way you work. In the next chapter, you'll learn how to create a macro to speed up performing repetitive tasks in Project.

# Chapter 21

## Speeding Up Work with Macros

## How to...

■ Record a macro

■ Run a macro

When you find yourself performing a task repetitively, consider creating a macro to speed up your work. A *macro* is a small program that contains the commands you want to perform; when you run the macro, the macro takes all the actions for you. Don't let the word "program" scare you, because you don't need to know how to write code to create a macro.

# Recording Macros

Visual Basic is the macro programming language that you use in Microsoft products, but you don't need to know Visual Basic to create a macro; instead, you can *record* a macro.

When you record a macro, Project memorizes the steps that you take to perform an action. You do whatever it is you want Project to do, and Project converts those actions into Visual Basic statements and stores the statements in a macro program. Later, when you want to take that action again, you run the macro to let Project take the steps for you.

The easiest way to record a macro properly is to run through the steps you take to perform the action—and maybe even write them down. That way, you are likely to record the macro correctly the first time you try.

Suppose that you find yourself using two different versions of the timescale on a regular basis. To get a more detailed look at a segment of the project, you want to view weeks on the middle tier and days on the bottom tier. And, to view the bigger picture, you want to switch to displaying months on the middle tier and weeks on the bottom tier. In this case, you'd create two macros—one for each version of the timescale that you use frequently. When you walk through the process, you find that you use the following steps to set up the big-picture macro (I'm providing these steps as an example here; in a moment, we'll follow these steps to record the macro):

1. Right-click the timescale and select Timescale to display the Timescale dialog box.

2. On the Middle Tier tab, choose Months for the Units.

3. On the Bottom Tier tab, choose Weeks for the Units.

4. Click OK.

You're ready to record a macro. We'll start by recording the big-picture macro, using these steps:

1. Choose Tools | Macro | Record New Macro to open the Record Macro dialog box.

2. Enter a name for the macro in the Macro Name box.

**TIP** *The first character of the macro name must be a letter, but the other characters can be letters, numbers, or underscore characters. You can't include a space in a macro name, so try using an underscore character as a word separator (for example, Big_Picture_Timescale) or capitalize the first letter of each word (BigPictureTimescale).*

3. (Optional) To assign the macro to a keyboard shortcut, type a letter in the Shortcut Key box. The letter that you assign can be any letter key on your keyboard, except numbers or special characters. You also can't assign a key combination that is already used by Microsoft Project. If you select a reserved letter, Project displays a warning message when you click OK.

**NOTE** *Keyboard shortcuts are only one of the ways that you can run a macro.*

4. Type a description of the macro or the function that it performs in the Description box. This description appears whenever you run the macro from the Macros dialog box.

5. Click OK, and Project redisplays your project. You don't notice any differences, but Project is now recording each action that you take.

6. Take all the actions that you want to record.

7. Choose Tools | Macro | Stop Recorder to stop recording your macro.

That's it—you just recorded a macro. If you're following along with my example, repeat Steps 1 to 7 to create the macro for the detailed view of the timescale.

# Running Macros

You can run a macro you recorded in a variety of ways:

- Using the Macros dialog box
- Using a keyboard shortcut
- Using a toolbar button
- Using a menu command

To run the macro from the Macros dialog box, choose Tools | Macro | Macros. Then, highlight the macro you want to run and click Run. Project runs the macro.

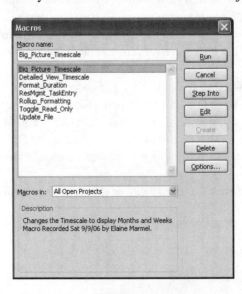

21

To run the macro using a keyboard shortcut that you assigned to it, press and hold the CTRL key and then press the key you assigned to the macro. Project runs the macro. If you didn't assign a keyboard shortcut to the macro, you can click the macro in the Macros dialog box and then click the Options button to assign one after the fact.

The last two techniques are very similar to each other; you add your macro to either a toolbar or a menu command as described in Chapter 20. Then, you click that toolbar button or menu command to run the macro. To find the macro to add it to a toolbar or a menu, choose Tools | Customize | Toolbars. Click the Commands tab and then scroll to the bottom of the Categories list. Click All Macros, and the macros you can assign to toolbars or menus appear on the right. Drag the macro onto a toolbar or a menu and close the Customize dialog box.

    *You can rename the macro using the Modify Selection pop-up menu as described in Chapter 20.*

# Index